Education and Social Change in China

This project received a grant from the
University of Hong Kong
Strategic Research in China Studies

Education and Social Change in China

Inequality in a Market Economy

Gerard A. Postiglione, Editor

Foreword by Stanley Rosen

An East Gate Book

M.E.Sharpe
Armonk, New York
London, England

An East Gate Book

Library of Congress Cataloging-in-Publication Data

Education and social change in China : inequality in a market economy / edited by
Gerard A. Postiglione.
    p. cm.
"East Gate Book."
"This volume arose from a panel organized for the annual meeting of the Association
of Asian Studies in New York City on the topic of education and social stratification
in China."
Includes bibliographical references and index.
ISBN 0-7656-1476-6 (cloth : alk. paper)
   1. Educational sociology—China—Congresses. 2. Educational equalization—China—
Congresses. 3. Education, Rural—China—Congresses. 4. Education and state—China—
Congresses. I. Postiglione, Gerard A., 1951–

LC191.8.C5E38 2006
306.43′20951—dc22   2005025788

Contents

Part IV. Urban Divisions: Migrants and the Middle Class

List of Tables and Figure

Tables

Figure

Foreword

The massive changes currently taking place in Chinese society have intensified the debate over the implications and consequences of those changes, especially for education. In recent years there has been a virtual cottage industry in academic and popular volumes published in China that document that nation's new patterns of social stratification. While some of the leading Chinese sociologists such as Sun Liping and Li Qiang have focused attention on the negative consequences that have emerged as the result of government policies to promote a "socialist market economy," including the cleavages that now rend Chinese society,[1] less academically-minded observers have produced best-selling books concerned not with warning government and Party leaders of the implications and dangers of an increasingly "fractured" Chinese society, but rather with how the educated reader can benefit from the opportunities that have become available as a result of the economic and social changes that have occurred.[2] In short, in a society that has produced and will likely continue to produce "winners" and "losers," unsurprisingly there are now guides to aid those who do not want to be left behind.

In addition to books, there are also popular magazines widely available at China's ubiquitous street kiosks that examine the "exotic" lifestyles not only of the rich and famous, but also of the middle and/or white collar class more generally. These magazines offer advice to the *nouveaux riches* who may not yet be sophisticated enough to understand proper behavior for someone of their station, while fueling the aspirations of those who have yet to make it, including some, such as migrant workers in urban areas, who have little hope of "making it."[3] Indeed, as a popular hostess—dubbed "China's Martha Stewart"—of a new lifestyle program on Chinese television put it, her show worked just as well on the level of fantasy as on the level of practical advice. "We are creating a dream for Chinese women who want comfort and elegance in their lifestyle. . . . For many viewers, this is already a familiar world, while others may never reach it. For them, there is no harm in dreaming."[4] But this is only one part of the story, the widely reported success of China's new urban middle class. One finds far less reporting of the other end of the spectrum—the details on the heavy costs of these new patterns of social stratification for those left behind. Some of the most revealing studies that *have* been published in China have been quickly suppressed for fear of the impact such revelations might have for social stability.[5]

While the educational system is not the central focus of this literature, it has not been completely ignored. Indeed, one of the most successful books—and greatest controversies–in recent years concerned the so-called "Harvard Girl," who was trained from birth by her parents to make it into Harvard University by the time she was eighteen years old.[6] Her success in gaining entrance to Harvard and three other prestigious American universities not only made the book the number one bestseller of 2001 and produced a sequel, but also led to countervailing volumes refuting the one-sided, materialistic values of the Harvard Girl's parents and even disputing the basic facts of the young lady's success.[7] Again, however, the high-profile "Harvard Girl Debate"—in which provincial education departments organized forums for parents on how to learn from Liu Yiting's achievement—focused attention on success strategies, with little interest in those who failed, and virtually no interest in those who were not in a position even to play the game.

What makes Postiglione's *Education and Social Change in China* so valuable is that it offers an extensively researched sociological study of the effects of government policies and market reforms on the educational system, with primary attention given to those who have generally been ignored in most other studies. It reveals better than any other work on this subject thus far the complexities and contradictions that rend China's educational system, and the unanticipated consequences and limitations that arise from even the most progressive educational reforms. Based on fieldwork and interviews in different regions of China, and in both urban and rural locales, the authors of the individual chapters collectively make a compelling case for the seeming intractability of educational reform, *by itself,* to be successful in reducing inequalities. While this conclusion would not be surprising to those familiar with the work done on inequalities in American schools, the present work is especially compelling because virtually every chapter, despite the different foci, reveals the failures of the educational system to ameliorate the inequalities that have been produced under the reform program. All offer policy prescriptions that strongly suggest that any educational reform strategy examine the likely consequences of that strategy for the types of outcomes desired by the consumers of the policy. Particularly in minority areas, there is even a real sense that the success of the state's educational strategies may have an impact on larger issues of political legitimacy.

Only Jing Lin's chapter on the new middle class deals with the clear beneficiaries of the reform. For the remaining authors, however, the commercialization of education has created challenges for which solutions have yet to be found. For some authors, such as Jin Xiao, state-mandated policies to revise the curriculum of rural schools in Yunnan province have not been successful because there remains a disconnect between the skills of the school graduates and the needs of the labor market; schools and local firms have different agendas. In a rather similar manner, Postiglione, Jiao, and Gyatso find that schools in Tibet have been unable to turn Tibetans into suitable competitors with outside migrants for the key positions offered by the developing market economy.

What also comes through in the cases studies are the complex interactions among state policies, market conditions, and traditional cultural patterns. Most authors therefore highlight the Chinese state's limited ability to solve educational problems. Perhaps Julia Kwong puts it best when she notes that the government has not intentionally discriminated against the migrant children; the problem stems largely from "the unanticipated nature and pace of social changes introduced by the market economy and the more liberal official stand on population and other social policies." Solutions to the problems plaguing the education system will necessarily be limited without an alteration of government priorities including, in the case of migrants, the final abolition of the *hukou* residential system. Yu and Hannum as well view a simple focus on education insufficient to solve existing problems. Because children's schooling is compromised by the poverty and ill health of the child or family, the primary state intervention must be in the public health sector. As with Yu and Hannum, Heidi Ross also suggests that state policymakers are not asking the right questions. Instead of measuring progress on female education solely by school access and participation ratios, they should be at least equally concerned with the purpose, the terms and the cost of school attendance. Among the authors, only Vilma Seeberg in her policy prescriptions seems to suggest that state policies, focusing on increased investment in the education of Tibetan girls, can in and of themselves, make the crucial difference. Taken together, *Education and Social Change in China* is likely to intensify the scholarly debate over the educational implications and social consequences of the rapid changes brought about by the market reforms in the Chinese economy.

Stanley Rosen
Director, East Asian Studies Center
University of Southern California
February 25, 2006

Notes

1. Sun Liping, *Duanlie: 20 shiji 90 niandai yilai de zhongguo shehui* (Cleavage: Chinese society since the 1990s) (Beijing: Shehui kexue wenxian chubanshe, 2003); Sun Liping, *Shiheng: Duanlie shehui de yunzuo luoji* (Imbalance: The logic of a fractured society) (Beijing: Shehui kexue wenxian chubanshe, 2004); Li Peilin, Li Qiang and Sun Liping, *Zhongguo shehui fenceng* (Social stratification in China today) (Beijing: Shehui kexue wenxian chubanshe, 2004).

2. *Ni zhongchan le ma?* (Are you part of the middle class?). (Beijing: Jingji ribao chubanshe, 2003). The title is translated in English on the cover of the book, along with the following questions (in Chinese): "In China, who belongs to the middle class? How far away From joining the middle class are you? How can you enter the middle class?" There is also a drawing of an overweight, self-satisfied golfer on the cover.

3. For examples, see *Renwu zhoukan* (VIP weekly), *Mingxing shidai* (Rich and famous), *Xin xiandai huabao* (Modern: For the luxury lifestyle), and *Qingnian caifu* (Young and wealthy). Note that the English translations for the first three appear on the magazines.

4. Howard W. French, "China's Martha Stewart, With Reasons to Smile," *The New York Times,* April 10, 2004, p. A4.

5. Chen Guidi and Chun Tao, *Zhongguo nongmin diaocha* (An investigation of China's farmers) (Renmin wenxue chubanshe, 2004). This runaway bestseller was banned by the Chinese government; however, in a striking indication of the decentralization and distribution of information, pirated copies flooded the market and interested buyers could purchase the banned book at around 80 percent off the original price.

6. Zhang Xinwu and Liu Weihua, *Hafo nuhai Liu Yiting: suzhi peiyang jishi* (Harvard girl Liu Yiting: The true story of her training) (Beijing: Zhongguo qingnian chubanshe, 2000) and its sequel, *Liu Yiting de xuexi fangfa he peiyang xijie* (Details of Liu Yiting's study methods and training) (Beijing: Zuojia chubanshe, 2004).

7. Zhou Hong, *Wo pingyong, wo kuaile* (I'm mediocre, I'm happy) (Taipei: Gaofu guoji wenhua gufen youxian chubanshe, 2002). The original edition was published by Guangdong jiaoyu chubanshe. A more vicious attack on the Liu Yiting case appeared in Xiao Yu, *Jiaoyu haizi xuyao da zhihui: 'Hafo nuhai liu yiting' zhenxiang* (Educating children needs great wisdom: The real story of 'Harvard Girl Liu Yiting') (Beijing: Zhongguo dianying chubanshe, 2004). This case is discussed in Stanley Rosen, "The Victory of Materialism: Aspirations to Join China's Urban Moneyed Classes and the Commercialization of Education," *The China Journal,* no. 51, January 2004, pp. 27–51.

Fieldwork Research Sites

Part I

Inequalities and Development Discourse

1

Schooling and Inequality in China

Gerard A. Postiglione

As a national issue, educational inequality continues to haunt China.[1] More than a half century after the Communist Revolution, the elimination of most educational inequality remains an elusive goal. Many households cannot afford to send their children to school. Rural Chinese counties continue to struggle over how to fund nine-year compulsory education.[2] Many villages went into debt when they tried to universalize nine years of compulsory education.[3] Even after tax reform, when the collection of education fees was curtailed, the debt in some areas could not be repaid and creditors blocked off local government buildings, sealed off school gates, and even roughed up teachers and principals.[4] Due to insufficient funds, a number of rural areas lack the basic conditions necessary for compulsory education, including desks and teaching aids such as chalk and paper.[5] The effect of insufficient funds has also devastated the teaching force as many teachers leave for counties and cities or cross the border, where conditions are better.[6]

Yet, access to schooling has never been more widespread in China.[7] China's accomplishment in making education available to its massive population has been nothing short of astonishing, especially when compared with other developing countries. Even with a low proportion of gross domestic product (GDP) allocated to education, China managed to push enrollment rates for primary and junior secondary schooling to levels above those of most other lower-income countries. Yet, educational inequalities continue to widen, compliments of a hot-wired market economy and the easing of pressure on the central government over the responsibility to ensure access and equity.

Although twelve years of schooling was virtually universalized in Beijing and Shanghai by the beginning of the twenty-first century, 20 percent of the country's populated rural areas had not attained the legally guaranteed nine years of education. By 2005, the figure had dropped to 10 percent. The education system in rural areas endures despite many rundown schools, inadequately prepared teachers, unattractive teaching materials, inefficient school

A primary school in the Linxia Hui Autonomous Prefecture of Gansu Province, where religious beliefs and practices have an influence on the classroom attendance ratios of girls to boys.

management, inadequate community participation and support, and high drop-out and repetition rates.[8] Whereas sixteen provinces in eastern China had an enrollment rate of 99.5 percent, those in the Northwest and Southwest remained below this mark. In Tibet, for example, the enrollment rate was 81.25 percent in 1998. Gender disparities also persist between the advanced coastal areas and the poor and remote areas of northwest and southwest China. Girls constitute 70 percent of the school-age children under eleven years old who are not in school. They also constitute 75 percent of the dropouts from primary school. Nine municipalities and provinces had already reached 100 percent universalization of nine-year compulsory education in 1998, whereas seven provinces and autonomous regions remained below 60 percent.[9]

These figures only tell part of the story. A study by the Central Party School published in 2005 found that officials regularly exaggerate enrollment figures. The number of students receiving nine years of education is much lower than government statistics suggest. The report casts doubt on the government claim that it provided free education to 2,598 counties, or 90 percent of the total, by 2002. Local officials see to it that names appear on the attendance roll for students who do not study in the school, and some schools sell diplomas to students who do not attend school. My own research in rural Yunnan in 1993 found junior secondary schools dispensing diplomas for a fee to the new entrants from inferior primary schools that "would not make it anyway." In this manner, schools actually save funds allocated for the registered students who depart early but remain on school records for the full three years. The Central Party School Report also confirmed that some schools borrow students for visits by the inspectors. Students in many towns and cities receive free education; students from rural areas—whose families and schools can least afford to—have to pay.[10] The widening gap between the rich and poor in educational standards has also prompted a group of leading academics and officials to point out to the government that it has never met the target of spending four percent of GDP on education. They also pointed out that despite a 60 percent rural population, less than a quarter of the funds for education went to rural areas. The former head of the Education Commission of Hunnan Province argued that education failed to pull people out of poverty and improve social equality.[11]

The hard reality is that within the new socialist market economy, it is the rural poor, ethnic minorities, girls, and migrants that have the monopoly on low enrollment and high dropout rates, leaving the urban middle class with dominion over the major indicators of school success. This volume is not an effort to judge China's efforts in providing educational access and equity, but rather to provide a sociological perspective on the educational inequalities that do exist. Although the chapters generally refrain from employing many familiar sociological concepts such as social reproduction, resistance, hegemony, and social capital, they do make one thing clear: contemporary education not only transmits China's heritage to the next generation, but also differentiates and stratifies, setting social trajectories early in life. The irony is that while the socialist market economy has increased the educational choices available, it has made these choices more a function of poverty, gender, and ethnicity than in the planned economy of the prereform period.

Education as a mechanism of social stratification is not new in China, a nation with a cultural heritage that includes the *keju,* a system of social selection based on examinations that test knowledge of the classic texts. It is the experience with market forces within an expanding global economy that continues to confound efforts to reduce the educational gap between rich and poor. China has learned to transform itself and its education system. However, in the process, markets often seem to matter more than Marxism in educational provision, though the latter continues to be a legitimizing force for state schooling. A great deal of legitimacy has also been gained through the popularization of nine-year compulsory education and the rapid expansion of postsecondary educational opportunities, the latter of which grew faster than anywhere on earth.[12] China is approaching a key historical educational juncture in education—the first time that children from nearly every family, region, and nationality in China will attend school. As schooling reaches into virtually all regions and households, it comes to play a larger role in determining China's social stratification. This is already apparent in the expanding university enrollments where, as more attend, the proportion of women and ethnic minorities in the top universities does not keep pace with the rate of expansion, and students from remote areas not only find themselves short of funds for tuition fees but also without the skills needed to survive and excel in an increasingly cosmopolitan university atmosphere.

As the chapters to come will show, the market economy has already transformed the equation of educational access and equity in rural China. Families can no longer rely with certainty on state-sponsored educational provision. As schooling has come to cost more, so also have basic foodstuffs and health care. Family incomes have become less stable, affecting the rural household environment and compelling some members to migrate to urban areas for work. As the profit motive of local enterprises have come to play a larger role in their decision about whom to hire, schools are being pressured to offer more vocational courses, while also inculcating new attitudes and dispositions for the production line. Markets also leave ethnic minorities in a quandary about how to maintain the traditional values that are the bedrock of their communities, while risking the dislocations brought on by mainstream consumer culture. Markets can also make the education of girls less valuable to many individual households, as well as unleash a wave of rural migration to urban areas where jobs may be found but where educational opportunities for children are inadequate. The poor rural villages of western China, including their girls, ethnic minorities, and urban migrants, remain underserved, both in terms of access and equity and in terms of the quality of the education they receive. This is not to deny the monumental gains made in educational access and equality under Chinese socialism. But the reforms launched since 1978, including administrative and financial decentralization, have placed the urban middle class at a distinct and seemingly insurmountable advantage.

At the very least, the following chapters illustrate a sharp contrast across regions and social categories. For example, whereas eastern China's urban children are schooled and well fed, many poor rural families in the Northwest exist on diets that stunt their children's growth and learning abilities. As rural schools in the Southwest strive to better equip children with skills that increase job prospects in new local enterprises, rural families in Tibet wonder how schools can help their children compete with outsiders for nonfarm labor jobs. Although urban girls are receiving more schooling than ever before, many rural households struggle to afford textbooks for their daughters—books that compound the problem by containing stereotyped gender roles. Finally, as waves of rural migrants descend on urban areas and find limited educational opportunities for their sons and daughters, many Beijing middle-class families are spending more than ever on private schooling for their children.

This chapter is followed by an examination of girls' education and the role of nongovernment organizations (NGOs). The rest of the volume's chapters are arranged by region (Northwest and Southwest), and by the divide existing between rural migrants and the urban middle class.[13] Chapter topics not only reflect the fact that most Chinese still live in rural areas and that western China has fallen far behind the rest of the country, but also that rural China is spilling into the cities, bringing the rural-urban divide to the doorstep of the new middle class.

Girls' Education and NGOs

Education for girls has been at the center of many policy debates about educational provision in China. At the turn of this century, about 70 percent of China's illiterates or semi-illiterates were women.[14] As the transition from a planned to a market economy got under way, China found that it had to place girls' education in a preferential position to ensure that enrollment rates increased year by year. In fact, by the beginning of the twenty-first century, the margin of increase in years of education received by women (over fifteen years old) had become larger than that received by men; the margin of decline in the female illiteracy rate was also larger than that for men. The gender difference narrowed. Yet, even with the feminization of agriculture due to men migrating in greater numbers for work, men remained the major beneficiaries of technical training courses. A gender gap remains in vocational education and curricula still reflect gender stereotypes. Girls typically learn service sector skills, including languages, secretarial tasks, hotel services, catering, waitressing, and housekeeping, whereas boys tend to study industrial trades. By the end of 2003, 47 percent of school enrollments for primary and junior secondary school were girls. The figure drops to 45 percent at senior secondary school and 44 percent at regular institutions of higher education. In higher education, women are represented more in provincial colleges and teacher training institutions than at national-level prestigious universities, and women are less in evidence than men in fields that lead to higher-paying jobs. Although girls' enrollment still lags, the gender gap is declining. By 2000, woman received an average of more than 6.5 years of education; the difference between adult men and women in terms of years of education was reduced to fewer than 1.5 years from 1.7 years in 1995.

Enrollment data may also mask high dropout rates, particularly for girls. As tuition fees became more the rule than the exception for rural families beginning in the mid-1990s, many parents took their daughters out of school to work at home. Such decisions are affected by the fact that upon marriage, many rural girls move to their husband's family, often in far-away villages. Thus, many households see little investment return for the fees they pay to schools. The employment available for teenage girls is also a factor in their dropping out of school. Expanded work opportunities are available as domestic helpers in well-off households as well as in rural townships and urban enterprises. Other factors that may cause parents in remote rural and ethnic minority areas to reconsider sending their daughters to school include safety, distance from home, lack of transportation, and a mostly male teaching force. Due to the significant number of female dropouts, many NGOs (nongovernmental organizations) have become active in addressing the problem.[15]

In chapter 2, Heidi Ross focuses on gender discrimination and how it is reproduced, maintained, and encountered. She looks specifically at affirmative action in girls' education. Distinguishing between equity and equality, Ross analyzes the discourses of policies and practices and how they are shaped by selective forces. She carefully deconstructs the discourse that surrounds girls' schooling and exposes the gender traps that reside within it. Ross notes how attendance rates increased in Beijing and Shanghai, where girls outnumbered boys in admission to tertiary education. Yet, she points out in stark contrast that three million girls have not completed five years of education and 70 percent of school dropouts are female. Ross opens up a way to understand how gender traps become nested within a tripartite formation that includes the logic of developmentalism, a naturalization of gender, and strong nationalism. Together, these reinforce an insidious form of gender stereotyping that reaches across family, school, and workplace. All this occurs against a backdrop of financial decentralization in which there is a passing of the buck and a failure to meet EFA goals. Ross demonstrates how the state has a monopoly on the framing of the conditions of social existence and how this affects the transnational alliances between foreign and national NGOs. Even with the growth of China's NGOs as a middle ground, a paradoxical social message directed at girls is clear: achieve, but take your role as men's subordinate. Ross presents a rich set of data that betrays an optimistic picture of the progress in people-centered development and calls for a thorough evaluation of the consequences for China's future. Drawing on her working experience with development NGOs, she highlights the multiple and contradictory processes of globalization at work. Examples include the Spring Bud Program's emphasis on getting girls into school and the Ford Foundation's supported effort to make schools recognize and address gender stereotyping in course textbooks and teaching materials. Ross's conclusion gets at the key issue of girls' schooling: for what purpose, on what terms, and at what cost?

The Northwest

The Northwest is one of the poorest regions of China. With twenty-five million people, Gansu Province has the largest population and is making the transition to a market economy with great difficulty. Despite its size, Gansu contributes less than one percent of GDP, and its net capital income is only 56 percent of the national average. At the turn of the century, forty-one of its eighty-six counties were designated as poor and deserving of special state and provincial financial assistance. In poor areas of rural Gansu, direct costs of education were estimated at between 15 to 30 percent of an average family's income (compared to the international norm of about 10 to 15 percent).[16] Before the end of the century, first-grade enrollment rates in elementary school were especially low for girls. National policies aim at achieving nine-year compulsory education for all school-age children, strengthening educational management at all levels, increasing government investment in basic education at all levels, continuous improvement of school conditions, and the enhancement of teaching quality.

Gansu also has two autonomous ethnic minority prefectures and five ethnic minority autonomous counties. The population in minority regions is 3,040,000, of which 2,330,000 (9 percent of the provincial population occupying 40 percent of the land of the province) are ethnic minorities.[17] By 1998, the ethnic minority autonomous regions of Gansu had 2,510 primary schools with 345,000 students and 14,000 teachers. The primary school enrollment rate for girls in Gansu was 91.45 percent but was only 87.4 percent for ethnic minority girls. There were only 147 middle schools with 73,000 students and 5,600 teachers. About 90 percent of the primary school teachers were qualified according to the required level of education; the figures were 71 percent for junior middle school and 40 percent for senior middle school. Of the twenty-one minority counties/cities in 1998, only four had popularized nine-year compulsory education, and only seven had popularized five-to six-year basic education. In some ethnic minority counties, the enrollment rate was only 50 percent, whereas for girls it was only 20 percent, and the dropout rate was over 60 percent.[18]

Since 2000, there has been much progress on all education indicators, but problems remain. In a demographic study of rural Gansu Province, Shengchao Yu and Emily Hannum point out in chapter 3 that the major obstacle to educational access in rural poverty-stricken areas is still health. Diets that lead to physical stunting do not bode well for education, and even if hungry children do go to school, they learn less. Moreover, their chance of staying in school for the length of compulsory schooling is greatly diminished. This is a direct result of the move to a market economy, because the rural cooperatives that provided inexpensive medical and health care have been dismantled. Financial decentralization has privatized not only school financing but also health costs. Poor health and poverty go hand in hand, but the nutritional environment, medical provision, and psychosocial health of households leave their mark on educational access and equity at the most basic level. In short, any examination of problems of educational access and equity in rural China has to begin with health, and this explains why Yu and Hannum's study of youth in Gansu appears early in this volume.

Yu and Hannum note that about 35 percent of schoolchildren in rural Gansu are at great risk of poor nutrition, as indicated by their stunting.[19] Height-for-age is a stronger predictor of school progress than weight-for-age. As an indicator of long-term nutritional status, stunting occurs across social categories such as gender and school dropouts. One of the major findings of their research is that the addition of nutritional environment to calculations of mathematics and language achievement reduces the effects of household expenditures on both of these. Moreover, short-term health problems can place dramatic stress on families' labor and finance as much as long-term disabilities do. Finally, Yu and Hannum also show that poor health has a broad meaning and includes a range of mental health problems experienced by young people in school, including symptoms of withdrawal, anxiety, depression, hyperactivity, aggression, and delinquency.[20]

The educational challenges of China's Northwest also need to be viewed against its indigenous cultural diversity. In chapter 4, Vilma Seeberg's anthropological fieldwork provides an insightful case study on Gansu's Tibetans. Her fieldwork clearly shows that educational reforms are affecting traditional ethnic patterns of life. Although the gendered division of labor continues to hold, girls in Tibetan regions are earning some comparative advantages due to their new position in the family and society. In this chapter, Seeberg suggests that "traditional" attitudes may not be as harmful to girls' education as is often assumed by development programs. Her research suggests that it is more important to understand the material conditions that present new opportunities and obstacles, and to study how ethnic girls and their families respond to them. It is in this interaction that culture is changed. In this research, conducted in 2004 to understand nomadic Tibetan ethnic minority girls' orientations to education, Seeberg argues convincingly that it is actually the relative lack of economic development that propels girls and women ahead, changes the construction of their identity and social relations, changes the context and meaning of education for them, and moves them into spaces of greater centrality and visibility. Throughout her chapter, Seeberg explores how culture, patriarchy, poverty, and economic decline circumscribe lives in these remote areas. Her research supports and optimism about new possibilities being explored by greater numbers of Tibetan girls and women, including higher attainment in education.

The Southwest

The Southwest has levels of poverty to rival the Northwest. Although not the poorest province in the Southwest, Yunnan faces many special educational challenges. With a total of 128 counties (cities or areas), Yunnan has 73 counties that are poverty-stricken and receive national support. Its 44,060-kilometer border with Vietnam, Laos, and Burma contributes to its large ethnic minority population, making it China's most culturally diverse province. In all, the ethnic minority population accounts for one-third of the total population. Its forty million people are spread over 390,000 square kilometers, 94 percent of which is mountainous. Poverty has been the main obstacle for the popularization of nine-year compulsory education in Yunnan. Strengthening basic education is also crucial to the campaign against drug abuse and the rapid rise in HIV/AIDS and related health problems. These challenges notwithstanding, Yunnan has attained some success in educational provision. Official figures show that over 97 percent of its ethnic minority school-age population has attended primary school.

Although 90 of Yunnan's 127 counties, including 52 ethnic minority autonomous counties, have achieved six-year compulsory education, only 34 counties have achieved the compulsory nine years of education (14 of which are ethnic minority counties). Under such conditions, there has been an effort to increase the relevance of schooling to the home economy by providing basic vocational skills beginning in upper primary and middle school.

As Jin Xiao notes in chapter 5 on schooling in rural Yunnan, there is a different set of problems in areas that have universalized basic education and where basic nutritional needs have been met. The pressure of the market economy is being felt in terms of the relevance of what is being taught. Five local primary schools, some in multiethnic localities with Yi and Hani minorities, were the focus of Xiao's fieldwork and interviews with teachers and students. She argues that classroom teaching is de-linked from the needs of the local firms that are supposed to lift the rural communities they serve out of economic stagnation. The key issue is the role of these particular schools in giving poor rural children a way out through learning that will get them jobs in rural firms where they can inject their skills and attitudes to help the firms succeed in the market economy and bring prosperity to the communities they serve. Although communities are being told that financial decentralization (and higher school fees) will be offset by the benefits of a market economy, Xiao's research points out that that the relevance of what is being learned in schools does not match the needs of new local enterprises. Through qualitative methods of research, Xiao clearly demonstrates that separate worlds exist. Local township industries want students that are open-minded, whereas school teaching methods generally promote closed minds. After interviews with rural firms that hire graduates from poor areas, Xiao points outs out that traits judged by local rural firms as important, including the ability to relate theory to practice, open-mindedness, initiative, and a sense of responsibility, are not being taught in schools.

Yunnan's Yi and Hani ethnic minorities are but two of China's fifty-six officially defined ethnic groups, many of whom remain underserved in education. Only ten of the fifty-five ethnic minority groups have education levels above the national average.[21] The challenge is to ensure equal opportunities, promote the economic development of ethnic minority regions, encourage ethnic groups to practice cultural autonomy, and build interethnic unity. However, state schooling is also charged with the responsibility to conserve ethnic minority cultures within a national context that places a premium on Han Chinese cultural capital. Schools are not thought of as creating an atmosphere that has positive institutional norms toward diverse cultural groups, or modifying their total environment to make it more reflective of ethnic diversity.[22] State policy does accord importance to the special cultural characteristics of ethnic minority regions; however, not enough is known about actual practice and, in particular, the way that they affect educational opportunities and social stratification. In-depth study of the schooling in particular ethnic communities is needed to measure the gap between the policy and practice of ethnic minority regional autonomy in education and to understand the manner in which ethnic communities innovate in their adjustment to state schooling. Ethnic autonomous regions, including Tibet, are authorized to develop their own educational programs, including levels and kinds of schools, curriculum content, and language of instruction. Special funds are allocated for education in ethnic minority areas. This could include funds for teacher training and bilingual education. Boarding schools have been established and stipends provided for students in pastoral, frontier, and mountainous localities.[23]

Tibet constitutes the largest area in Southwest China. It is the most geographically remote, ethically homogeneous, broadly religious, and economically poor of China's five nationality autonomous regions, and, before 1951, it had more autonomy than the others. It covers 12.5 percent of the country but contains only 0.002 percent of the population.[24] Its residents possess a distinctive culture dating back over a thousand years, with a complex religious tradition and writing system. Tibetans are dispersed beyond the Tibetan Autonomous Region (TAR) in four adjoining provinces, where most live.[25] All told, they occupy 3.8 million square kilometers of China—about half the size of the United States. The ethnic composition of the TAR was 95.5 percent Tibetan in 1990, and this declined to 92 percent in 2000.[26] Tibet has generally been several steps behind other ethnic minority regions of China in the development of state schooling.[27] Despite its rich cultural tradition, it has the lowest education levels of any provincial entity in China. By 1990, less than 20 percent of the TAR Tibetans had a primary education, and few had much more than that. Until the mid-1990s, most villages had only popularized two to three years of education. At the end of the twentieth century, illiteracy and semiliteracy stood slightly above 50 percent and enrollment in junior secondary school stood below 25 percent. Urban areas, where most non-Tibetans reside, have higher enrollment rates; many remote regions have only universalized three-year compulsory education. At the close of the twentieth century, Tibet had managed to have about a third of its counties institute nine-year compulsory education.

The poverty of the TAR and the distribution of its population make popularizing education a daunting task for far-away Beijing. Cultural dimensions of ethnic minority education, particularly language and religion, increase the complexity of the task at a time when globalization has inflated the salience of regional cultures.[28] As rural minorities struggle to achieve a better living standard, they face the problem of how to make state-sponsored education work in effective ways so that it can become a valued part of family and community life. Chapter 6 by Gerard Postiglione, Ben Jiao, and Sonam Gyatso is based on data gathered in villages of two TAR counties. It examines how home, school, and community factors affect school participation. The main theme concerns the interaction between economic development and cultural vitality, as it relates to education's perceived role in improving life within a rapidly changing Tibet. The authors argue that despite the abolition of school fees and the provision of boarding schools, the dropout rates in rural Tibet remain high due largely to the inability of schools to provide villagers with competitive jobs after graduation. This chapter examines the development, problems, and adaptations of rural education in Tibet. The case of Tibet is special not because of its status as a nationality autonomous region of China, but because it is so culturally different. Indeed, there is no entity as large as Tibet in China that stands out so clearly as culturally distinct from the rest of China. Rural Tibetans would support state schooling more, even accepting many acculturation sacrifices, if they could see a direct economic return for their households. Yet, the problems of education confronted by rural Tibetans are not unlike those in other transition economies. Although willing to enter the nonfarm labor sector, Tibetans want schools to provide the skills needed to compete with the influx of outsiders.

Urban Divisions

Migrants

The planned economy meant a steady population structure for China. However, the unleashing of market forces on rural China has led to more stress on the urban education system as a way to integrate rural children into the urban mainstream. The increased flow of people is actually an education system in itself in that it creates a system of communication that not only transmits increased knowledge about employment, markets, and related opportunities but also communicates knowledge about cultural and social transformations. Starting in the 1980s, rural people migrated to cities in great numbers to look for jobs. Although only 2 million rural people migrated to cities at the beginning of the 1980s, it is estimated that the number of surplus laborers in rural areas grew to about 200 million, and 80 to 100 million eventually migrated to the cities.[29]

The rural domicile system was established in the 1950s. The system divided people along lines of being agricultural or nonagricultural and basically prevented people in rural residences from moving to the city, cutting down on their access to urban employment and causing a large gap in income between urban and rural residents. People with an urban *hukou* could find jobs in cities and reside there. There were three stages of migration management. The first stage, from 1949 to 1957, was a free migration period in which people were permitted to migrate between countryside and cities. It is estimated that rural-urban migration accounted for 60 percent of the increased urban population from 1950 to 1957. The second stage, from 1958 to 1984, was a period of controlled migration. At first, authorities responded with measures to halt the massive shift to urban areas, and by the late 1950s large numbers of demobilized military personnel and others were transferred to rural areas. This continued during the Cultural Revolution, especially with sent-down youth and re-education. Between 1969 and 1973, ten to fifteen million urban secondary school leavers were resettled in rural areas and deprived of the documents to return. The third stage occurred after 1984, when the national residence identification card rule was published. It was also a time when many of the sent-down youth returned to their urban residences. By 1988, the *hukou* became less important. The floating population grew larger and began to stay longer, with many becoming permanent residents. Population mobilization to metropolitan areas can no longer be easily controlled.

In Beijing, family units make up about a third of all migrants. These families stay for longer periods of time, and, as is the case in other parts of the world, family units have less of an intention to return than do individual migrants. [30] Beginning in 1992, migrant families began to organize education for their children. This usually amounted to tutoring or holding classes in shanties or vegetable sheds and later in homes and abandoned buildings. These "illegal" schools were banned or demolished. However, as the population grew, there came to be over 200 migrant schools in Beijing with over 40,000 children. [31]

It is estimated that the average stay in Beijing is about two years, with 72 percent staying more than six months. Twenty-two percent stay for up to a year, 22.4 percent reside for between one and three years, 9.4 percent for three to five years, and 9 percent stay longer than five years. Many rural migrants who bring families stay more than ten years. [32] The floating population in Beijing is estimated at around 2.5 million. These people stay for more than half a year and account for 83.3 percent of the whole floating population in Beijing. Those who live in Beijing for more than half a year become Beijing citizens in the statistical classification. The increased rate of in-migration accounts for 67.7 percent of the total population increase. The natural birthrate accounts for 10.4 percent, and the formal migration rate accounts for 21.9 percent. The massive movement of people from rural to urban areas will continue to be a major challenge for decades to come.

While many rural migrants bring their families with them, others start families in their temporary urban homes. As the need for schools has grown, migrant encampments attract teachers from the home communities to deal with the unwillingness of many local schools to admit migrant children. Julia Kwong explores the Beijing situation in chapter 7. She argues that rural children who are brought to Beijing or born there will likely receive an inferior education and be stereotyped, as well as being more likely not to graduate from secondary school and avoid unlawful activity. Without a household registration, many migrants and their children will live a second-class existence, marginalized and stereotyped. Such discrimination has a way of perpetuating the difference between migrants and local Beijing residents. Kwong's chapter raises a key issue for Beijingers and other "*hukou*ed " urbanites. Rural migration to urban China will continue into the middle of the twenty-first century and will inevitably lead to a radical increase in the cultural diversity of the urban landscape. Although the decision has been made to capitalize on the human labor capital dimension of the equation, no serious consideration has been given to how schools can capture the cultural capital embedded within the texture of life in migrant communities and their home regions. The degree of social integration of second-generation migrants in urban middle-class schools could increase or decrease, depending on the gap between popular perceptions and the long-term national vision.

The Middle Class

In chapter 8, Jing Lin provides the contrast for the other chapters of this volume that focus on the rural poor, ethnic minorities, and new migrants. She does this by examining education and the rise of the middle class in Beijing and other major Chinese cities. These cities act as magnets to migrants, and by 2020, 400 million people will flow into mainland cities, half into the affluent areas on China's east coast.[33] The three east coast regions of the Pearl River Delta, Yangtze River Delta, and Bohai Rim account for 3 percent of the country's land, 12 percent of the population, and 40 percent of the nation's GDP. Nevertheless, rural migrants to these regions find themselves largely excluded from middle-class urban lifestyles, including the educational opportunities available to the children of the middle class. Lin stresses the increasing ability of middle-class residents to secure a place for their children in expensive *minban* schools outside of the regular school system. Although these so-called private schools are not private in the same sense as their counterparts in other parts of the world, they share much of their elitist character.

Minban schools arose for a number of reasons, including economic reform, growing prosperity, an inadequacy of many regular government schools, and a differentiation of demands. The *minban* education movement quickly became characterized by uneven development across regions, the influence of market forces, and a variety of forms of ownership. The pace of development shot far ahead of regulations that tried to shape the evolution of these schools. Many issues plagued their development, including whether they should be able to make a profit, rights over their property, and assessment of quality. Although the central government still exerts control over *minban* schools through a national policy framework, local governments can tailor policies to their particular situations. A key difference from their counterparts in the public sector is that *minban* schools focus on the demands of particular interest groups and draw their funds from the respective social sectors. The quality of education offered and the fees charged have a great deal to do with the economic resources, donations, and ways to generate new funds. Tuition and fees are the major source of funds, so the schools are greatly driven by type of clientele and enrollment expansion. They keep costs low by hiring part-time and retired teachers. Many investors in these schools are motivated by profit making.[34] They advertise, and some invite celebrities to be members of their board to promote their reputation. Their governance is usually centralized, with low participation by stakeholders in decision making.[35]

In December 2002, the Standing Committee of the National People's Congress passed the Minban Education Promotion Law. The point of this action was to vigorously encourage *minban* schools to operate as long as they abide by legal guidelines for management. However, the most important aspect of this law—and the reason it was delayed several times—was the confirmation by government that *minban* schools could generate reasonable profits, an issue that was highly contested by those who believe that a profit motive has no place within the business of running educational institutions.[36]

Lin notes the suffocating effect of rising tuition fees in the urban *minban* schools on the general population. These schools provide, in many cases, not only an education superior to most public schools but also access to social networks on which families can capitalize later in terms of further schooling or job selection. The rise of the middle class in the market economy has propelled private schools that can offer better facilities, better teachers, and a better environment for learning. Yes, as Lin makes very clear, rural migrants and the urban working class both lack the resources, especially personal savings, to make it possible to capitalize on new educational opportunities.

Conclusion

The financial disparity across regions has widened, and with this has come a deepening educational chasm. The income gap between eastern and western regions widened from 2.1 to 3.2 times between 1990 and 2003, leading the government to set aside 15 billion yuan for fighting rural poverty.[37] At the same time, calls have grown louder for the government to further increase expenditure on education in rural areas as a way to lift people out of poverty.[38] A number of measures have been advanced to accelerate efforts to address the problem of inequality and rural education. The State Council held the first national working conference since 1949 to formulate plans for the development of education in rural areas. The document that resulted from the meeting, "Decisions of the State Council to Further Strengthen Education in Rural Areas," reaffirmed the importance of education in rural areas to the construction of a well-off society and proposed to strengthen efforts to achieve the "two basics" and improve the quality of nine-year compulsory education in 372 counties in western China within five years. It also reaffirmed the role of vocational and adult education to solve problems of agriculture in rural areas. Among the more specific measures proposed are the implementation of a county-centered management system of compulsory education to improve the mechanism that guarantees education funds and the establishment of a sound system that provides full sponsorship for the education of poor students and protects the right of school-age children in rural areas to receive compulsory education. The document further specified that by 2007, all poor students receiving compulsory education would be exempt from miscellaneous fees and textbook charges and would receive lodging allowances. The "Decision" also included provisions to speed up the reform of personnel systems in schools, improve teacher quality, implement distance-education programs, strengthen leadership, and mobilize society to support rural education.

Yet, the problems of rural and migrant education remain critical. A survey of one medium-level county in each of six provinces or autonomous regions at various economic levels has shown that the dropout rates of rural junior high schools were as low as 3.66 percent and as high as 54.05 percent. The survey suggests that beyond food and clothing, there are a number of reasons for dropping out. Among them are a loss of confidence and interest in continuing education at the initial stage, too much money required for textbooks, monotonous school life, tense relationships between students and teachers, poor food and lodging, inconvenient transportation, and rising costs of school lodging.[39]

In 2003, the government published "Suggestions to Provide Better Compulsory Education to the Children of Migrant Workers in Cities."[40] Among its provisions were that public primary and junior secondary schools should take the major responsibility to educate the children of migrant workers. It also stated that enrollment rates among the children of migrant workers should reach the local level and should be included in the urban social development plans. It also specified that children of migrant workers should be charged the same amount of tuition and fees as local students and that no fee should be charged for the transfer of migrant children to other schools. However, according to the fifth national census of 2000, there were twenty million such children, and the dropout rate among them was as high as 9.3 percent.[41]

More systematic research is needed in the coming years to assess the result of such new decisions and policies aimed at addressing educational inequalities for rural and migrant children. The study of educational inequality in China has attracted greater attention, especially among economists of education focusing on equity in school finance and resource allocation.[42] However, the sociological study of educational inequality has often fallen between the cracks of the ambiguous relationship between sociology and educational studies. Though sociology of education was reestablished in 1979, the dozen or so textbooks published since then place less stress on educational inequality and stratification than one might expect for a market economy.[43] Despite this, Chinese sociology is turning with more frequency to the topics of inequality, stratification, and mobility.[44] With the largest student population and fastest growing market economy in the world, China could take a greater lead in studies of educational inequality and social stratification. Yet there is a shortage of research on these topics at a time when policies aimed at alleviating rural poverty and educational inequality could benefit from closer examination. The following chapters provide case studies aimed at gaining a wider perspective on social change and educatioal inequality, a complex topic that deserves more attention in the coming years. This volume is a modest attempt to contribute a set of empirical studies and new fieldwork data to considerations about the multilevel processes that create and produce educational inequalities in China. It brings to light the plight and perspectives of underserved rural groups of girls, minorities, and migrants within the context of a transition economy and national policies that aims to provide universal access to schooling within a transition economy. The outline of a process is most clearly visible in the case of girls' access to education by the contrasting patterns of development mediated by state schooling, indigenous perspectives, and transnational alliances of local and foreign NGOs. That process cuts across a spectrum that includes the struggle for access to education amid poverty and malnutrition, and to the struggle between top-down and bottom up decisions about how to make schools relevant to cultural values, household economy, and community development. There is little doubt that the transformation processes in rural China will continue to become heavily affected by the migration to urban areas. In this context, access to education in both urban and rural areas becomes a factor. As long as the availability and quality of urban schooling for migrant children remain questionable, and the rewards of urban schooling become dependent on who can pay for a school place, there will also be a tendency for migrant parents to leave children in rural areas or even to send them back to attend poor rural schools.[45] Either way, the consequences are unattractive and a pattern of resistance by dropping out of school early will continue to reproduce educational inequalities. Schooling in China's socialist market economy has to better ensure that educational choices are not only improved by market forces but also more widely and fairly accessible to underserved groups, if it is to stay in line with the socialist values that underlay the system.

Notes

1. Yang Dongping, *Jiannan de richu: Zhongguo xiandai jiaoyu de 20 shiji* (The long awaited sunrise: China's contemporary education in the twentieth century) (Shanghai: Wenhui chubanshe, 2003); Wu Degang, *Zhongguo quanmin jiaoyu wenti yanjiu: Jianlun jiaoyu jihui pingdeng wenti* (A study of education for all in China: Concurrently on equal educational opportunity) (Beijing: Jiaoyu kexue chubanshe, 1998); Yuan Zhenguo, *Zhongguo jiaoyu zhengce pinglun 2001* (Commentary on China's

educational policy 2001) (Beijing: Jiaoyu kexue chubanshe, 2001); Zhang Renjie, *Zhongguo jiaoyu 2004* (Education in China 2004) (Guangzhou: Guangdong jiaoyu. chubanshe, 2005); Zhu Xiaoman, *Duice yu jianyi 2003–2004 niandu jiaoyu redian, nandian wenti fenxi* (Countermeasures and opinions 2003-2004: Hot educational issues and analyses of difficult problems) (Beijing: Jiaoyu keue chubanshe, 2004); Guojia faxhan yanjiu zhongxin, *Zhongguo jiaoyu lupi shu 2003* (Green paper on education in China 2003) (Beijing: Jiaoyu kexue chubanshe, 2003); Zhongguo jiaoyu kexue janjiusuo, *Zhongguo jichu jiaoyu fazhan yanjiu baogao* (A report on the development of basic education in China 2004/2005) (Beijing: Jiaoyu kexue chubanshe, 2004); Li Lanqing, *Jiaoyu fangtanlu*, (Interviews on education with Li Lanqing) (Beijing: Renmin jiaoyu chubanshe, 2004); Min Weifang, Yang Zhoufu, Li Wenli, *Wei jiaoyu tigong chongzu de ziyuan: Jiaoyu jingjixue guoji yantaoyui lunji* (Raising adequate resources for education: Proceedings of an international conference on the economics of education) (Beijing: Renmin jiaoyu chubanshe 2003); UNESCO, *Report on the International Symposium on Rural Education*, volumes I and II, Baoding, Hebei, January 20–23, 2003 (Beijing: UNESCO Office, 2003).

2. Liu Yarong, Zhang Jie, and Yu Jingtian, "Jiaoyu juzhang yanzhong de jiaoyu jingfei–dui 302 ge quanguo di (shi), xian jiaoyu juzhang de diaocha," (An investigation into the view on education fees of 302 heads of education bureaus of districts [cities], and counties) in Zhu Yongxin, *Zhongguo jiaoyu lan pi shu 2004 nian*, (China education blubook 2004) (Beijing: Gaodeng jiaoyu chubanshe, 2005), pp. 362–370.

3. According to Ren Yuling, a member of the Chinese People's Political Consultative Congress (CPPCC), the campaigns to make nine-year compulsory education universal brought great debt: about 2.1 billion yuan to Hubei, 1.5 billion to Shaanxi, 140 million to Xinyang in Henan, and 130 million to Bazhong in Sichuan; cited in Yang Dongping, *Zhongguo jiaoyu lan pi shu (2003) nian* (China's education in 2003: From growth to reform) (Beijing: Higher Education Publishing Company, 2004).

4. In Tuanfeng County, Hubei alone, twenty-one schools were shut down. See Zhang Yulin, "Zhongguo shinianlaide jiaoyu touru yu muqian nongcunde jiaoyu weiji" (China's past ten years of educational spending and the current crisis in rural education). *Zhanlue yu guanli* (Strategy and management), 2004, no. 4.

5. See Yang Dongping, *Zhongguo jiaoyu lan pi shu (2003) nian*. He noted that a school survey in rural western regions indicated that 38 percent did not have enough desks and chairs, 22 percent had unsafe classrooms, and 33 percent did not have enough funds to buy teaching aids (i.e., ink, chalk, and other supplies). Yang Dongping believes that tax reform has actually worsened the funding for compulsory education. Although the reform helped alleviate farmers' burdens, it also reduced township government revenue. The agriculture ministry reported that the percentage of public funds for compulsory education in rural areas in total expenditure declined consecutively, from 22.98 percent to 19.75 percent, and then to 18.4 percent, down by 4.94 percentage points (www.agri.gov.cn/jjps/t20031220_37712.htm). *Zhongguo qingnian bao* (China youth daily), on September 30, 2003, noted that revenue of many towns in Hebei in 2002 was down by 46 percent and one was down by 68 percent. Also, according to Yang Dongping (*Zhongguo jiaoyu lan pi shu [2003] nian*, p. 22), Wang Bintai and 375 other deputies proposed a bill to speed up the amendment of the Compulsory Education Law at the first meeting of the Tenth National People's Congress held in early 2003. The law would be revised so that funds for compulsory education would be shared among governments at various levels. This reflects the fact that more people are calling for free compulsory education in rural areas.

6. Many teachers left schools due to low salaries and lack of security. Luotian, Hubei, lost over 100 teachers. Xinyan, Henan, and Xianfan, Hubei, lost over 300 and 600 teachers, respectively. For more information, see www.people.com/cn/GB/kejiao/40/20030406/964244/html as cited by Yang Dongping, *Zhongguo jiaoyu lan pi shu (2003) nian*, p. 22. According to the survey conducted by *Xinhua Viewpoint* correspondents of Xinhua News Agency, Jichun County, Hubei Province lost more than 800 teachers. Most left for counties and large and medium cities. See also Hu Pingping, "Clarify Legal Channels for Education Input," *Remin zhengxie bao* (CPPCC post), September 11, 2003. Since 2002, some primary and junior secondary school teachers in border areas of Yunnan Province crossed over into Vietnam to teach. See "Help Compulsory Education in Rural Areas to Cast Off Poverty," *Zhongguo jiaoshi bao* (Chinese teachers post), March 12, 2003.

7. Official statistics (*China Education Daily,* March 2, 2005, www.jyb.com.cn/gb/2005/03/02/zy/jryw/2.htm) show that by the end of 2004, the coverage rate of nine-year compulsory education had reached 93.6 percent, 1.8 percent higher than the previous year, and the overall school distribution rate had been adjusted, with a decreased scale in primary and secondary education and an increase in senior secondary education. By 2004 there were 16,000 ordinary senior secondary schools, with 37.92 percent of the students in secondary technical schools. In 2004, over twenty million students were studying in higher institutions, and the gross enrollment rate reached 19 percent, 2 percent higher than the previous year. Postgraduate education increased rapidly by 21.35 percent; 326,300 postgraduates were recruited. The gross enrollment rate of kindergartens was 40.75 percent, an increase of 3.35 percent. *Minban* education has played a more important role since the law promoting private education was implemented. In 2004, the number of China's *minban* schools at different levels was 78,500, and the number of students studying in *minban* schools was 17,693,600 (3,529,600 more than the previous year) Around 2,045,800 illiterates received preliminary education, and the illiteracy rate among young people was about 4 percent.

8. See World Bank Group data (www.worldbank.org.cn/English/content/683u1148366.shtml), December 24, 2004.

9. Tibet was at only 18 percent.

10. See Josephine Ma, "Many Rural Pupils Cheated of Their Right to Schooling: Survey Finds Counties Struggling to Fund Nine Year Compulsory Education," *South China Morning Post,* January 15, 2005, p. A4. Also see "Zhu Qingshi weiyuan: Jiaoyu gongping jixu zhidu baozhang" (Committee member Zhu Qingshi: Educational equality needs an institutional guarantee), *Zhongguo qingnianbao* (China youth news), March 5, 2005 (www.news.ustc.edu.cn).

11. See also Jane Cai, "Education Policy Closes Door on Poor: Nation Has Missed Spending Target and Ignored Rural Areas, Says Group of Returned Officials," *South China Morning Post,* February 3, 2005, p. A6.

12. See "World University Students Surpassed One Hundred Million for the First Time, China Listed on the Top." *China Education Daily*, August 3, 2003. UNESCO Report showed that China ranked top in the world, exceeding the United States in university enrollments (www.jyb.com.cn/gb/2003/08/03/zy/jryw/12.htm).

13. These regions and categories are not meant to be exclusive. Regions can be problematic in that the inequalities within provinces may be greater than those among provinces. Educational standards in Lanzhou or even a county seat in rural Yunnan may be higher than in a village of eastern Anhui Province. Social categories are also complex. The average education level of children of Han Chinese officials in rural

Qinghai may not be as high as that of an ethnic minority Korean family in Yanbian. Regional and social categories also overlap. Being a village girl from a devout Muslim family of Dongxiang in a mountainous area of western China can be an overlapping pattern of great disadvantage.

14. See World Bank figures (www.worldbank.org.cn/English/content/gender-en.pdf), December 20, 2004.

15. In particular, the Spring Bud Program. See, for example, China Education and Research Network, "35,000 Gansu Girls Return to Schools" (www.edu.cn/20010101/21791.shtml).

16. See information about the Gansu-England Basic Education Project at www.gbep.org.

17. *Zhongguo minzujiaoyu wushi nian* (Fifty years of ethnic education in China) (Beijing: Hongqi chubanshe, 1999), p. 495.

18. *Zhongguo minzujiaoyu wushi nian*, pp. 516–517.

19. The figure for urban Beijing is 1 percent.

20. Access to eyeglasses is also limited. For example, in 2000, the Gansu Survey of Children and Families showed that among the 2,000 sample children ages nine to twelve, only 7.9 percent reported wearing eyeglasses, whereas 20.1 percent reported having difficulties seeing the blackboard or doing homework due to poor vision. Many rural children have difficulty doing homework because of the difficulty of seeing in poor light. This holds true even for many classrooms in remote areas. Such an environment would lead to more myopia in rural areas.

21. The State adopted several measures regarding educational development for ethnic minorities. In July 2002, the State Council published the "Decision on Deepening the Reform and Accelerating Education for Ethnic Minorities," and in early 2004 the "State Plan to Basically Universalize Nine-Year Compulsory Education and Basically Eliminate Illiteracy Among the Young and Middle-Aged Population in the West (2004–2007)" was implemented with 10 billion yuan of planned input from the central budget. See, for example, Mou Benli, Vice Minister of the State Ethnic Affairs Commission, at the press conference sponsored by the State Council Information Office, titled "New Progress in the Cause of Ethnic Unity and Advancement in China," May 30, 2005 (www.china.org.cn/e-news/news050530–2.htm).

22. Gerard Postiglione, *China's National Minority Education: Culture, Schooling and Development* (New York: Falmer, 1999); Judith Liu, Heidi Ross, and Donald P. Kelly, *The Ethnographic Eye: An Interpretive Study of Education in China* (New York: Falmer Press, 2000); see also Ha Jingxiong and Teng Xing, *Minzu jiaoyuxue tonglun* (A general survey of ethnic minority educational studies) (Beijing: Jiaoyu kexue chubanshe, 2001).

23. Guo Fuchang and Wei Pengfei, *Sheng shi zizhiqu shaoshu minzu jiaoyu gongzuo wenjian xuanpian 1977–1990* (Province, city, autonomous region ethnic minority education work documents 1977–1990) (Chengdu: Sichuan minzu chubanshe, 1995).

24. T. Zhang, *Population Development in Tibet and Related Issues* (Beijing: Beijing Foreign Language Press, 1995).

25. The 1990 census counted 4,289,000 Tibetans in China, of which 2,096,700 were in the TAR.

26. Robyn Iredale, Naran Bilik, Wang Su, Fei Guo, and Caroline Hoy, "Tibet and the Movement of Tibetans" in *Contemporary Minority Migration, Education and Ethnicity*. (Aldershot, UK: Edward Elgar, 2001) pp. 138–139, www.jyb.com.cn/gb/2001/05/30/zhxw/jyzx/3.htm.

27. *Zhongguo minzu jiaoyu wushi nian* (Fifty years of ethnic education in China) (Beijing: Hongqi chubanshe, 1999), p. 49.

28. Anthony D. Smith, "Toward a Global Culture," and Jonathan Friedman, "Being in the World: Globalization and Localization," in *Global Culture: Nationalism, Globalization and Modernity,* ed. Michael Feathermore (London: Sage Publications, 1997).

29. www.unescap.org/esid/psis/population/database/chinadata/beijing.htm, December 28, 2004.

30. Beijing Migrant Population Census Office, *1997 Census of the Migrant Population in Beijing Municipality* (Beijing: China Commercial Printing House, 1998).

31. See Han Jialing, "Beijing shi liudong ertong yiwu jiaoyu zhuangkuang diaocha baogao" (Report on investigation of Beijing City transient children compulsory education situation) *Zhongguo qingnian yanjiu* (Youth studies), no. 8 (2001), pp. 1–7.

32. Zou Lanchun, *Beijing de liudong renkou* (Beijing's floating population) (Beijing: Zhongguo renkou chubanshe, 1996).

33. See comments of Wang Yiming, Vice President of the National Development and Reform Commission, in *South China Morning Post*, May 26, 2005, p. A6.

34. Liu Wanyong, "Commissioners Call for the Formulation of an Education Investment Law," *Zhongguo qingnian bao* (China youth daily), March 8, 2003.

35. "Minban Education in China: Background and Current Situation," Fengqiao Yan and Xiaoying Lin Graduate School of Education, Peking University, March 2004 (www.tc.columbia.edu/centers/coce/pdf_files/b5.pdf).

36. The law was finally passed after four readings of the Standing Committee of the National People's Congress in eight years. Moreover, the law came into effect in September 2003, shortly after the government released the "Regulations on Sino-Foreign Joint Ventures in Education." By this time, the government had already approved over 700 Sino-foreign educational joint ventures.

37. See report in *South China Morning Post*, May 26, 2005, p. A6, about a paper (title not provided) delivered by Gao Guangsheng at the International Forum on Urban Development, Beijing.

38. Among the many voices in 2005 was that of Nobel Laureate James Mirrlees at the International Forum on Urban Development, Beijing, May 26, 2005.

39. Sheng Lianxi and Xue Kang, "Primary Education in Rural Areas: Investment Is Not Everything," *Remin zhengxie bao* (CPPCC post), June 26, 2003 (cited in Dongping, *Zhongguo jiaoyu lan pi shu [2003] nian).*

40. "Migrant workers to benefit from new policies" (2003-10-02 11:11) (Xinhua) www.chinadaily.com.cn/en/doc/2003-10/02/content_269126.htm; "Sunnier city life for rural children" (2003-11-06 08:58) (China Daily HK Edition) www.chinadaily .com.cn/en/doc/2003-11/06/content_278905.htm.

41. Alan de Brauw and John Giles, "Migrant Opportunity and the Educational Attainment of Youth in Rural China," www.econ.yale.edu/seminars/trade/tdw05-06/de%20Brauw_paper.pdf; Wenfei Winnie Wang, "Urban-Rural Return Labor Migration in China: A Case Study of Sichuan and Anhui Provinces," www.iir.ucla.edu/research/grad_conf/2004/wang.pdf.

42. See, for example, Min Weifang, Yang Zhoufu, and Li Wenli, eds., *Raising Adequate Resources for Education: Proceedings of the International Conference on Economics of Education* (Beijing: People's Education Press, 2002).

43. See, for example, Wu Kangning, *Jiaoyu shehuixue* (Sociology of education) (Beijing: Renmin jiaoyu chubanshe, 1997); Ma Hemin and Gao Xuping, *Jiaoyu*

shehuoxue yanjiu (Research in the sociology of education) (Shanghai jiaoyu chubanshe, 1998); Bo Songshou, *Jiaoyu shehuixue xinlun* (The new sociology of education) (Hebei: Hebeidaxue chubanshe, 1997). Educational inequality is seldom a main theme of national conferences in the sociology of education.

44. See, for example, Li Peilin, Li Qiang, and Sun Liping, eds., *Zhongguo shehui fenceng* (Social stratification in China) (Beijing: Social Science Documentation Publishing House, 2004); Lu Xueyi, *Dangdai Zhongguo shehui liudong* (Social mobility in contemporary China) (Beijing: Social Science Documentation Publishing House, 2004).

45. Wun Ni, *Zhongguo nongcun liushou ertong wenti yanjiu* (The problem of China's left behind rural children) (Beijing: Zhongyang jiaoyu kexue yanjiusuo [China National Institute of Educational Research], 2005).

2

Challenging the Gendered Dimensions of Schooling

The State, NGOs, and Transnational Alliances

Heidi Ross

Introduction: The "Wicked" Contexts of Girls' Schooling

> Schooling may be a subversive or a conservative activity, but it is certainly a circumscribed one. . . . The faith is that despite some of the more debilitating teachings of culture itself, something can be done in school that will alter the lenses through which one sees the world; which is to say that nontrivial schooling can provide a point of view from which what is can be seen clearly.[1]

This chapter presents a modest attempt to reveal the "what is" of gender discrimination in China by exploring how it is (re)produced, maintained, and sometimes countered through schooling. The contexts for analysis include two programs designed to enhance girls' educational opportunities. The first program, a "Spring Bud" partnership between an international nongovernment organization (NGO) and the Shaanxi Province Women's Federation (SWF), funds education for 1,000 girls. The second program, a research effort supported by the Ford Foundation, examined gender content in China's formal and implicit school curricula.

The projects represent affirmative action for girls at opposite ends of China's educational spectrum, the materially disadvantaged rural and the privileged urban. From these divergent vantage points, each project sheds light on what Margaret Sutton has called the ABCs of girls' education: access to schooling, benefits of schooling, and constraints to full participation in schooling.[2] Both projects aim for educational equity rather than equality. If equality is the

Girls inside the school wall waiting for classes to begin.

same education, equity is the right education. This definition contrasts sharply with the state's deficit model of girls' education, in which achieving gender parity is problematized as an issue of poverty alleviation.

Each project helps us answer two questions critical to understanding the gendered project of Chinese schooling. What discourses of female education inform school policies and practices? How are these discourses shaped by top-down forces of state policies and agencies, bottom-up forces of communities and women's groups, external forces of international NGOs and donor agencies, and middle forces, bridging civil society and state, of domestic NGOs, particularly the All China Women's Federation (ACWF)?

Gender socialization and discrimination neither begin nor end at the school gate. Nelly Stromquist has characterized gender issues as "wicked problems," "complex, interrelated, and less amenable to technical or scientific solutions since they depend primarily on value preferences."[3] Formal education is but one of several institutions (and policy arenas) that make up the fluctuating, wicked environment that genders human beings. The family (marriage, property, and population policies), the economy (employment and market policies), and culture (values and preferences regarding appropriate roles and aspirations for sons and daughters, fathers and mothers) are sites of gender construction that influence a female's ability to receive and use formal education.

Reforms associated with market socialism have transformed these institutions, simultaneously enhancing women's opportunities and reconfiguring barriers to women's full participation in society.[4] During the Maoist years, "women" barely registered in public discourse, because the achievement of socialism and the achievement of male and female equality were thought to share the same trajectory. Of course, this assumption proved false. A persistent gender gap in school participation, earnings, and political representation favoring men in both revolutionary and reform periods challenges "the state-as-equalizer model just as it challenges the market-as-equalizer model."[5]

Since 1978, as the Communist Party and state approved the end of collective farming, allowed private ownership, implemented strict population control policies, broke the iron rice bowl of employment and urban social safety nets, and gradually opened China's market, media, and culture to global influence, "what counts as work, what counts as household, and what constitutes properly gendered behavior"[6] have been transformed. Women's expanding educational and occupational opportunities and liberating explorations of identity, femininity, and sexuality in high and popular culture have been accompanied by the feminization of agriculture, discrimination in the job market, disproportionately high layoffs of "surplus" women, and a skewed male/female birth ratio resulting in "missing" girls. In this contradictory context, schools are necessary but far from sufficient to secure for girls and women productive and equitable positions in their communities.[7]

A comprehensive international review of state policies on women between 1975 and 1998 indicated that the most important predictors of strong and effective state action on behalf of females were "(in addition to contact with transnational networks) the proportion of women in ministerial positions, the degree of democracy in the country, and the extent to which women had similar access to men for secondary education."[8] Given low levels of democracy in China and low numbers of Chinese women at top levels of government, progress in providing females access to formal education remains the state's primary means for making good on its commitment to equal opportunity. The truth about the ABCs of Chinese schooling is that girls and women have made greater strides there than in employment or in political participation.

The two case studies in this chapter illustrate how gender relations and discrimination are intimately tied to China's increasing integration into the global economy. Educational challenges facing girls and women are simultaneously national and international, and their exploration requires coming to terms with the "dialectic of the global and the local."[9] Recently, theorists have used this insight to create the neologism "glocalization," sometimes explained as globalization through localization. Policies that look like and often are responses to globalization are also "pursued within the context of managing state-building and economic growth in a state-directed (or government-directed) paradigm of governance."[10] In fact, how the moral authority of state policy is challenged by globalization is evident in Chinese discourses on girls' education. Anthropologist Kathryn Anderson-Levitt describes such processes as global models inhibiting and inhabiting local practices.[11] The "global" is not an autonomous space, but rather a "terminal point" for educational signs or targets such as the "girl child." Unattached from any specific context, these signs and targets circulate through the global educational community, ready for appropriation. Thomas Popkewitz has envisioned this process with the metaphor of "indigenous foreigners" (John Dewey, for example), who when locally appropriated "take on the characteristics of that context before they move on to other contexts and become the target of further interpretations and reinterpretations."[12] The girl child as mother of development has become one of the world's most recognized "indigenous foreigners."

China's Discourse of Developmentalism and the International Consensus on Girls' Education

In 1990, leaders from 180 countries convened a World Education for All (EFA) conference and set three strategic objectives: universalize primary education, eliminate illiteracy, and end educational inequality between men and women—by the end of the decade. China became a high-profile player in female education as one of the Summit of Nine, along with other most-populated countries with high illiteracy rates: Brazil, Bangladesh, India, Egypt, Indonesia, Mexico, Nigeria, and Pakistan. Girls and women accounted for two-thirds of the world's out-of-school children and adult illiterates, figures that closely matched the Chinese experience in 1990. Female education was declared the single most important investment a country could make in enhancing household income; improving family health and nutrition; reducing infant mortality; improving the skills and knowledge of agricultural workers (the majority of whom are women); democratizing decision making at household, community, and national levels; and alleviating poverty. In short, female education became the magic bullet of development.

Despite an almost fetishistic celebration of girls' education throughout the 1990s, EFA goals went unmet worldwide, as both the number of children in school and the number of children without access to school climbed.[13] Recognizing the failure of many nation-states to act decisively on behalf of basic schooling, new EFA targets were set in 2000. The United Nations reaffirmed EFA commitments by approving eight Millennium Development Goals to be achieved by 2015. Millennium Development Goal 3, gender parity in primary and secondary education, was considered crucial to the success of the other seven goals. Consequently, its target date for achievement was pushed up to 2005, and a flurry of international reports heralded the importance of girls' education to global development, sustainability, and well-being.[14]

By 1990, Chinese schools were grappling with the consequences of decentralization of school funding, which began just as compulsory schooling was expanded through junior secondary school. The collision of these two policies precipitated retrenchment of village schools and declining enrollment rates. Nevertheless, a decade later the number of girls with no access to primary school decreased in China from 1,712,900 to 554,200; the national percentage of school-age girls able to enter primary school increased from 96.31 percent to nearly 99.1 percent; and the percentage of primary school age girls attending five years of school increased from 82.2 percent in 1995 to over 94.5 percent.[15] In fact, female enrollment increased at every level of formal schooling. For the first time, the proportion of female students in colleges exceeded 40 percent (in contrast to 19.8 percent in 1949 and 24.1 in 1978), and girls have come to outnumber boys as first-year college students in Shanghai and Beijing.

Nevertheless, a recent report on China's EFA policies offers a sobering picture of low expenditures on education, inaccurate reporting of enrollment rates, failure to eliminate the financial obstacles to schooling faced by China's poorest children, and use of legal guarantees as "the end rather than merely a means for human rights protection."[16] I take the last criticism to mean that state policy must do more than merely signal the need to right pressing social wrongs. Declaring basic education for all girls and boys a target without setting a plan of action does not "unleash energies in the amount and form necessary" to achieve it.[17]

China currently ranks 99 out of 177 countries in terms of gross domestic product (GDP) per capita and educates nearly 25 percent of the world's students. Doing much with little, China has made steady progress in educating its children. However, three million girls are not completing five years of primary school, and 70 percent of dropouts are female.[18] China did not meet Millennium Development Goal 3 in the year 2005.

Chinese EFA policies hinge on two utilitarian narratives that define girls (and women) as "important mediators in the modernization process."[19] First, state policy rests on the premise that education provides the master key to poverty alleviation and to development. Second, China's embrace of the global consensus on girls' education has been constructed through the logic of developmentalism. Educated girls become valued as mothers of development and the means for reducing poverty, containing population growth, engendering public health, and strengthening the nation. In the discourse of developmentalism, girls are assumed to be both recipients and agents of development, not its victims. However, this version of agency is built on a narrowly utilitarian assessment of female lives, lives rarely considered as ends in themselves. Developmentalism thus reflects a "gender trap within the market solution" of neoliberal development policies.[20]

Two additional gender traps, the "naturalization of gender" and "strong China nationalism," constrain girls' education. The naturalization of gender is a central motif in China's postsocialist allegory.[21] The allegory reads that the Maoist state repressed natural distinctions between males and females through egalitarian discipline and labor. In the era of opening and reform, women reclaimed their sexuality and the family and men their virility and the state. Schools and the public now further the discourse of natural difference just as they previously furthered the discourse of egalitarian sacrifice and productive labor. In the post-Mao era, the naturalization of the gender paradigm for human relationships and abilities "holds out hope and excitement; it celebrates national strength and private pleasures; it appears to move beyond the regulatory politics of Maoist socialism; it seems to carve out a space separate from the state."[22] Accepting this paradigm, however, reinforces gender stereotyping in Chinese families, schools, and the workplace.[23]

Linking expanded opportunities for girls and women to the cause of strong China nationalism has provided a strategic cover of respectability for activists working on behalf of gender equality. Yet it also weakens the possibility for transnational alliances on women's rights. Many transnational feminist NGOs seek to moralize citizenship not in terms of specific cultures or nations but in terms of women's (and men's) common humanity. Any exclusion of Chinese women from the dialogue on women's rights as human rights means a loss to women around the world.

Arenas of Discourse and Action on Behalf of Girls' Education: The State, Transnational Alliances, and the Women's Movement

China's agenda for educating females is created in three arenas: the state's education bureaucracy, which sets school policy and funding paths; domestic and transnational NGOs, including women's studies groups, which use, accommodate, and resist state policies to provide education for females; and international aid and cooperation agencies that help the state and social organizations educate females. Although overlapping relations among these arenas are in flux, the state is paramount, mobilizing the nonstate sector in order to finance and regulate education.[24] The state also directly influences the key government-organized NGO representing Chinese women, the ACWF.

The Indispensable State

One of the common explanations for the rising disparities in education that impact negatively on China's most vulnerable populations is the decentralization of educational funding and provision begun in the 1980s.[25] Since 1978, the state's reorganization of education has been primarily to support economic policies associated with market socialism. As funding was gradually decentralized to lower levels of government, provincial and local governments were allowed to retain part or most of their revenues and decide how to spend them. Furthermore, taxation reform a decade ago codified legitimate authorities of taxation and helped stabilize incomes of central and subcentral levels of the government.[26] Educational policies promoting decentralization expanded to include (1) the reduction of the central state's regulation, provision, and subsidies of education service; (2) the devolution of responsibility and power to localities; (3) the diversification of resources, (i.e., the encouragement of multiple channels of funding, including cost recovery measures such as tuition); and (4) enhanced flexibility and autonomy in governance of education institutions.

That the state continues to play a strong guiding role in a decentralized educational market will surprise few readers who have followed the processes and conditions of decentralization worldwide. Decentralization defined as the redistribution of power and responsibility does not necessarily mean that states do less.[27] It does mean that their role as "education service providers" changes "from carrying out most of the work of education itself to determining where work will be done, by whom and how."[28] Indeed, the Chinese state's legitimacy increasingly depends on whether it successfully organizes the education system.

In general, the state has garnered public support for its ability to guide educational expectations and futures with a deft, pragmatic hand. However, stresses in the system and the public's faith in it are apparent, particularly around the issues of increasing costs of schooling at all levels; unequal educational opportunities for minority, rural, working-class, and migrant children; and scandals involving enrollment bribes, illegal school fees, and land grabs by private universities and local university complexes.

Comparative educators and glocalization theorists argue that "there exists much more political and even financial space for governments to condition the way globalization is brought into education than is usually admitted. . . . That states generally choose not to be responsive to more equitable versions of knowledge production is at least partly the result of ideological preference rather than helplessness in the face of new competitive pressures and new, globalized thinking."[29] China presents a case in point. Devolution of authority in the governance of education has increased educational flexibility. But it has also allowed the state to pass the buck on social justice issues.

The international literature on girls' education provides abundant evidence that many of the most important changes affecting gender relations have been generated not by the state but by women themselves, often in the form of actions and programs organized through NGOs at local levels before they became issues incorporated in national policies.[30] Ethnographic accounts of contemporary Chinese society detail how two decades of reform have eroded the state's monopoly on "framing the conditions of social existence."[31] One intriguing argument is that while the state's partial withdrawal from individual and community life worlds has precipitated a confusing, corruption-inviting lack of moral authority at the local level, paradoxically "widespread changes in Chinese society have formed a moral space at large, making possible a new grounding for social interaction and individual experience."[32] Extending anthropologist Xin Liu's argument about community life to schooling, the "lack of a moral economy in communal life in conjunction with the emergence of a moral space at large"[33] has provided a crucial condition for the development of China's educational NGOs.

The Middle Ground of NGOs

The rise of NGOs in China has produced a large body of divergent commentary regarding their ambiguous relation with the state.[34] When they first appeared in China in the 1980s, NGOs were seen as one more example of decentralization—a way to release the state from social welfare burdens. Some Chinese social scientists remain skeptical of the extent to which China has a civil society.[35] In contrast, others document the state's encouragement of NGOs because they serve areas the state cannot reach without unleashing potentially uncontrollable social forces. In his analysis of how China developed markets for educational institutions and various international development assistance organizations, David Zweig explains how resistant but opportunistic bureaucrats came to support transnational exchanges critical to civil societies in a global age.[36] Lisa Rofel has argued that when the Maoist state was rejected, policies of state feminism were also questioned.[37] The logical consequence was that supporters of women's rights looked elsewhere, spurring the development of the nonstate public sphere.[38]

There is now a tangible NGO and nonprofit foundation community in China, receiving well over $100 million each year in project funding directly from or channeled through 500 groups. With the exception of environmental NGOs, the most visible education-related NGOs, such as Project Hope and the Spring Bud Program, are involved in poverty reduction.[39] These NGOs and nonprofit social organizations reflect a diverse set of assumptions about the purposes of development, and many are aligned with state policies of global economic integration and strengthening.

While Chinese NGOs seem to retain as their guiding principle "Do not criticize government policy" and emphasize constructive and mutually dependent relations between society and state, their memberships are also asking questions about political purposes and consequences.[40] A decade ago, prominent activists in the women's movement favored keeping their eyes on China's structural inequalities and called the possibility of an effective grassroots women's movement "absurd."[41] This assessment has been refuted on the ground. In at least four ways, NGOs in China create supportive conditions for thinking and acting on behalf of girls and women. They facilitate women's right of association in a political culture where such a right had not been practiced for decades.[42] They increase women's consciousness of citizenship and community participation, and they nurture female leadership and significant learning about lobbying and mobilization. Finally, their actions widen the state's definition of acceptable *renquan*, which can mean basic human rights or grassroots people power.

In the two projects discussed in this chapter, NGO action takes place in a semiautonomous, middle ground for change that serves to mediate between international support, community advocacy, and state interests. The Ford Foundation project allows educational researchers to construct a middle ground by reaching down to teachers and principals, up to supportive policy makers and textbook publishers, and outward for international funding and collaboration with international scholars specializing in the gendering processes of school curricula. Community-based action flows in the Spring Bud program through a network of homeroom teachers and principals (who serve as parents' representatives), local and provincial SWF representatives, and members of an international NGO. SWF representatives have played a pivotal role in mediating potential conflicts among various government units, school officers, and the international NGO. This is no small task given the scope of the project—1,000 girls and their families; twenty-one village schools; county and city educational officers; county, city, provincial, and national women's federation representatives; and international NGO members. In championing the significance of the project while ensuring its accountability, the SWF has had to act like both a grassroots organization and a state agency. From a comparative perspective, the SWF's attempt to walk on two legs, one the state's and one civil society's, complicates the international finding that "there are very few cases of alliances between women's groups and the state education sector."[43]

Women's Activism and Women's Studies

Women's studies emerged contemporaneously with NGOs, likewise propelled by economic reforms of the post-Mao era.[44] Heightened inequalities between men and women as a result of market socialism coupled with more freedom in social life created space for critical reappraisal of party/state advocacy for women. Li Xiaojiang and Liang Jun summarize the beginning of the contemporary Chinese women's movement in three periods.[45] A "theoretical exploration" period between 1980 and 1985 brought professionals in the ACWF and in academe together to explore women's problems associated with economic and social transformation. In 1982 the name "women's studies" was introduced to conceptualize these activities. In 1983 the ACWF announced its "four-selfs" slogan. Twenty years later, a version of that slogan —"self-respect, self-support, self-confidence, and self-strengthening"— remains the dominant paradigm for female education.

In 1985, the Society of Women's Studies was founded, and the first women's studies symposium was convened in Zhengzhou. The same year Li Xiaojiang, often described as one of the mothers of Chinese women's studies, taught courses at the Henan Provincial Institute for Women Cadres. Her proposals for a women's studies curriculum were published and widely circulated. *Zhongguo funu,* the official women's magazine of China, ran a year-long dialogue about whether women should leave the workforce for home.

The years 1986 to 1988 witnessed the growth of popular women's magazines, the establishment of NGOs dedicated to female equality, the continued growth of women's studies at Chinese universities, and increased collaboration between the ACWF and scholars in those programs. As access to social services, including schooling, deteriorated in rural China, the ACWF became more proactive in seeking aid for women. However, the ACWF's identity as a government-organized NGO constrained its direction, funding, and purposes. Academics pursued a "post-Federation" women's studies agenda just as the ACWF established the Institute of Women's Studies.

From 1990 to 1993, the economic and social dislocations of market socialization experienced by women was headline news. In 1990 the State Council established the Women and Children Work Committee and passed the Law on the Protection of the Rights and Interests of Women. Faced with growing evidence that market socialism advantaged some women and disadvantaged others, the ACWF sponsored research on the social status of females that disaggregated the category of women and recognized the particular concerns of ethnic minority groups. Women's studies centers were founded in Zhengzhou and Peking Universities, and in 1993 an influential exchange conference, "Engendering China: Women, Culture, and the State" brought together Chinese and U.S. women's studies faculty at Harvard University, Wellesley College, and the Massachusetts Institute of Technology. The same year at a seminar in Tianjin, scholars introduced the concept of *shehui xingbie* (gender, or social sex) to articulate how males and females are socially constructed.

After the United Nation's Fourth World Conference on Women, held in Beijing in 1995, China's women's movement was no longer directed primarily by the state or the party but by diverse groups of women concerned with the "mutual promotion and encouragement of social development and women's progress."[46] A decade of "separatism," when Chinese scholars remained relatively isolated from the international women's movement and intentionally distant from state policy on women, had ended.

Scholarship on Chinese women's relations to the state since the 1980s has shifted from strong critique[47] to more positive interpretations of limited agency across region and political level[48] to analyses that contrast the state's proactive efforts on behalf of women from the 1950s to the 1970s with reversals during the reform decades.[49] Fifteen years ago, Marilyn Young described Chinese women as the vehicle through which the state deploys and constrains its population. As the previous analysis of the state, NGOs, and women's organizations has illustrated, new social spaces have emerged to expand transnational collaboration and women's social imaginations. What has not changed, apparently, are the paradoxical social messages directed at girls and women from families, schools, media, and the state. With the substitution of globalization for the four modernizations, Marilyn Young's summary of these messages applies nearly as well to 2004 as it did to 1989:

> Women should learn the arts of adornment, but refrain from their undue exercise; women should be filial toward parents and in-laws, but modern, independent, antifeudal; women should certainly follow dictates of state population policy and are of course the primary child-rearer, but they must learn, from professional experts, how to avoid spoiling the single child; women should fully participate in the drive to realize the four modernizations (in agriculture, industry, science and technology, and defense), but they might just want to take three, four, or even ten years maternity leave as well. Romantic love is an acceptable socialist notion, but women are responsible for controlling their own and male sexual behavior and sex itself should be indulged in only after marriage and strictly within its confines.[50]

The Shaanxi Spring Bud Project: Educational Reform Through Transnational Alliance[51]

Project Context and Purpose

Mapping the contours of girls' opportunities is an exercise in sorting through contradictions. The girls who participate in the Shaanxi Spring Bud program stand on the downside of what sociologist Sun Liping calls China's "cleavage" and what the *New York Times* calls China's "great divide." This divide is being reshaped by a "tidal wave" of migration of people from the countryside to the city.[52] Over 114 million people have left China's countryside, and that number may swell to 300 million in fifteen years. The difficulties rural communities face in accommodating the mammoth social, economic, and cultural dislocations associated with this shift have a direct and powerful impact on the abilities of those communities to provide schooling for their children.[53]

For the first time in two decades, rural incomes during the past year rose faster than urban incomes. Nevertheless, rural income is still one-third, child mortality is still double, and maternal death is still five to ten times higher than in coastal metropolitan areas. In 1985, the disposable income of urban citizens was on average 1.89 times higher than those of the rural population. By 2003, the disparity had reached 3.1. And while life expectancy continues to rise in China and over 95 percent of children have been immunized against the full range of infectious diseases, the World Health Organization ranks China's health care system as one of the worst in the world. Recent research indicates that over 40 percent of children in poor rural areas are stunted in their physical growth and that child malnutrition impairs children's opportunities to perform well at school. From 1986 to 2000, fifty million students (almost all rural) never entered junior high school, even though junior high school was by law compulsory for all Chinese students. In 2000, over 55 percent of urban students, compared with 20 percent of rural junior high school graduates, could enter high school.

China's rural development challenges have finally appeared on the policy maker's radar screen. Led by the economic aims of China's Western Development Strategy, rural-based EFA initiatives, survey research, and international assistance are guided by four developmentalist principles for poverty alleviation, including comprehensive planning, sustainability, targeting, and participation. The endorsement of participation appears to be drawn from a current orthodoxy in international development that participatory activities produce promising results in rural schooling. Advocacy for participatory development is contradicted, however, by the State Council's 2003 "Decision on Further Strengthening Rural Education." The document states that the fundamental aim of rural education is to promote urbanization, reflecting the same utilitarian developmentalism that characterizes girls' education.

The Chinese government's newest slogan for addressing rural poverty is "giving more while charging less." Working with the United Nations Children's Fund, the government has just begun to provide textbooks for students in rural families in twenty-two regions and provinces in western and central China. Such assistance cannot come too soon. According to state figures, eighty-five million people in China live on an annual income of U.S.$104. The Asian Development Bank calculates that 533 million Chinese citizens live on less than U.S.$2 a day. The cost for sending one child to a rural primary school, at least U.S.$24 a semester, does not include "hidden" school fees, a topic so controversial that few principals will speak openly about it. Even "all-in-one" payment systems used in many cities to ensure transparency of school costs fail to address this issue. It is too early to know whether new policies to help rural families afford schooling represent a breakthrough or a symbolic band-aid.

Intersecting gender discrimination with rural poverty provides a challenging context for achieving educational equity. Fifty million women have left the Chinese countryside to work in cities. Although this shift is often positively correlated with increased female wage-earning capacity, educational attainment, and status within the family, it also separates vulnerable young women from protections they traditionally receive from their natal families. Whereas 39 percent of China's paid workforce is female, 50 to 60 percent of those laid off during the past decade have been women. Attempts by the ACWF to help unemployed women find jobs as housekeepers and nannies place more women in unregulated working conditions.

Finally, women's (and men's) futures are profoundly influenced by China's skewed sex ratio, which averages above 120 males born for every 100 females. Some scholars are so alarmed by this destabilizing trend that they suggest it could "tip the scales toward war."[54] Concerns about the trafficking and kidnapping of females have penetrated to the villages of Shaanxi, where Spring Bud parents and leaders worry about the safety of girls walking to school. Dubbing China's "missing girls" phenomenon "gendercide" may sensationalize a profoundly complex social issue, but the Chinese government is taking the problem seriously enough to launch a "girl care" program and to begin paying rural parents U.S.$144 per year as a bonus for having one child, two girls, or a disabled child, when they reach sixty years of age.

No easy solutions for narrowing the divide between China's haves and have-nots will be found within the school. Nevertheless, education is the first place anxious leaders turn for an answer, and this Spring Bud story is primarily about the affirmative power of education to bridge divides.

The Spring Bud project was initiated in 2000 by the 1990 Institute, a U.S.-based NGO.[55] Described as the largest international NGO Spring Bud initiative, it is also considered one of the most successful and is promoted as a model by the SWF, the China-based partner for the project. The 1,000 girls participating in the project are Han Chinese and from impoverished and in most cases remote mountainous villages in the administrative regions of Shang Luo and Ankang cities.[56] Per capita income of the villages ranged from under

U.S.$100 to U.S.$125 in 2000. The girls' lives have been beset by material and social hardships, including devastation of land and home by flooding, the deaths of parents, and severe illness. Each of the 1,000 girls was out of school when selected by the SWF (using low household income to measure greatest need) to receive 1990 Institute funds to attend fourth grade in the autumn of 2001.

Taking Identity Work Seriously

> I was born into a poor farming family. I have several sisters, and parents aged and weakened by years of hard work. Three years ago we had a most unfortunate surprise. Father's liver had hardened to an advanced stage. This added substantially to the family's burden. Mother bravely hid her constant tears, but we knew things needed to change. Older sister quit school to earn money to help pay for Father's treatments. To lessen the financial strains on the family, I too left school to help out at home. The instant I stepped out of the schoolyard for what I thought was forever, tears streamed down my face.
>
> —a Spring Bud girl

The state's developmentalist approach to girls' education and to poverty alleviation implies that children spend their time in schools responding only to dominant lessons. The problem with this sort of modernization theory is that it imagines becoming modern as unidirectional, something that happens to individuals only from the outside. In contrast, the assumption that "educated persons" have agency[57] influences this analysis of how collective ideas about what is modern and what is "traditional," "local," "rural," or "cultural" emerge in how girls imagine themselves and their futures.

Multiple and sometimes contradictory processes of globalization dig deep into Spring Bud girls' identities and recognitions of social place and status. The transnational support they receive to go to school makes this inevitable. Images projected by the mass media and the "urbanization" of township life also teach girls lessons about the space they occupy in the status hierarchy of China. Girls who watch village friends go to school when they cannot experience the humiliation and sadness of rural inequalities (which are now larger than inequalities within urban areas).

Interviews with Spring Bud girls highlight the contradictory consequences of schooling for rural children and depict with utter clarity how much "economic reforms have introduced global space as a source for social imagination."[58] Schools get formulated in rural spaces "as a civilizing practice that implies and confers proximity to the modern."[59] Rural education operates through a discourse of lack, a discourse of compensatory education designed to take girls who hear themselves called low-quality (*suzhi di*),[60] backward (*luohou*), poor (*pinchong*), unenlightened (*yumei*), and ignorant (*wuzhi*) and make them modern. Rural girls are confronted with an ideal of success and of quality that is defined through market and modernity. If their parents were not driven by those discourses, then whose fault is it? Poverty becomes their parents' marker, their "culture." Just like that, poverty is explained away by culture, the state is absolved from its obligation to provide compulsory education, and the school is empowered to further the state's development program by making sure rural girls are remediated to live up to twenty-first-century standards of quality.

Just as modernization is used to dilute ethnicity in minority schools in China, it stakes out ignorance in rural schools. Most programs in China created to widen educational access for (usually rural, female, and minority) children of "poor and backward regions" are firmly rooted in progressive, nationalistic, and universalistic definitions of modernity that by design or default denigrate local cultural practices and knowledge.[61] They are run on the premise that schools can and should align local communities with urban/global forces and that this interface is a relatively unproblematic cultivation of human capital.

One of the most successful elements of this Spring Bud program is its careful attention to the selection of homeroom teachers (many of whom were raised in local communities) who recognize that modern schools produce both knowledge and ignorance. Teachers help girls evaluate and counter the exclusionary, urban-centric categories (of what is progressive and what is backward, for example) that are the inevitable outcome of market socialism. Put a different way, what anchors the moral politics of the Spring Bud program is taking identity work seriously as a way of empowering girls.

> It was a hot summer day three years ago, unusually hot. Suddenly dark clouds rolled in, thunder struck and lightning streaked. Rain poured, driven by strong winds. In an instant one could not distinguish where the sky ended and the earth began. Water was everywhere. In that engulfing darkness, our home swayed as if it were ready to crumble. At Father's command, we ran out to seek safe refuge. But then Father remembered that the ginger that Mother and I had crisscrossed mountains and valleys for so many days to dig up was still in the house. That ginger was to pay for the fees of my next school term. The moment Father went back into the house, it collapsed. The rain gush washed away our home. It carried Father away.
>
> —a Spring Bud girl

Spring Bud students commonly introduce their school experiences with stories about the precariousness of life. In contrast to interviews with students attending privileged schools, which are characterized by entitlement and optimism as well as weariness at the pressures of schooling, Spring Bud girls are painfully earnest, yearning for recognition, articulate about the costs of market socialism (particularly to their mothers), and truly grateful they attend a school that actually cares about them. They are also aware of the opportunity costs of schooling, which they describe as adding to the intense demands rural life makes on their parents. School fees mean sacrificing family welfare and parental health. They (and their parents) perceive "success in school" as an overwhelmingly positive yet contradictory resource, one that will produce skills, desires, and associations that will both complicate and enhance their future identities, family relationships, and career opportunities. International scholarship on girls' education indicates that parents "calculate" both the costs and the benefits of their daughters' schooling from their own points of view rather than from the point of view of their daughters.[62] One of the findings from the Spring Bud program is that fathers and mothers perceive their daughters' schooling as a sound investment for the family's future.

Local officials in Shangluo and Ankang, and now parents of girls in the Spring Bud project, have a favorite saying: "*zhi yu mian qiong*" (to alleviate illiteracy in order to be free from poverty)—reaffirming the state's narrative that education is the key to alleviating poverty. In fact, education and poverty are interrelated in much more complex and compounding ways. Gender, economic, and cultural factors all influence household educational decisions.

Research on rural schooling in China indicates that parents want education for both boys and girls, but they believe it is more useful for boys, who will later support families and elderly parents.[63] Some studies conclude that the son preference persists in the face of sweeping economic and social change and that urbanization, female education, and employment only slowly change incentives for sending girls to school.[64] Still other researchers agree that patriarchy (son preference, for example) still matters but that it is being more quickly weakened by economic development.[65]

Interviews with Spring Bud parents suggest that "traditional" attitudes (such as son preference) no longer erect severe barriers to girls' education, and placing too much weight on "culture" obscures equally or more important material obstacles with which girls and their families contend. Parents hold relatively egalitarian attitudes toward their daughters and sons, although their educational and employment aspirations for sons are higher. However, participation over three years in the Spring Bud project has raised parents' expectations for their daughters—and raised the aspirations of girls well beyond what their families would be able to support without 1990 Institute funding. Finally, the Spring Bud project has created a local ethos of the importance of girls' education in their villages, prompting local leaders to seek more out-side funding to help out-of-school children "return to the school gate."

> [We] girls established a "Love Bank" to further the spirit of the 1990 Institute. We pool together what we can save of our pocket money and make loans to those among us who need it most. . . . Unfortunately, all around us, there are still many students who cannot afford schooling. I have thought about this a great deal, and have made a vow. When I grow up I will work very hard and help those who have lost the opportunity to learn because of their poverty, so that like us they will swim carefree in the ocean of knowledge. My friends, let us shoulder-to-shoulder and hand-in-hand build a "Great Wall of Love," and spread the spirit of the 1990 Institute.
>
> —a Spring Bud girl

The national Spring Bud logo is inscribed with a diagonal line representing the power of hands, symbolic of social mobilization. While helping hands from afar are not always welcomed in a postcolonial world, one of the transformational consequences of the Spring Bud project is the extensive network of social capital it has extended to participating girls and their families. Girls (and their teachers) are seen and see themselves as part of a larger enterprise of training China's future female leaders. In this sense, the influence of schooling on girls' lives lies in what schooling signifies locally, not just in its literal content.

> I knew that this special opportunity was a rare gift. . . . Whenever I regressed I seemed to hear the American grandaunt and aunties saying, "Child, don't slack off, go back to work!" Every time I earn less than perfect marks I see the American grandaunt and aunties appear before me, looking at me with gentle but firm eyes. . . . Rest assured that with your help, under the guidance of my teachers, I will study hard, make progress, and grow up to be a valuable member of our society. Finally I would like to say, "Love and family can be found all over this country; love and family can be found all over the world."
>
> —a Spring Bud girl

How the Spring Bud girls frame themselves as passionately hard-working, honor-bound students recalls MaryJo Benton Lee's interviews with minority students in Southwest China.[66] Successful minority students feel compelled to work hard to succeed in school out of obligation to and gratitude for the sacrifices of parents and hometown supporters. With the currency of their college degrees, students then confer honor and service on family, village, and ethnicity. A cycle of high expectations, success, obligation, achievement, and empowerment creates social capital. "Teachers, neighbors and parents of successful minority students expect them to go on to college—and tell them so repeatedly. Finally, those minority students, who are repeatedly defined as achievers by significant others, begin to see themselves the same way and to share these same expectations."[67]

The Spring Bud program entered Phase 2 in the autumn of 2004 when all 1,000 of the girls participating in the project received funding raised by the 1990 Institute to attend junior high school,[68] perceived as a critical stage in Chinese schooling that "serves as the bridge to higher learning and the alleviation of intergenerational poverty."[69] Phase 2 will provide a timely opportunity for assessing the impact of schooling on girls' aspirations, life chances, and family well-being in the context of a growing but contradictory set of findings from girls' educational access projects in different regions of China.

Gender in the School Curriculum: Educational Reform Through Women's Studies[70]

Project Context and Purpose

A recent review of girls' schooling worldwide identified two research areas in urgent need of investigation: "the context in which girls live and learn, and the experiences of girls within the schools."[71] Without rigorous, microlevel studies that include girls' responses to curricula and improvement in girls' enrollment and attainment, rates are not good enough measures to ensure educational equity for girls' schools.[72] The Ford Foundation project "Analytical Gender Study of Teaching Materials in China's Kindergartens, Elementary Schools, Secondary Schools, and Adult Literacy Courses" was premised on these conclusions.

The project team, consisting of twenty researchers from Chinese research institutes, universities, and publishing houses, employed diverse methodologies, including analyses of textbook content, observations of classroom interaction, and interviews with students and teachers about girls' gender socialization through the formal school curriculum.[73] The conceptualization of curriculum was limited to formal education but defined broadly enough to include not only the intended curriculum (textbook content) but also how textbook content interacts with the school's informal or hidden curriculum of gendered messages and construction. The project also attended to the enacted curriculum—teachers and students doing something with textbook content. The project touched minimally on the received curriculum—the values and knowledge students take away from their classroom experiences.

Three primary objectives guided the study. First, its designers hoped the project would heighten awareness of gender issues among educational workers who would then make gender equity a key criterion for assessing teaching materials and practices. Second, the designers wanted to provide state officers concrete recommendations for implementing guidelines that were already inscribed in state policy. China's "Program for the Development of Chinese Women (2001–2010)," for example, explicitly states that, "The primary objectives of women's education shall be incorporated in the state's plan for education," and "social gender awareness shall be incorporated into training courses for teachers during the reform of courses, educational content, and teaching methods." Finally, project designers hoped to build a research and teaching community of precollegiate and college educators dedicated to gender-responsive schooling.

The Gendered Lessons of Schooling

The case-based studies associated with the project illustrated that teaching materials for preschool, elementary, and secondary school pupils present a distinct imbalance in the proportion of male to female characters and references. Females appear in very young children's reading materials, whose content consists primarily of scenes from family life. Male appearances in young children's books outnumber female appearances only when activities described involve "acquiring knowledge," "learning to calculate," and misbehaving children.

As the social settings in teaching materials widen beyond the family, the proportion of male appearances in texts increases from 48 percent to 61 percent; 20.4 percent of characters in elementary school language teaching materials are female, and this number decreases with each passing grade. The number of females and males in social studies teaching materials is approximately equal, but only 5 percent of characters who are named or central to a storyline are female. In a reformed mathematics textbook, not only do males appear more frequently than females in the texts (males 1,023 times, females 542 times), but males also appear in privileged settings and occupational roles that by contrast implicitly derogate female mathematical abilities.

Analyses of the content of social studies texts indicate that messages regarding the gendered division of labor and role patterns are most clearly manifested in young children's reading materials. One hundred percent of scientists, workers, peasants, and soldiers are males, whereas 100 percent of teachers and 75 percent of service personnel are female. Even prominent female leaders who have shaped the course of Chinese history are depicted in domestic or supportive roles, mending clothes instead of making policy. Elementary-school pupils could easily describe male characters from their lessons, whether they were leaders and heroes or "little people"—the ticket seller who liked to study, the sentry who stuck to regulations. In contrast, neither boys nor girls could recall female characters.

Classroom interaction mirrored gendered roles. For example:

> A female kindergartener, Wang Zhan, is playing at being a mother. She pretends that a chair is a car and runs around the classroom driving it. A female classmate, Dong Xiaofei, complains to the teacher that Wang Zhan does not act like a mother and has made a mess of the home.
>
> Teacher: What should mothers do?
>
> Dong: Mothers don't run around, driving cars.
>
> Teacher: Right, mothers should cook dinner. They should tidy up the rooms, sweep the floor, and tell stories to their children. Look how untidy your house is! Nobody comes anymore. Stop driving and running around!
>
> Wang Zhan lowers her head and begins to tidy up the room as the teacher has requested.

In primary school mathematics classes, researchers noted that interaction between teachers and boys was direct, casual, continuous, and extended. Teachers spoke with girls, on the other hand, gently, mildly, and from a cautious distance. The striking disparity between teachers' "polite, avoidance-based" interaction with girls and "natural, focused" interaction with boys worked its way into students' interrelationships. In one classroom session, girls and boys were paired against each other in a mathematics contest. The boys dominated the game, interrupting girls when they tried to speak. The teacher's questions were simple, and both boys and girls knew the answers. After class the researchers asked the girls to explain what happened.

> Researcher: Did you all have replies when the teacher asked you the questions?
>
> Girl 1: Yes, we did.
>
> Researcher: Then did you speak up?
>
> Girl 1: The boys spoke up faster than we did. They were absolutely faster than we were.
>
> Girl 2: They are more eager to win.
>
> Girl 1: Right, we feel that all that's necessary is to know the answer. We all like to know things. But they are so eager to win. They always want to come out on top. They insist on being better than us girls in all things.

The girls accepted their "loss" with considerable equanimity. Girls do not "lose face" when they lose out to boys, but they do lose face and risk ridicule if they give a wrong answer.

> Girl 1: [If a girl gives a wrong answer] the teacher certainly will not criticize you. But those boys are such a pain. For example, if there is a question you cannot answer, the teacher will at most ask another student to help you by adding or correcting things. But those boys will say, "Look! You have lost face

for the girls again!" That makes me feel very bad, and the next time I won't dare to speak up again. I will think, "This has nothing to do with me anyhow." But if I do answer and make a mistake, those boys will pick on me, and the bit of confidence I have managed to build up will disappear. And if the boys pick on me a second time, I will never speak up again.

Girl 2: Being picked on and looked down on by the boys makes us feel especially bad.

The Ford Foundation project reflects an attempt to distinguish between a nonsexist curriculum (free of stereotypes and distortions) and an antisexist curriculum (one that actively attempts to dismantle stereotypes and construct a new way to perceive and establish social relations between men and women). One way in which this effort might have lasting impact is by influencing ongoing efforts to reform China's basic education curriculum. Lead editors of educational publishing houses joined project participants in 2001 for a review of the project's findings. These were met with great interest as well as skepticism. Skeptics wondered whether the public desired the kind of gender transformation called for by presenters. Wasn't gender equity of the sort being advocated working against the grain of the way most parents wanted their children socialized? Whether project participants can be persuasive in the face of such questions remains an important question and medium-term goal of the project. A small but influential network of Chinese girls' school principals and teachers has taken note of the Ford project's findings and has launched evaluations of the "gender culture" of their own curricula.[74]

Conclusion: Developmentalism vs. People-Centered Development

The real question for girls in China today is not whether to attend school but rather to attend for what purpose, on whose terms, and at what cost. Both projects described above engaged participants constantly in such questions and in doing so offered students, teachers, and local leaders significant opportunities to reflect on and debate the gendered nature of schooling and expectations and aspirations for girls.

In contrast to these programs, the state has measured progress on female education almost solely by school access and participation ratios. In 1999 I was assured by a policy maker that educators in many regions of China had "no need to worry about gender issues," as gender gaps in enrollment and attainment had disappeared. Bolstered by the global consensus on girls' education, the discourse of developmentalism will be difficult to dislodge.

Nevertheless, China's "reform and opening" era has been characterized as a struggle to balance the needs of two civilizations, one spiritual and one material. Education has been conceptualized as part of spiritual civilization, an underpinning of a new social ethos that could ameliorate the negative social consequences of the strong nation, getting-rich-is-glorious forces of market socialism. Much has been made recently in the Chinese and international press of the pains President Hu Jintao has taken to represent the Chinese government as more caring. Progress is to be measured not in terms of growth but in terms of "people-centered development" (*yi ren wei ben*).

A significant lesson from global educational initiatives is that to succeed, "an educational agenda must be accompanied by a political agenda."[75] Now might be the time for supporters of equity in Chinese schooling to appropriate the state's discourse on people-centered development and engage in a thorough evaluation of the consequences of developmentalism for China's future.

Notes

1. Neil Postman, *The End of Education* (New York: Vintage Press, 1996), pp. ix–x.

2. Margaret Sutton, "Girls' Educational Access and Attainment," in *Women in the Third World: An Encyclopedia of Contemporary Issues,* ed. Nelly P. Stromquist (New York: Garland Publishing, 1998), pp. 381–396.

3. Nelly P. Stromquist, "The Intersection of Public Policies and Gender: Understanding State Action in Education," paper presented at the Comparative and International Education Society annual conference, Salt Lake City, Utah, March 2004, p. 5.

4. Lisa Movius, "Cultural Devolution," *The New Republic,* vol. 1 (2004), pp. 116–121; Grace C.L. Mak, ed., *Women, Education and Development in Asia* (New York: Garland Publishing, 1996).

5. Yanjie Bian, John R. Logan, and Xiaoling Shu, "Wage and Job Inequalities in the Working Lives of Men and Women in Tianjin," in *Re-drawing Boundaries, Work, Households, and Gender in China,* ed. B. Entwisle and G. Henderson (Berkeley: University of California Press, 2000), pp. 111–133.

6. Barbara Entwistle and Gail Henderson, "Introduction," in *Re-drawing Boundaries: Work, Households, and Gender in China,* ed. B. Entwisle and G. Henderson (Berkeley: University of California Press, 2000), p. 11.

7. Nelly P. Stromquist, "Women's Education in the Twenty-First Century: Balance and Prospects," in *Comparative Education* (2nd ed.), ed. Robert F. Arnove and Carlos Alberto Torres (Lanham, MD: Rowman and Littlefield, 2003), pp. 176–203.

8. Stromquist, "Women's Education," p. 196.

9. Robert F. Arnove and Carlos Alberto Torres, eds., *Comparative Education* (2nd ed.) (Lanham, MD: Rowman and Littlefield, 2003).

10. Ka-Ho Mok, ed., *Centralization and Decentralization: Educational Reforms and Changing Governance in Chinese Societies* (Hong Kong: Comparative Education Research Centre, University of Hong Kong, and Kluwer Academic Publishers, 2003), p. 213.

11. Kathryn Anderson-Levitt, "Reading Lessons in Guinea, France and the U.S." *Comparative Education Review,* vol. 48, no. 2 (2004), pp. 229–253.

12. Kenneth Hultqvist and Gunilla Dahlberg, eds., *Governing the Child in the New Millennium* (New York: Routledge Falmer, 2001), p. 11.

13. Harvey Goldstein, "Education for All: The Globalization of Learning Targets," *Comparative Education*, vol. 40, no. 1 (2004).

14. UNESCO, *Gender and Education for All, The Leap to Equality, EFA Global Monitoring Report 2003–2004* (Paris: UNESCO Publishing, 2003); World Bank Gender and Development Group, *Gender Equality and the Millennium Development Goals.* (Washington, DC: World Bank, 2003); UNICEF, *The State of the World's Children Report, 2004, Girls' Education and Development* (New York: UNICEF, 2003).

15. Ministry of Education, *2002 nian jiao yu tong ji bao gao* (2002 Statistical Report on Education) (Beijing, 2003) (www.moe.edu.cn/stat/tjgongbao/).

16. Katarina Tomasevski, *United Nations Report on Economic, Social, and Cultural Rights: The Right to Education* (New York: United Nations, 2003) (www.unhchr.ch/Huridocda/Huridoca.nsf/e06a5300f90fa0238025668700518ca4/d2a0154274b5f3f3c1256dff002ff8f4/$FILE/G0317038.pdf).

17. Stromquist, "The Intersection of Public Policies and Gender," p. 7.

18. These are estimates for out-of-school girls. See Ministry of Education, *Statistical Report of National Education Development Affairs* (Beijing: Ministry of Education, 2004) (www.moe.edu.cn/edoas/website18/inf05103.htm).

19. Stromquist, "Women's Education in the Twenty-First Century," p. 177.

20. Marilyn Young, "Chicken Little in China: Women After the Cultural Revolution," in *Promissory Notes: Women in the Transition to Socialism,* ed. Sonia Kruks, Rayna Rapp, and Marilyn B. Young (New York: Monthly Review Press, 1989), pp. 233–247.

21. Lisa Rofel, "Museum as Women's Space: Displays of Gender in Post-Mao China," in *Spaces of Their Own: Women's Public Sphere in Transnational China,* ed. Mayfair Mei-Hui Yang (Minneapolis and London: University of Minnesota Press, 1999), pp. 116–131.

22. Lisa Rofel, *Other Modernities: Gendered Yearnings in China After Socialism* (Berkeley: University of California Press, 1998), p. 255.

23. See Heidi Ross and Jing Lin (guest eds.), "Educating Girls in a Different Way: Teaching and Learning in Chinese Girls' School," *Chinese Education and Society,* vol. 34, no. 1 (2001).

24. Mok, *Centralization and Decentralization,* p. 208.

25. Ibid., p. 210; Lin Jing and H. Ross, "The Potentials and Problems of Diversity in Chinese Education," *McGill Journal of Education,* vol. 33, no. 1 (1998), pp. 31–49.

26. Kai-ming Cheng, "Reforms in the Administration and Financing of Higher Education," in *Higher Education in Post-Mao China,* ed. Michael Agelasto and Robert Adamson (Hong Kong: Hong Kong University Press, 1998), pp. 11–28.

27. Mok, *Centralization and Decentralization*; Mark Bray, "Control of Education: Issues and Tensions in Centralization and Decentralization," in *Comparative Education,* ed. Arnove and Torres, pp. 204–228.

28. Mok, *Centralization and Decentralization,* p. 213.

29. Martin Carnoy, *Globalization and Educational Reform* (Paris: UNESCO, 1999), p. 83.

30. Regina Cortina and Nelly P. Stromquist, eds., *Distant Alliances: Promoting Education for Girls and Women in Latin America* (New York: Falmer, 2000).

31. Erik Mueggler, *The Age of Wild Ghosts, Memory, Violence, and Place in Southwest China* (Berkeley: University of California Press, 2001), pp. 4–5.

32. Liu Xin, *In One's Own Shadow: An Ethnographic Account of the Condition of Post-Reform Rural China* (Berkeley: University of California Press, 2000), p. 182.

33. Liu Xin, *In One's Own Shadow*, p. 183.

34. NGOs are variously referred to as "people's organizations" (*minjian zuzhi*), "nongovernmental organizations" (*feizhengfu zuzhi*), or "social organizations" (*shehui tuanti*). Additionally, the term "private nonprofit organization" (*minban fei qiye zuzhi*), or *minfei,* provides an even more expansive definition. Another type of organization characteristic of China is the "quasi-governmental NGO" or "government-organized nongovernmental organization," commonly known as the "GONGO" (*banguanfang zuzhi*). The ACWF is an example. It is said that 80 to 90 percent of Chinese NGO funding comes from international sources.

35. See Yunxiang Yan, *Private Life Under Socialism* (Stanford, CA: Stanford University Press, 2003).

36. David Zweig, *Internationalizing China: Domestic Interests and Global Linkages* (Ithaca, NY: Cornell University Press, 2002).

37. Rofel, "Museum as Women's Space."

38. Quisha Ma, "The Governance of NGOs in China Since 1978: How Much Autonomy?" *Nonprofit and Voluntary Sector Quarterly,* vol. 31, no. 3 (2002), pp. 305–328.

39. James Yardley, "The New Uprooted," *New York Times,* September 12, 2004, Section 4, p. 6.

40. See *China Development Brief,* no. 5 (2002–2003), p. 3.

41. Yiyun Chen, "Out of the Traditional Halls of Academe: Exploring New Avenues for Research on Women," in *Engendering China: Women, Culture, and the State,* ed. Christina Gilmarten et al. (Cambridge, MA: Harvard University Press, 1994), pp. 69–79.

42. Ma, "The Governance of NGOs in China Since 1978."

43. Cortina and Stromquist, *Distant Alliances*, p. 82.

44. Dongchao Min, "The Development of Women's Studies: From the 1980's to the Present," in *Women of China: Economic and Social Transformation,* ed. Jackie West et al. (New York: St. Martin's Press, 1999).

45. Li Xiaojiang and Liang Jun, "Women in China," in *Women in the Third World: An Encyclopedia of Contemporary Issues,* ed. Stromquist, pp. 593–600.

46. Li Xiaojiang and Liang Jun, "Women in China," p. 596.

47. Judith Stacey, *Patriarchy and Socialist Revolution in China* (Berkeley: University of California Press, 1983); Margery Wolf, *Revolution Postponed* (Stanford, CA: Stanford University Press, 1985).

48. Neil Diamant, *Revolutionizing the Family* (Berkeley: University of California Press, 2000).

49. Deborah Davis and Stevan Harrell, eds., *Chinese Families in the Post-Mao Era* (Berkeley: University of California Press, 1993).

50. Young, "Chicken Little in China," p. 244.

51. China has two national EFA-related projects. The first program, Project Hope, was launched in 1989 by the Chinese Communist Youth League to solicit donations for primarily rural children too poor to attend school. By its tenth anniversary, Project Hope had helped over two million poor students return to school. The Spring Bud Plan, sponsored by the China Children and Teenagers' Fund (CCTF), was established in 1981 as the nation's first national-level welfare fund organized through a nonprofit organization. In 1992 CCTF formally established the Spring Bud Plan under the guidance of the ACWF to assist impoverished girls in returning to school. By the end of

2003, U.S.$65 million had been raised and 1.35 million dropout girls had been sponsored to go back to school.

52. Yardley, "The New Uprooted," p. 6.

53. See Gregory E. Guldin, *What's a Peasant to Do? Village Becoming Town in Southern China* (Boulder, CO: Westview Press, 2001); Perry Link et al., eds., *Popular China: Unofficial Culture in a Globalizing Society* (Lanham, MD: Rowman and Littlefield, 2001).

54. See Valerie M. Hudson and Andrea M. den Boer, *Bare Branches: The Security Implications of Asia's Surplus Male Population* (Cambridge, MA: MIT Press, 2004); Felicia A. Lee, "Engineering More Sons than Daughters," *New York Times,* July 3, 2004, p. A17.

55. Building on school achievement data, teacher assessments, and student essays and interviews collected during the first three years of the Spring Bud program, I am beginning a three-year longitudinal study to understand whether, how, and in what ways participating in the project improves girls' lives and futures (and by extension the lives and futures of their family members and communities).

56. Shangluo is a city with 2.4 million residents spread across seven counties and 2,800 villages. Each county supports an average of seven high schools and twenty-eight junior middle schools. About 30 percent of Shangluo's ninth-grade graduates can enter high school, which is 10 percent less than the provincial average. An Kang is home to 1,000 of the 25,000 primary school girls out of school in Shaanxi Province.

57. See Bradley Levinson, Douglas E. Foley, and Dorothy C. Holland, eds., *The Cultural Production of the Educated Person* (Albany: State University of New York Press, 1996).

58. Aihwa Ong and Donald M. Nonini, eds., *Ungrounded Empires: The Cultural Politics of Modern Chinese Transnationalism* (New York: Routledge, 1997), p. 102.

59. Lyn Jeffery, "Placing Practices," in *China Urban: Ethnographies of Contemporary Culture,* ed. Nancy N. Chen et al. (Durham, NC: Duke University Press 2001), pp. 23–42, quote on p. 25.

60. Who has the right to define quality is a contentious issue. See Rachel Murphy, "Turning Peasants into Modern Chinese Citizens: 'Population Quality' Discourse, Demographic Transition and Primary Education," *The China Quarterly,* no. 177 (2004), pp. 1–20.

61. See, for example, Mette Halskov Hansen, *Lessons in Being Chinese* (Seattle: University of Washington Press, 1999).

62. C. Colclough, "Education and the Market: Which Parts of the Neo-liberal Solution are Correct?" *World Development,* vol. 24, no. 4 (1996), pp. 589–610.

63. Emily Hannum, "Poverty and Basic Education in Rural China: An Analysis of Community and Household Influences on Girls and Boys Enrollment," *Comparative Education Review,* vol. 47, no. 2 (2003), pp. 141–159.

64. See Danke Li and Mun C. Tsang, "Household Decisions and Gender Inequality in Education in Rural China," *China: An International Journal,* vol. 1, no. 2 (2003), pp. 224–248.

65. See Ethan Michelson and William L. Parish, "Gender Differentials in Economic Success: Rural China in 1991," in *Re-drawing Boundaries,* ed. B. Entwisle and G. Henderson, pp. 134–156.

66. MaryJo Benton Lee, *Ethnicity, Education and Empowerment: How Minority Students in Southwest China Construct Identities* (Aldershot: Ashgate Publishing, 2001).

67. Lee, *Ethnicity, Education and Empowerment,* p. 19.

68. Since 2000, only ten girls have dropped out of the project. With the exception of one "over age" student, these girls moved away from the project area with one or both parents seeking work. Two hundred of the girls are attending key junior high schools. The 1990 Institute's thirteen-year project is committed to funding all qualified girls through college.

69. Cortina and Stromquist, *Distant Alliances,* p. 191.

70. See Jinghuan Shi and Heidi Ross (guest eds.), "Entering the Gendered World of Teaching Materials, Part I," *Chinese Education and Society,* no. 35 (2002) p. 5.

71. Sutton, "Girls' Educational Access and Attainment," p. 395.

72. Mak, ed., *Women, Education and Development in Asia.*

73. Gender socialization is defined here as the process by which girls take up gender-specific values, norms, expectations, beliefs, and behaviors in a society and form their attitudes and expectations toward their multidimensional roles in that society.

74. See China Contemporary Girls Research Network: www.cgedu.net.

75. Stromquist, *Comparative Education,* pp. 196–197.

Part II

Rural Northwest

3

Poverty, Health, and Schooling in Rural China

Shengchao Yu and Emily Hannum

As is widely recognized, China's transition to a market economy since the early 1980s has brought remarkable growth in per capita income and reductions in poverty. Despite these favorable developments, many of China's youth who live in poor rural areas continue to experience problems associated with poverty; basic health concerns and barriers to education persist.[1] Regarding health, for example, whereas child malnutrition declined in rural areas in the late 1980s and early 1990s, physical stunting remains common in some poor rural areas.[2] Regarding education, although overall levels of access are rising, significant shortcomings exist in poor rural areas. For example, among the 201 million illiterate people in 1997, 90 percent lived in rural areas and 50 percent lived in eight western provinces with a population of only 10 percent of the country's total.[3] Discontinuation and dropout rates of students in rural areas have been high, and although basic-level enrollments continued to rise through the 1990s, official statistics suggest that the discontinuation rate of middle school students in rural areas has increased slightly.[4]

Further, some of the reforms that have emerged in the health and education sectors in recent years have heightened concerns about access for China's poorest children. In the health sector, the dismantling of the rural cooperative medical system, together with fiscal decentralization and the privatization of costs, has diminished the role of the state in the provision of health care and increased the reliance on individuals' out-of-pocket spending.[5] As a result, many poor rural people are increasingly excluded from the pay-for-service medical system.[6] Access to health insurance among children and youth remained extremely limited through the 1990s.[7] At the same time, parallel changes in education—fiscal decentralization and privatization of costs— have mobilized new resources to support schooling, but have increased the financial burden on poor families and families in poor regions.

A teacher gathers students together for singing within the walled schoolyard of a rural school in Yuzhong County, Gansu

Although there is general recognition that rural children in China are particularly vulnerable to poverty, ill health, and educational barriers, research has generally not explored linkages between these three issues. Conceptually, these linkages are important: Poor families may have a hard time affording health care, making their children particularly vulnerable to poor health. Limited access to, or high costs associated with, health care can mean that ill health pushes families further into poverty, making them unable to pay for their children's schooling. There could also be a direct effect of ill health on children's ability to perform in school, and thus their educational attainment.[8] Poor educational attainments, in turn, can lead to further poverty and ill health, whether through setting the stage for a disadvantaged position in a labor market that increasingly rewards credentials or by limiting access to knowledge about health care.

In this chapter, we examine evidence about the linkages between poverty, health, and educational outcomes in rural China. Our discussion highlights two points. First, poor health coincides with poverty: children in poor households tend to be children afflicted with health problems. Second, evidence suggests that poor health could have an important influence on schooling in and of itself. In the examples we present here, where multivariate analyses are possible, indicators of health predict schooling outcomes net of conventional measures of socioeconomic background.

We focus on three aspects of health: child malnutrition, parental health, and psychosocial health. For each topic, we discuss available evidence regarding links to poverty and educational outcomes. We then discuss additional health issues that may be particularly significant for education but for which empirical data from China are not available, namely, nutritional deficits associated with micronutrient deficiencies and helminthic (parasitic) infections, myopia, and communicable diseases. We close with a discussion of the implications of findings about the relations between poverty, health, and children's schooling.

Child Malnutrition

We begin with a discussion of malnutrition and consider two approaches to research on nutrition: anthropometrics and food security/food environment. For each approach, we discuss the link between poor nutrition and poverty in China. Then, considering evidence from China and, where relevant, from other settings, we discuss the linkage between nutrition and school outcomes.

Anthropometrics

Anthropometrics, or height and weight measures, are among the most commonly used measures of long-term malnutrition. In China, anthropometrics show an important association with poverty and levels of economic development. For example, Jamison found that about 35 percent of schoolchildren in rural Gansu, a poor western province, were stunted, whereas less than 1 percent of children in urban Beijing were stunted.[9] Because poorly nourished children are more likely to drop out of school, Jamison also suggests that the differences in stunting that emerge in his sample of enrolled schoolchildren might well underestimate the real disparities in malnutrition among all children, including nonenrolled children.

Jamison's work used data from 1979, but more recent analysis of the nutritional status of children using 1989 and 1993 data from the China Health and Nutrition Survey (CHNS) paints a consistent picture of nutritional disparities associated with geography and also with household socioeconomic status.[10] For example, among children ages seven to twelve in 1993, children's height-for-age and weight-for-age[11] varied significantly by household per capita income and by residence location: children living in poorer families (bottom quintiles of per capita income) were generally lighter and shorter than those living in richer families (top quintiles of the per capita income), and children living in urban areas were better nourished than those living in rural areas (Table 3.1). Table 3.1 also suggests that weight-for-age varied

Table 3.1

Nutritional Status by Household Income and Residence

	Percentage of the median value of NCHS standards*	
	Height-for-age	Weight-for-age
Per capita income		
First quintile (lowest)	92.31	82.42
	(5.79)	(16.59)
Second quintile	92.20	82.70
	(6.04)	(17.47)
Third quintile	93.91	86.02
	(5.84)	(23.94)
Fourth quintile	95.46	87.70
	(5.52)	(19.66)
Fifth quintile (highest)	94.92	90.22
	(8.26)	(19.46)
F value	34.38	24.70
Prob>F	0.00	0.00
Residence		
Rural	92.93	83.35
	(6.23)	(17.14)
Urban	96.24	93.31
	(6.52)	(25.22)
F value	50.04	55.05
Prob > F	0.00	0.00

Source: 1989 and 1993 CHNS data. See note 10 for details.

Note: Standard deviations shown in parentheses. NCHS = National Center for Health Statistics.

*These values are expressed as a percentage of the median value for a large sample of U.S. children surveyed, to establish standards, by the U.S. NCHS.

with household per capita income more consistently than height-for-age. The rural-urban divide was also particularly wide for weight-for-age, with urban students ages seven to twelve about 10 percent closer to the median value of the U.S. National Center for Health Statistics (NCHS)[12] standard than their rural counterparts.

Other studies have similarly found evidence of dramatic regional variation in nutritional indicators, with physical stunting remaining a significant problem among some poor rural areas.[13] By some estimates, the rate of severe malnutrition of children in poor rural areas is about three times that in urban areas.[14]

In short, malnutrition is clearly linked to poverty in China, as it is in many other places in the world. The next question to consider is whether malnutrition can be linked to educational outcomes. Early, severe, and long-lasting protein-energy malnutrition can lead to substantial impairment of physical

Table 3.2

Comparison: Regression of Grades Behind on Nutritional Status

	Grades behind[a]	
	Jamison (1986)	CHNS Estimates
Height-for-age	−0.029	−0.015
	(11.39)***	(4.45)***
Weight-for-age	−0.004	−0.003
	(4.22)**	(2.35)*
Control variables	Child's age, sex, geographic location[b]	Household per capita income, parental education, number of siblings, child's age and sex, geographic location,[c] and residence

Source: Column 1: Adapted from Table 3 of Dean T. Jamison, "Child Malnutrition and School Performance in China," *Journal of Development Economics,* vol. 20 (1986), pp. 299–309. Column 2: 1989 and 1993 CHNS data. See note 10 for details.

Notes: T values are shown in parentheses; * $p < 0.05$. ** $p < 0.01$. *** $p < 0.001$ (two-tailed test).

[a]Grades behind is calculated by the grade a child should be in, given his or her age, minus his or her actual grade.

[b]Provincial coverage: Beijing, Gansu (Lanzhou), Gansu (rural), Jiangsu (Nanjing), Jiangsu (rural).

[c]Provincial coverage: Liaoning, Jiangsu, Shandong, Henan, Hubei, Hunan, Guangxi, Guizhou.

growth and possibly irreversible brain damage, and therefore may inhibit intellectual development and contribute to poor school outcomes.[15] Many studies in developing countries have found associations between malnutrition and school outcomes.[16]

In China, Jamison's study, described earlier, was the first to estimate the impact of children's malnutrition on schooling. Using data on 3,000 elementary school children ages seven to fifteen from five different locations, Jamison found that both height-for-age and weight-for-age affected children's grade attainment. In other words, better-nourished children were significantly less far behind in school than children with poorer nutrition (Table 3.2). Jamison's study did not incorporate information about children's home environment, and it should not be generalized without caution due to its limited sample. However, this study offered the first provocative suggestion that child malnutrition in China could be linked to school outcomes.

Jamison's analysis used data from 1979, prior to the dramatic improvements in quality of life seen in the 1980s and 1990s. To test whether his conclusions remained valid in more recent years, we replicated Jamison's work using the same nutrition and school performance measurements, that is, height-for-age, weight-for-age, and grades behind, but we used more recent and comprehensive data from the 1989 and 1993 CHNS.[17] The children in our analysis were ages seven to twelve in 1993.[18] Our models are not directly comparable to Jamison's, as our sample drew from different provinces and we incorporated more home background factors, such as household per capita income, parental education, and number of siblings. However, inferences regarding the significant negative effects of malnutrition on age-adjusted grade attainment are consistent with those from Jamison's earlier study: shorter and lighter children were significantly further behind the expected grade.[19] Our results also suggest that height-for-age is a stronger predictor of school progress than weight-for-age. This result is consistent with Jamison's finding and is unsurprising, as height-for-age is generally considered to be a better indicator of long-term nutritional status.[20]

Food Security/Home Nutritional Environment

As we discussed earlier, previous studies of health and schooling often use anthropometry as an indicator of nutritional status. Although useful, this approach is often criticized because of the fact that parents with a propensity to invest in children's schooling are likely to also have a propensity to invest in children's health, which causes methodological problems in statistical models of the impact of health on education.[21] In addition, anthropometry measures do not capture information on shorter-term nutritional status, such as recent household food environment, which may be as influential as earlier nutritional status in affecting school outcomes. We are not aware of studies in China on this issue, but studies in the United States suggest that household food insecurity may adversely affect children's attention, interest, and learning, even when it is not linked to physical size measures.[22] Consistent with the importance of considering more short-term nutrition measures, studies in developing countries find that children receiving high-energy diets perform better in school through better attendance and concentration on stimuli in the learning environment.[23]

Using data on 2,000 children and households in rural Gansu, China, we examined the effects of household nutritional environment on children's school experience.[24] We measured family nutritional environment using a scale derived from food frequency questions that indicates a household's access to a variety of nutritious foods in the previous year (see notes for Table 3.3).[25] We first show that socioeconomic status is closely linked to nutritional environment in rural China (Table 3.3). Across the models in Table 3.3, annual household expenditures positively predict family nutritional

Table 3.3

Regression of Nutritional Environment on Household Economic Status

	Nutritional environment	Nutritional environment	Nutritional environment
Log expenditures	0.723 (0.04)***	0.648 (0.04)***	0.622 (0.04)***
Mother's education		0.070 (0.01)***	0.068 (0.01)***
School/village fixed effects			—
Constant	−3.245 (0.39)***	−2.841 (0.38)***	−2.596 (0.38)***
Observations	2,000	2,000	2,000

Source: Adapted from Table 3 in Yu and Hannum (2003).

Notes: The Gansu Survey of Children and Families asked mothers of sample children a series of questions regarding the frequency with which their families consumed a variety of foods (meats, aquatic products, rice, eggs, fresh vegetables, fresh fruits, and dairy products) in the previous year. Using principal components analysis, we obtained the best-performing scale (according to the "eigenvalue greater than 1" criterion), which we employed as our indicator of nutritional environment (Yu and Hannum 2003).

Standard errors are in parentheses; $*p < 0.05$. $** p < 0.01$. $*** p < 0.001$ (two-tailed test).

environment, indicating that poorer children have significantly reduced access to nutritious foods, even net of school and community effects. Consistent with our discussion of anthropometry, these results indicate that poorer children tend to be more vulnerable to risks of poor nutrition.

These risks may have educational implications. In Table 3.4, we show that school performance, measured by mathematics and language (Chinese) scores on end-of-semester examinations, is predicted by household nutritional environment. We regressed end-of-semester test scores on children's socioeconomic and demographic background characteristics and nutritional environment. First, we note that poor children are disadvantaged at school: Household economic status, measured by household expenditures in the past year, significantly predicts math and language scores, even net of all of the control variables (Table 3.4).

Second, poor nutrition shows negative impacts on children's school performance. In Table 3.4, Model 2 shows that our nutrition measure exerts a statistically significant impact in the most conservative specifications of the language and math models, which control for household expenditures, other factors, and school fixed effects. For example, each 1-point increase along the 8-point nutrition measure scale is associated with a 1.16 point (0.08 standard deviation) increase in math scores (Table 3.4).

Table 3.4

Regression of End-of-Semester Test Scores on Nutritional Environment: Language and Math

	Chinese Model 1	Chinese Model 2	Mathematics Model 1	Mathematics Model 2
Nutritional environment		0.972 (0.33)**		1.159 (0.37)**
Log expenditures	2.371 (0.61)***	1.781 (0.64)**	2.584 (0.68)***	1.878 (0.71)**
Mother's education	0.450 (0.09)***	0.398 (0.09)***	0.444 (0.10)***	0.383 (0.10)***
Control variables	Child's age, sex, number of siblings, books at home, parents' help with homework			
Constant	53.182 (6.21)***	55.538 (6.25)***	54.493 (6.89)***	57.336 (6.94)***
Observations	1,915	1,915	1,921	1,921

Source: Adapted from Tables 4 and 5 in Yu and Hannum (2003). All models are school/village fixed-effects models.

Notes: Standard errors are in parentheses; $* p < 0.05$. $** p < 0.01$. $*** p < 0.001$ (two-tailed test).

Finally, comparing the household expenditures effects in the models with and without the nutrition measure (Model 1 and Model 2) reveals that the addition of nutritional environment reduces the effects of household expenditures in both math and language models. In other words, Tables 3.3 and 3.4 show that poorer households are more likely to have poor nutritional environments, and poor nutritional environment appears to explain part, but of course not all, of the relation between family economic status and school achievement. The Gansu Survey of Children and Families also sheds light on a possible mechanism of impact: nutritional environment may influence children's school performance through ability to concentrate and energy levels. For example, bivariate results suggest that children living in households with a better nutritional environment report better ability to concentrate and higher energy levels. In turn, children reporting better abilities to concentrate and higher energy levels perform better in school.[26]

Parental Health

Most studies of health effects on education have focused on children themselves. Another potentially important perspective, and one that to our knowl-

Table 3.5

**Percentage of Children with Parental Health Problems by
Family Wealth Quintile**

	Disability[a]	Sickness[b]	Hospitalization[c]
Family wealth			
First quintile (lowest)	9.66	22.73	7.63
Second quintile	3.14	14.78	7.79
Third quintile	4.53	12.22	5.10
Fourth quintile	2.10	8.44	3.21
Fifth quintile (highest)	1.46	7.78	4.74
Pearson chi-square value	98.60	117.53	26.70
Probability	0.00	0.00	0.00
N	4,617	4,605	4,607

Source: 2000 Gansu Survey of Children and Families.

[a]Either parent reported disability, including deafness and muteness, blindness, bodily disability, mental illness, or retardation.

[b]Either parent reported sickness that prevented him or her from working in the past three months.

[c]Either parent reported being hospitalized in the past year.

edge is unstudied in China, is the health of children's parents. The effects of parental health on schooling could be direct or indirect. Parental illness may directly interfere with children's school performance if a sick parent cannot help with children's schooling or asks a child to spend additional time on household chores rather than schoolwork.

Indirectly, there are a number of paths by which children's schooling could be affected. For example, parental illness can cause poverty if parents cannot work on the farm or participate in labor migration, or if their medical bills are high; poverty in turn affects both children's opportunities to attend school and their performance in school. Poor parental health may also impose negative effects on children's psychosocial well-being, affecting their ability to focus at school, or may have negative impacts on children's health.

Unfortunately, although anecdotes of parental ill health leading to children dropping out of school abound, there are no empirical studies of this issue. We provide one piece of illustrative evidence using data on 4,617 children in all sampled households from the 2000 Gansu Survey of Children and Families.[27] Tables 3.5 and 3.6 depict the association of parental health, measured by disability, a long-term measure of parental health status, sickness in the past three months, and hospitalization in the past year with family wealth[28] (Table 3.5) and children's school outcomes (Table 3.6), measured by current enrollment status and whether the child is behind the expected grade.

Table 3.6

Percent Currently Enrolled and Behind Expected Grades by Parental Health

	Currently enrolled			Grades behind
	Ages 7–16	Ages 7–12	Ages 13–16	Ages 7–16
Disability[a]				
No	90.80	97.82	72.09	34.67
Yes	84.62	96.64	55.56	48.12
P value (chi)	0.01	0.39	0.06	0.001
N	3,938	3,052	783	3,614
Sickness[b]				
No	90.67	97.89	71.68	33.75
Yes	89.56	96.95	70.00	44.40
P value (chi)	0.43	0.24	0.74	0.000
N	3,929	3,044	782	3,605
Hospitalization[c]				
No	90.61	97.85	71.91	34.43
Yes	89.25	96.41	64.44	45.88
P value (chi)	0.51	0.22	0.28	0.001
N	3,931	3,046	782	3,607

Source: 2000 Gansu Survey of Children and Families.

[a]Either parent reported disability, including deafness and muteness, blindness, bodily disability, mental illness, or retardation.

[b]Either parent reported sickness that prevented him or her from working in the past three months.

[c]Either parent reported being hospitalized in the past year.

Table 3.5 shows the distribution of children by parental health status and family wealth quintile. Just as we showed above that children's own physical health is associated with poverty, Table 3.5 shows that children's parental health is associated with poverty: The percentages of parents reporting disabilities and sickness decline with increases in family wealth. Parents reporting more hospitalizations also tend to be from poorer households, although the relation appears less strong as the financial ability to pay for hospitalization may play a role.

Table 3.6 addresses the question of whether parental health status has implications for schooling. In Table 3.6, disability, sickness, and hospitalization are all dichotomous variables in which "No" means neither of the parents is disabled or sick or hospitalized and "Yes" means that one or both parents report being disabled or sick or hospitalized. Information on current enrollment status is measured by asking if the child is currently enrolled in school. Here, grades behind indicates whether a child is behind his or her expected grade based on the standard primary school enrollment age of seven.

Grades behind may be caused by late enrollment or grade repetition or both. We include children ages seven to sixteen in this table.

There are several interesting findings in Table 3.6. First, different dimensions of parental health do not all seem to be associated with children's school outcomes to the same degree. For instance, disability is significantly associated with children's current enrollment status among all children, but the disparity appears concentrated among those ages thirteen to sixteen, where fees are higher and enrollment rates are lower. Among those ages thirteen to sixteen, the percentage of currently enrolled is only 56 when either parent is disabled, whereas the percentage is 72 among those whose parents are not disabled (the p value, however, is only marginally significant for this subgroup). Neither short-term sickness nor prior year's hospitalization shows a significant association with current enrollment status. Given that short-term health problems may not bring dramatic stress, either on family finance or labor needs, as much as long-term disabilities might, we think this differential association across different measures of parental health reasonable.

When we consider grades behind, we find a more consistent, significant association with parental health, by all measures. In general, when parents do not report a health problem, about one-third of children are behind the expected grade. When parents do report a problem, about 44 to 48 percent of children are behind their expected grade.

These results must be interpreted with caution, because our sample consists of children in rural households with at least one nine- to twelve-year-old child and because the cross-sectional data preclude a convincing multivariate analysis due to temporal problems.[29] However, Table 3.5 and Table 3.6 do provide suggestive evidence that poor children are more likely to experience parental illness and that parental illness may be an important conditioning factor in children's school outcomes.

Psychosocial Problems

Another dimension of health that is not yet widely investigated in studies of education in China is mental health. A significant number of children and young people in school are experiencing a range of mental health problems, including symptoms of withdrawal, anxiety, depression, hyperactivity, aggression, and delinquency.[30] Studies show that symptoms of psychosocial problems such as anxiety and depression are not uncommon in urban or suburban Chinese children, but studies of psychosocial well-being are few among children in poor rural areas of China.[31]

We conducted a regression analysis of psychosocial welfare indicators on household socioeconomic status using data from rural Gansu.[32] We employed scales created to tap into two kinds of psychological problems: internalizing and externalizing problems.[33] Results in Table 3.7 indicate that psychosocial health, like other dimensions of health, is directly linked to economic status: children from wealthier families experience fewer psychosocial health problems. Associations are consistent and significant for both internalizing and externalizing problems, net of the effects of all other relevant factors and school fixed effects.

We then investigated the relation between psychosocial well-being and children's school achievement while controlling for a full range of resources that might affect children's educational achievement (Table 3.8). In this analysis, children's school achievement was measured by standardized mathematics and language (Chinese) tests. Of course, children's prior achievement probably conditions their psychosocial welfare, and these models partially address this problem by controlling for the feedback children have received in the form of end-of-semester test scores.[34] The negative coefficients for psychosocial well-being in Table 3.8 demonstrate that children's psychosocial well-being significantly predicts their school achievement: children with fewer psychosocial problems achieve higher scores in both language and math tests than those with more psychosocial problems. These findings hold in models that consider household socioeconomic status, children's demographic characteristics, family sibling structure, and home learning environment, as well as end-of-semester scores and school fixed effects. In sum, our results suggest that in rural China children from wealthier families suffer from fewer psychosocial problems and that children with fewer psychosocial problems perform better in school.

Additional Health Concerns

The particular health issues that we consider here are illustrative and of course do not represent the full range of potential health-related barriers to schooling for poor children in China. Additional issues, for which we were not able to present empirical evidence, are probably also worthy of consideration, and we outline a few of these here.

One important example is nutritional deficits associated with micronutrient deficiencies and helminthic infections. Although these problems may be correlated with anthropometric measures or food security type measures, it is unlikely that such measures serve as very precise proxies. In China, micronutrient deficiency disorders have been widespread in rural areas, and helminthic infections are a major public health problem.[35] In other countries, micronutrient deficiencies and helminthic infections have been convincingly linked to either poor school performance or to symptoms that plausibly im-

Table 3.7

Regression of Psychosocial Well-Being (Internalizing and Externalizing Problems) on Household Expenditures

	1A Internalizing	2A Internalizing	3A Internalizing	1B Externalizing	2B Externalizing	3B Externalizing
Log household expenditures	−0.369 (3.69)**	−0.299 (2.98)**	−0.321 (3.17)**	−0.393 (3.37)**	−0.303 (2.60)**	−0.333 (2.83)**
Control variables	Mother's education, age and sex of child, number of books in the home, number of siblings, parents' help with homework	1A + previous semester's test scores on language and math	2A + school/village effects	Mother's education, age and sex of child, number of books in the home, number of siblings, parents' help with homework	1B + previous semester's test scores on language and math	2B + school/village effects
Constant	12.244 (12.18)**	13.777 (13.42)**	13.979 (13.36)**	12.981 (11.06)**	15.086 (12.62)**	15.374 (12.64)**
Observations	1,954	1,914	1,914	1,954	1,914	1,914

Source: Adapted from Table 2 in Shengchao Yu, Emily Hannum, and Xiaodong Liu, "Poverty, Psychosocial Well-Being, and School Performance in Rural China" (work in progress).

Notes: Standard errors are in parentheses; * $p < 0.05$. ** $p < 0.01$. *** $p < 0.001$ (two-tailed test).

Table 3.8

Regression of School Achievement on Psychosocial Well-Being
(Internalizing and Externalizing Problems)

	Chinese score	Chinese score	Math score	Math score
Internalizing problems	−0.729 (2.46)*		−0.933 (2.44)*	
Externalizing problems		−0.818 (3.15)**		−0.859 (2.66)**
Control variables	Household expenditures, mother's education, age and sex of child, number of books in the home, number of siblings, parents' help with homework, end-of-semester test scores			
Constant	−22.925 (1.62)	−21.363 (1.53)	−0.793 (0.04)	0.768 (0.04)
Observations	987	987	930	930

Source: Adapted from Tables 5 through 8 in Shengchao Yu, Emily Hannum, and Xiaodong Liu, "Poverty, Psychosocial Well-Being, and School Performance in Rural China" (work in progress, 2004). Models are all school/village fixed-effects models.

Notes: Standard errors are in parentheses; * $p < 0.05$. ** $p < 0.01$. *** $p < 0.001$ (two-tailed test).

pede school performance,[36] suggesting that these health problems are worthy of attention as a barrier to schooling in rural China.

An additional health issue likely to be a significant barrier to school performance is poor vision. In China, a survey of 250,000 students conducted in 1980 found that 29.4 percent of students in urban middle schools and 19.1 percent of students in urban primary schools had poor vision.[37] In rural middle schools and primary schools, the rates were 15.5 percent and 18.6 percent, respectively.[38] Access to glasses appears to be limited in poor rural areas. For example, in 2000, the Gansu Survey of Children and Families showed that among the 2,000 sample children ages nine to twelve, only 7.9 percent reported wearing eyeglasses, whereas 20.1 percent reported having difficulties seeing the blackboard or doing homework due to poor vision (our calculations, not shown).

Although there are not, to our knowledge, studies of vision and school outcomes in China, one recent study in rural Brazil directly assessed visual acuity and indicated that vision problems were a key factor influencing both persistence and achievement in school.[39] Because of this evidence, and because of the very direct impact of poor eyesight on ability to complete homework and opportunities to learn in the classroom, especially given the poor lighting conditions prevalent in many rural homes and schools, we believe that vision problems are a significant topic for further research on educational inequalities in China.

Finally, a third health issue worthy of scrutiny is communicable diseases. Analyses of recent Global Burden of Disease Project data show that communicable diseases are the world's biggest killers of children and among the top causes of death of adults in the developing world. About half of all deaths in children under age five are due to five preventable and treatable communicable diseases such as pneumonia, diarrhea, measles, malaria, and HIV/AIDS.[40] Although China has an impressive track record of fighting many communicable diseases, there are some old and emerging diseases that are important to consider, including tuberculosis (TB), HIV, and hepatitis B (HBV).

Each of these illnesses is linked to poverty. The TB problem is most severe in rural populations in the most disadvantaged counties and among migrant workers in areas of high economic activity. In poor rural areas of China, the rate of TB is nearly three times higher than in economically developed urban areas.[41] A major mechanism of HIV spread in China has been blood-selling by impoverished peasants; poverty and the dislocation of poor rural migrants have also contributed to the rising sex industry and to the spread of disease.[42]

Regarding HBV,[43] there is a high prevalence of the infection, despite its being vaccine-preventable: 10 to 14 percent of the total population are HBV carriers.[44] An official survey in 1999 revealed an average coverage rate of three doses of HBV vaccination of 70.7 percent, and this rate was higher in urban areas than in rural areas.[45] One study found that of about 2,000 persons surveyed in 1992 in Guangxi Province, one of the poorest provinces in China, only 5.6 percent reported receiving HBV vaccination.[46] Poverty and poor health services also contribute directly to HBV infections because of unsafe medical injections, which are primarily experienced by the poor.[47]

It is reasonably evident that micronutrient deficiencies, helminthic infections, myopia, and communicable diseases pose particular problems for China's rural poor. What is not empirically established is whether the presence of these problems detracts from school achievement. However, given the nature of these health problems, it is probably safe to speculate that they, like the health problems discussed earlier for which more direct evidence is available, exacerbate the educational barriers faced by poor rural children.

Discussion and Conclusions

In this chapter, we have considered evidence about linkages between health, poverty, and schooling in China, focusing on examples of malnutrition, parental health, and psychosocial health. While each of these dimensions of health is unique, the story that emerges is consistent. Across these dimensions of health, we find evidence, sometimes suggestive and sometimes strong, that the poor tend to face heightened risks of ill health and that ill health predicts school outcomes for children.

The coincidence of ill health and poverty and the apparent consequences of ill health for education have significant implications. First, and most generally, health may be an important unobserved determinant of educational acquisition in China. Second, ill health may be a significant mechanism— largely ignored in empirical research—by which poverty operates on educational outcomes and subsequent life outcomes. Our findings suggest a vicious intergenerational cycle for poor families experiencing ill health. Children's schooling is compromised as a result of poverty and ill health of the child or family, and the lack of schooling serves as a barrier to children's own subsequent ability to avoid poverty and ill health.

More constructively, these findings point to the need for policies or interventions designed to promote children's schooling among the poor to more fully consider how to address potential barriers associated with ill health. This conclusion, of course, pertains particularly to China, but it can be placed in a broader context. In recent years, health has increasingly been recognized as a key component of human capital.[48] Improving public health is now a leading strategy undertaken by development agencies to lift populations out of poverty. Yet, a recent review of global research on public health and education comes to the conclusion that the correlation between education and health outcomes is widely observed, but an understanding of these relations does not appear to influence public policy in a meaningful way.[49] In China, at least, this state of affairs is a significant problem. Health issues appear worthy of additional attention for members of the policy community interested in promoting education for underserved populations.

Notes

1. Emily Hannum and Jihong Liu, "Adolescent Transitions to Adulthood in Reform-Era China," in *The Changing Transitions to Adulthood in Developing Countries*, ed. Cynthia B. Lloyd, Jere R. Behrman, Nelly P. Stromquist, and Barney Cohen, pp. 270–319 (National Academy of Science, 2006).

2. Chunming Chen, "Fat Intake and Nutritional Status of Children in China," *American Journal of Clinical Nutrition*, no. 72, supp. (2000), pp. 1368S–1372S; Albert Park and Sangui Wang, "China's Poverty Statistics," *China Economic Review*, no. 12 (2001), pp. 384–398. In remote poor areas, the infant mortality rate exceeds 100 per 1,000, at least twice the national average; *Poverty in China* (United Nations, 2001) (www.unchina.org/about_china/html/poverty.shtml).

3. Xiaohua Liu, "Overview of Educational Needs and Philanthropic Opportunities in China," 2002 (www.icfdn.org/aboutus/publications/China%20Education%20Needs.doc).

4. Jennifer Adams and Emily Hannum, "Children's Social Welfare in Post-Reform China: Access to Health Insurance and Education 1989–1997," *The China Quarterly*, 181 (March): 100-121; Dongping Yang, "2000 Educational Evolution in China (I): Educational Evolution and Reform," China Education and Research Network, 2000 (www.edu.cn/20010101/22290.shtml).

5. William Hsiao, Dean T. Jamison, William P. McGreevey, and Winnie Yip, "Financing Health Care: Issues and Option for China," World Bank Report No. 17091, September 30, 1997 (Washington, DC: The World Bank).

6. G. Bloom and X.Y. Gu, "Introduction to Health Sector Reform," *IDS Bulletin*, vol. 28, no. 1 (1997), pp. 1–23; H. Yu, S.H. Cao, and H. Lucas, "Equity in the Utilization of Medical Service: A Survey of Poor in China," *IDS Bulletin*, vol. 28, no. 1 (1997), pp. 16–23.

7. Adams and Hannum, "Children's Social Welfare in Post-Reform China."

8. Outside of China, a substantial body of research in the social sciences demonstrates the close relation of childhood health and school outcomes in developing countries. See, for example, Jere R. Behrman and V. Lavy, "Children's Health and Achievement in School," Living Standards Measurement Study Working Paper No. 104 (Washington, DC: The World Bank, 1994); Paul Glewwe, Hanan G. Jacoby, and Elizabeth M. King, "Early Childhood Nutrition and Academic Achievement: A Longitudinal Analysis," *Journal of Public Economics*, vol. 81 (2001), pp. 345–368.

9. Jamison's data were from 1979, which predated the large-scale emergence of the floating population. Thus, we do not believe that these figures refer to the children of the floating population in 1986.

10. The data used in Tables 3.1 and 3.2 come from the China Health and Nutrition Survey (CHNS). This survey covers eight provinces, Guangxi, Guizhou, Henan, Hubei, Hunan, Jiangsu, Liaoning, and Shandong, which vary substantially in geography, economic development, public resources, and health indicators. The analysis included children who were aged from seven to twelve in 1993 and who had ever enrolled in primary school, with a maximum sample size of 1206 for analyses. We show grades behind measured in 1993 and nutritional status and other characteristics of children and their households measured in 1989. Measures included in the tables are described below:

School Performance. In the CHNS household survey, the years of formal education and age were collected for each member in the selected households. Like in Jamison's 1986 study, grades behind is simply the grade a child should be in, given age, minus actual grade. The criterion used to measure grades behind in school is based on the national standard of seven years old for entering Grade 1.

Nutritional Status. Children received detailed physical examinations in the CHNS survey that included weight and height. Height is measured as centimeters in the survey and in this analysis we construct height-for-age using height, age, and sex for the purpose of standardization. Height-for-age is expressed as percentage of the median value for a large sample of U.S. children of the same age and sex surveyed by the U.S. National Center for Health Statistics (NCHS), referred to as the NCHS standard. Similarly, weight-for-age is constructed in the same way as another indicator of children's nutritional status.

Other Variables. We use per capita income as an indicator of family wealth. Income was constructed by summing all sources, including wages, home gardening, farming, raising livestock, fishing, small business, and so on. As a measure of parental human capital, we use mother's and father's years of schooling. As demographic controls, we use measures of gender, age, and siblings in the age range of seven to twelve. Urban-rural and regional differences in living standards and public resources in China are significant and increasing with rapid economic development; we also include in our analyses measures of urban-rural residence and province of residence.

11. These measures are defined as percentage of the median value for a sample of U.S. children surveyed by NCHS standards. For example, height-for-age/weight-for-age 100 means that the nutritional status is equivalent to the NCHS standards. The smaller the value, the worse the nutritional status compared to the NCHS standards.

12. See Note 8.

13. Chunming Chen, "Fat Intake and Nutritional Status of Children in China"; Albert Park and Linxiu Zhang, "Mother's Education and Child Health in China's Poor Areas," unpublished manuscript (University of Michigan, Department of Economics, 2000); Y. Wang, B. Popkin, and F. Zhai, "The Nutritional Status and Dietary Pattern of Chinese Adolescents 1991 and 1993," *European Journal of Clinical Nutrition*, vol. 52 (1998), pp. 908–916.

14. United Nations Children's Fund, "At a Glance: China," 2004 (www.unicef.org/infobycountry/china.html).

15. Beryl Levinger, *Nutrition, Health and Education for All* (New York: Education Development Center and United Nations Development Programme, 1996) (www.edc.org/INT/NHEA/index.html).

16. See, for example, Ernesto Pollitt, *Malnutrition and Infection in the Classroom* (Paris: UNESCO, 1990). Other examples include the following: In the Philippines, Florencio concluded that the academic performance of pupils with good nutritional status was significantly better than that of pupils with poor nutritional status, although the relation varied by grade level and subject matter. See Cecelia Florencio, "Child, School, Home: Determinants of Academic Performance," excerpt from Edukasyon, vol. 1, no. 2 (1995), A Quarterly Monograph Series of the University of the Philippines Education Research Program (ERP). See also Harold Alderman, Jere R. Behrman, Victor Lavy, and Rekha Menon, "Child Health and School Enrollment—A Longitudinal Analysis," *Journal of Human Resources*, vol. 36, no. 1 (1997), pp. 185–205. Alderman and his colleagues suggested that children's health and nutrition were three times more important for enrollment than suggested by the assumption that children's health and nutrition are predetermined or exogenous. In rural northeast Brazil, a study showed that students' nutritional status affected school performance; a recent study on a large sample of Filipino children also suggested a causal link between nutrition and academic success; see Glewwe, Jacoby, and King, "Early Childhood Nutrition and Academic Achievement."

17. See note 10 for more information on the analysis using CHNS data.

18. Our approach links the 1989 and 1993 CHNS data, using 1989 data on predictors and 1993 data on outcomes. One rationale for linking the two years' data is that household per capita income in 1993 may influence household decisions on both nutrition and schooling. However, this simultaneous decision is very unlikely to have been made in 1989, when most of the children in our analysis had not yet entered school. In addition, this strategy reduces the problems of interpretation associated with the fact that children who were behind in 1993, in many cases, started to fall behind earlier than 1993.

19. See, for example, Dean T. Jamison, "Child Malnutrition and School Performance in China," *Journal of Development Economics*, vol. 20 (1986), pp. 299–309. To maintain a parallel analysis to Jamison, our outcome variables are calculated for children currently in school. Enrollment rates are 91 percent among the seven- to twelve-year-olds in the sample, so we believe that the selection problem is small. However, if those who were not in school were out due to health problems, our results could underestimate the effects of malnutrition on schooling.

20. Height is generally preferred because weight is more subject to short-term fluctuations, while height is a relatively stable indicator. See, for example, Yu and Hannum,"Child Malnutrition and School Performance in Rural China." Interestingly, Yu and Hannum find more consistent variations of weight-for-age with socioeconomic status than height-for-age using CHNS data (Table 3.1); weight-for-age does not show stronger impacts on school outcomes. This inconsistency may suggest that nutritional status is not simply a proxy for poverty's influence on school performance, and nutritional status itself may exert impacts on school outcomes net of poverty level. It is important to acknowledge genetic differences in stature, independent of nutritional status. We are not able to incorporate controls for these differences.

21. The common problem is endogeneity, caused by households' simultaneous decision making on nutrition and schooling.

22. See Levinger, *Nutrition, Health and Education for All*; Joshua Winicki and Kyle Jemison, "Food Insecurity and Hunger in the Kindergarten Classroom: Its Effect on Learning and Growth," *Contemporary Economic Policy*, vol. 21, no. 2 (2003), pp. 145–157; American Dietetic Association, "Position of the American Dietetic Association: Domestic Food and Nutrition Security," *Journal of the American Dietetic Association*, vol. 102, no. 12 (2002), pp. 1840–1847. For example, using an eighteen-item food security module in the Early Childhood Longitudinal Survey, Winicki and Jemison demonstrated significant negative effects on math achievement and on growth in math achievement among kindergarteners in households with even the most marginal levels of food deprivation. Similarly, a study using the Third Annual Health and Nutrition Examination Survey showed that six- to eleven-year-old food-insecure children had significantly lower math scores, significantly more grade repetition, and significantly more behavioral problems. See also Katherine Alaimo, Christine M. Olson, and Edward A. Frongillo, Jr., "Food Insufficiency and American School-Aged Children's Cognitive, Academic, and Psychosocial Development," *Pediatrics*, vol. 108, no. 1 (2001), pp. 44–53. The U.S. case is dissimilar to China in many ways, and the scope of estimated effects in the United States cannot be generalized to China. However, the relations documented in the United States do indicate an important mechanism of educational advantage and disadvantage that is likely to have parallels in China.

23. Pollitt, *Malnutrition and Infection in the Classroom*; Levinger, *Nutrition, Health and Education for All*. In one study in the Philippines, Florencio concluded that attendance in school, ability to concentrate in class, and/or study habits at home were not independent of participation in supplementary feeding, breakfast skipping, feeling of hunger in school, and/or health and nutritional status. See Florencio, "Child, School, Home."

24. Shengchao Yu and Emily Hannum, "Food for Thought: Poverty, Family Nutritional Environment and Children's School Performance in Rural China" unpublished manuscript (2003).

25. In this sample in Gansu, 98 percent of respondents are Han Chinese, and thus these particular results are unlikely to be confounded by religious practices. Food questions are asked about the previous year, in hopes of avoiding issues of seasonal-

ity. In Gansu, it is possible that there may be regional differences in availability of particular types of foods, which could be substituted by other types. However, within the broad categories of our scale, we believe that regional disparities would represent real regional contributions to differential nutritional status of children.

26. Yu and Hannum, "Food for Thought."

27. This sample includes all children in the 2000 households of nine- to twelve-year-old children that were sampled for the survey.

28. Family wealth is constructed from detailed measures of household assets, including the value of housing, fixed capital, and household durable goods. It is the sum of the current value of all household durable goods (furniture, appliances/machines, and tools, etc.) and the current value of housing.

29. Specifically, there is a lack of an appropriate lag time between illness measures and current enrollment, and there is a temporal ordering problem with parental illness measures and the grades behind data, because, in many cases, children became behind due to having started late or repeated early school grades.

30. See Shengchao Yu, Emily Hannum, and Xiaodong Liu, "Poverty, Psychosocial Well-Being, and School Performance in Rural China" (work in progress). In this study, the indicators for the internalizing and externalizing problems are summative scales from thirty-six items, eighteen items for each, reported by the children. Internalizing problems cover numerous questions that address symptoms of unhappiness, feelings of being unloved, mood swings, feelings of worthlessness, and feelings of being withdrawn (exact wording for questions is available at www.ssc.upenn.edu/china). Externalizing problems assess children's acting out, truancy, fighting, and delinquency.

31. Xiaodong Liu, "Parenting Practices and the Psychological Adjustment of Children in Rural China," doctoral dissertation, Harvard University Graduate School of Education, 2003.

32. Yu, Hannum, and Liu, "Poverty, Psychosocial Well-Being, and School Performance."

33. Xiaodong Liu, "Parenting Practices."

34. The tests were designed by experts at the Gansu Educational Commission to cover the range of official primary school curriculum.

35. Chorching Goh, "An Analysis of Combating Iodine Deficiency: Case Studies of China, Indonesia, and Madagascar," OED Working Paper Series No. 18 (2001); Peter J. Hotez, Zheng Feng, Longqi Xu, Minggang Chen, Shuhua Xiao, Shuxian Liu, David Blair, Donald P. McManus, and George M. Davis, "Emerging and Reemerging Helminthiasis and the Public Health of China," *Emerging Infectious Diseases*, vol. 3, no. 3 (1997), pp. 303–308; and United Nations Children's Fund, "At a Glance: China."

36. Iron-deficiency anemia, iodine, and vitamin A deficiency are among the most concerning micronutrient deficiency disorders in the developing world. Iron deficiency can lead to anemia, and anemia reduces energy necessary for playing and learning in children and leads to poor motor skills and delayed speech and reading. School-age children who are iron deficient exhibit reduced levels of alertness, attention, and concentration in class and display less aptitude. These traits hinder the development of children's ability to learn and cause poor school performance. See, for example, Levinger, *Nutrition, Health and Education for All*; also see J. Larry Brown and Ernesto Pollitt, "Malnutrition, Poverty and Intellectual Development," *Scientific American* (February 1996), pp. 38–43. Although the mechanisms that iron-deficiency anemia affects behavioral dysfunction are not understood, previous studies demonstrate that iron-deficiency anemia directly impedes educational efficiency. See, for example, Pollitt, *Malnutrition and Infection in the Classroom*.

Similarly, iodine deficiency can cause mental and physical handicaps, such as reduced intelligence, psychomotor retardation, mental and neurological damage, and cretinism. The consequences of iodine-deficiency disorder were found to be significant in terms of school outcomes. In 1990, Pollitt reviewed studies dealing with the consequences of iodine deficiency and noted that children who suffer from iodine deficiency disorder may have impaired visual-perception organization, visual-motor coordination, speed of information-processing, and hearing. Poor perception, motor skills, hearing, and so on constitute major obstacles to satisfactory school achievement. Vitamin A deficiency causes blindness and also leads to night blindness and limited peripheral vision. Because of its close association with an impaired immune system and therefore reduced resistance to acute respiratory infection, diarrhea, and measles, direct examinations on vitamin A deficiency alone and school outcomes are few, although poor vision itself is obviously a barrier for students who cannot see well in the classroom. Helminthic infection, or parasitic worm infection, is another type of childhood health issue that has significant impact on school outcomes. Some studies found evidence of this relation. For instance, see Edward Miguel and Michael Kremer, "Worms: Identifying Impacts on Education and Health in the Presence of Treatment Externalities," *Econometrica*, vol. 72, no. 1 (2004), pp. 159–217. In this recent study in Kenya, Miguel and Kremer found that deworming drugs increased school attendance and was by far the most cost-effective method of improving school attendance among a series of educational interventions implemented in the larger study. Another study in the American South showed increased school enrollment and school attendance with hookworm infection treatment. However, whether helminthic infections directly cause cognitive deficits is a matter of debate. See Hoyt Bleakley, "Disease and Development: Evidence from Hookworm Eradication in the American South" (Population Research Center, NORC, and the University of Chicago, 2002).

37. C.B. Shi, P.F. Zhu, and Z.Q. Zhou, "People's Republic of China: Perspectives in School Health," *Journal of School Health*, vol. 60, no. 7 (1990), pp. 349–350.

38. Shi et al., "People's Republic of China."

39. João Batista Gomes-Neto, Eric A. Hanushek, Raimundo Hélio Leite, and Roberto Cláudio Frota-Bezzera, "Health and Schooling: Evidence and Policy Implications for Developing Countries," *Economics of Education Review*, vol. 16, no. 3 (1997), pp. 271–282.

40. Son Nguyen, Prabhat Jha, Shengchao Yu, and Fred Paccaud, "Indirect Estimates of Avoidable Mortality in Low and Middle Income Countries," Commission on Macroeconomics and Health Working Paper Series, Paper No. Working Group 5: 21 (Geneva: World Health Organization, 2001).

41. World Bank, "Combating Tuberculosis in China" (Washington, DC: The World Bank, 2002) (http://web.worldbank.org/WBSITE/EXTERNAL/NEWS/0, content MDK:20041881~menuPK:34457~pagePK:34370~piPK:34424~theSitePK:4607,00.html).

42. Bates Gill, Jennifer Chang, and Sarah Palmer, "China's HIV Crisis," *Foreign Affairs* (March/April 2002), pp. 96–110.

43. Such a low rate of HBV vaccination results from the fact that there is no universal HBV vaccination program and the fact that parents have to use personal resources to pay for their children's vaccination. See Zhuo Jiatong, Guoyu Tao, Shahul H. Ebrahim, Shusheng Wang, Zhongbin Luo, and Haitao Wang, "The Relationship of Hepatitis B Virus Infection Between Adults and Their Children in Guangxi Province, China," *Journal of Hepatology*, vol. 33 (2000), pp. 628–631. High costs of service are still among the challenges facing poor rural children today, although the Ministry of

Public Health of China planned to incorporate HBV vaccination into the nationwide Expanded Program of Immunization starting January 1, 2002. See Z. Sun, L. Ming, X. Zhu, and J. Lu, "Prevention and Control of Hepatitis B in China," *Journal of Medical Virology*, vol. 67, no. 3 (2002), pp. 447–450. Even when the immunization program claims to be free, parents often have to pay all kinds of added costs such as administration fees and payment for needles and syringes, which poor people cannot afford.

44. A. Kane, J. Lloyd, M. Zaffran, L. Simonsen, and M. Kane, "Transmission of Hepatitis B, Hepatitis C and Human Immunodeficiency Viruses Through Unsafe Injections in the Developing World: Model-based Regional Estimates," *Bulletin of the World Health Organization*, vol. 77, no. 10 (1999), pp. 801–807. Zhao Shoujun, Zhiyi Xu, and Ying Lu, "A Mathematical Model of Hepatitis B Virus Transmission and its Application for Vaccination Strategy in China," *International Journal of Epidemiology*, vol. 29 (2000), pp. 744–752.

45. Sun et al., "Prevention and Control of Hepatitis B in China."

46. Zhuo Jiatong et al., "The Relationship of Hepatitis B Virus Infection."

47. In China, the common means of HBV transmission is dirty needles, because a large percentage of health facilities reuse needles and syringes without sterilization only to cut costs. See Hitoshi Murakami, Makoto Kobayashi, Xu Zhu, Yixing Li, Susumu Wakai, and Yasuo Chiba, "Risk of Transmission of Hepatitis B Virus Through Childhood Immunization in Northwestern China," *Social Science and Medicine*, vol. 57 (2003), pp. 1821–1832. In their model-based estimate, they suggest that at least 135–3,120 among 100,000 fully immunized children are infected with HBV due to unsafe immunization injections. This study reveals that immunization injections pose a significant public health risk for the transmission of HBV in northwestern China. Even when the health facilities are willing to switch to use auto-disable syringes, they may face the challenges of insufficient supply of equipment and training, as well as the resistance to behavior change of vaccinators.

48. United Nations Development Programme, *Human Development Report 2000* (New York: Oxford University Press, 2000).

49. Ruth Levine, "Better Health Through More Education: Getting to Win-Win Policy," American Academy of Arts and Sciences Working Paper, April 4, 2004. One exception to this statement is a nutritional intervention project in Gansu sponsored by the British Department for International Development. We thank the editor of this volume for alerting us to this project.

4

Tibetan Girls' Education

Challenging Prevailing Theory

Vilma Seeberg

In recent years I have gathered stories of girls clamoring for an education in remote corners of the People's Republic of China (PRC). The desire for education in this population has not only come to my attention but has made headlines nationally and internationally.[1] When I funded a small scholarship for girls in a remote mountain village of Shaanxi Province, the girls wrote passionate letters promising eternal gratitude for enabling them to return to school. They told heart-wrenching stories of economic hardship and illness in their families, of having to give up their place in school to a younger brother, and their unyielding determination to stay in school despite it all.[2] Heidi Ross, author of another chapter in this book, had a similar experience with scholarship girls in a neighboring county in Shaanxi.[3] The girls' stories revealed a resolute faith, seemingly held together by a mere thread of hope, that schooling would open new worlds, keep them from suffering the fate of their parents, and allow them to repay the latter for their sacrifices.

I wondered about the source of the determination these village girls showed. They were standing up against deep-seated patriarchal systems and values and were taking on or demanding that their families take on crushing financial burdens. What hopes do these strong-minded girls harbor, and what potential force and endowment do they represent to their country?

A reconceptualization of the role of girls and women in development can come out of the above understanding of the girls' will and capacity to envision a new path or future. Directing educational interventions accordingly might begin to deconstruct the deep-seated traditions and barriers to education often cited in international reports. These girls' acts of courage represent

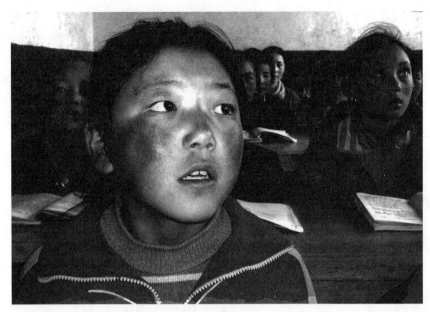

Eager students in a primary boarding school on the open high mountain plains in a Tibetan Autonomous Prefecture of Qinghai Province

a direct assault on such encompassing hindrances as patriarchy and poverty. Enabling girls to complete their schooling, by definition, will change the culture and, in the long run, will decrease material poverty as well. Both poverty and patriarchy are targets of Education for All (EFA), an international movement born in 1990 at the World Conference on Education for All in Thailand. The participants pledged to provide primary education for all children and massively reduce illiteracy by the end of the decade. Perhaps girls are the most active allies EFA has in the struggle to overcome impediments to education and development.

It is commonly thought that national economic development will improve the quality of life across the board, like boats on a rising sea, not equitably for sure, but ultimately inclusive of minority peoples and women. According to Assie-Lumumba and Sutton,[4] summarizing research on gender and education and economic and cultural forces of globalization has "encouraged higher educational aspirations among girls, women, and some historically marginalized boys and men, while at the same time changing the context and meaning of educational attainment."[5]

Research I conducted in the fall of 2004 in northwest China's Qinghai and Gansu Provinces confirms those theories—but with a twist. I found that it is rather the relative lack of economic development that propels girls and women ahead, changes the construction of their identity and social relations, changes the context and meaning of education for them, and moves them into spaces of greater centrality and visibility. The process and spaces vary by ethnicity because gender roles bear the mark of age-old traditions. Patriarchy and poverty still define lives in the remote areas we visited, but new spaces have opened up possibilities that are being explored by girls and women in greater numbers, and this includes their participation and higher attainment in education.

Poverty and Lagging Development in the Northwest

This chapter looks at Tibetan[6] girls and their schooling in a section of the vast northwest Chinese "hinterland," remote, high, cold, and poor, stretching about 2,000 miles westward into Central Asia. Though the area constitutes 78 percent of China's land surface, less than 22 percent of its gross domestic product is produced here, and approximately 34 percent of China's population lives here. Except for a few plains and river basins, the land is mountainous and largely infertile and harbors unknown mineral wealth and extreme poverty, especially among the ethnic minority people[7] living in these areas. Tibetan nomadic herders have occupied the northern plateau region, where they have pastured their sheep and yaks, constantly moving the herds and settling only for the coldest of the winter months. For most of the discussion that follows, I use the Chinese term for Tibetan, *Zang*.

The heartland of China lies below, a land of fertile and intensively cultivated plains sustaining a dense population along the eastern coast of China, only 150 to 600 miles wide.[8] China's "gold coast" (*yanhai*), its most modern and wealthy economy, stretches along the shore of the Pacific Ocean. This is the "miracle China" that has become a supply center of manufacturing for globalization. The growing chasm between the eastern gold coast and the western hinterland indirectly or directly affected every family and individual I met in the Northwest in the fall of 2004. Sweeping change in China's gold coast has affected schooling for the people in minority regions of the Northwest.

At the same time that the chasm has widened, financing of education has become increasingly decentralized by central government mandates, resulting in growing educational disparities.[9] Control of educational administration and content remains in the central government.[10] However, under the central government's "Open the West" development policy, schooling has been expanding in this previously neglected region.[11] Extra support has come not only from the central government but also from international agencies such as the World Bank, bilateral government agreements such as the United Kingdom–China Gansu Basic Education Project, several Hong Kong philanthropists, and nongovernmental philanthropic organizations such as Save the Children–Hong Kong.

Extensive survey-based, representative, baseline data have been collected on the state of the economy and education in parts of northwest China. Excellent sociological analyses and interpretations have been published in English by Bray,[12] Hannum,[13] and Löfstedt,[14] and in Chinese by Xiao[15] and Zhou,[16] available in English translation. The studies have identified common determinants of relatively poor enrollment and high dropout rates as harsh natural conditions, grinding poverty, historic lack of educational development, sociocultural attitudes and patriarchy, and the high cost of schooling from the households' perspective. Girls were everywhere are reported to bear the brunt of the burden of these conditions and hardships.

How, under these crushing conditions, were some girls rising up and demanding an education?[17]

In this chapter, I hope to transmit some of the perspectives I gleaned from observing and talking with children, families, and school personnel in Huangnan Tibetan Autonomous Prefecture in Qinghai Province and Gannan Tibetan Autonomous Prefecture in Gansu Province. Tibetans constitute the majority population in these areas.[18] The lingua franca is Tibetan, and only higher-level educators, university graduates in leading staff positions in schools, and townspeople involved in commerce spoke some amount of standard Chinese (*putonghua*).[19] Although I focus specifically on Tibetan issues, many of the economic and natural conditions similarly affect all of the twelve ethnic groups in the area, but some of the patterns of responses to these conditions are culturally specific.[20]

Big Picture: Educational Attainment of Girls and Women in China

We begin this discussion with a look at the bigger picture of educational participation in order to put local conditions into perspective. Although China mandated compulsory ninth-grade education in 1985, in 2002, the Chinese government reported that illiteracy among young and middle-aged women remained "excessively high."[21] The absolute number of female illiterates was increasing annually as was their proportion among all illiterates. Every year approximately one million new illiterates emerged throughout the country, the great majority of whom were girls who dropped out of school.[22] High female illiteracy proportions are typical across the developing world.[23] However, the EFA Committee of China (2000) admitted that no statistics exist, in the census data or elsewhere, that would allow for an assessment of either gross or net primary intake rates, not to mention disaggregated data by gender. Because of strict population control policy[24] and the Compulsory Education Law, gross and net enrollment figures locally are a volatile topic in the hinterland of the PRC.

Rural ethnic minority birth figures, especially in nationality autonomous prefectures or counties, must be considered speculative. In rural areas of autonomous regions, families more easily avoid reporting their children on the household registries (*hukou*).[25] In the towns I met young families with fewer than three children, but in the rural areas almost all the children I interviewed had three or more siblings. The parental generation of these school-age children and education bureaus staffs, ages twenty to forty, usually had four or more siblings. University educators joked that birth number is "the biggest secret in the village."[26]

Schooling for Zang Girls

Given speculative birthrates and numbers, we could only guess at school enrollment rates. Given traditional boy preference, enrollment rates for ethnic minority girls were even more uncertain. What we could observe or find out was what proportion of the student body was constituted by girls as compared to boys and if their proportions and numbers had been increasing.

In my fall 2004 fieldwork in Zang area primary schools, I observed near parity of girls and boys in classes. Educators gave me conflicting views on proportion and attainment of girls; some higher education teacher trainers reported fewer Zang girls than boys in basic education;[27] others reported equal enrollment proportions in basic education.[28] Rural elementary school teachers and principals often stated that there was near equality in enrollment and that Zang girls would finish primary education. According to them, the junior high school entrance was the "gate" through which they could not pass. Town primary school teachers placed the gate after junior secondary school.[29] My own observations confirmed more or less equal gender proportions in basic education[30] but markedly decreasing total enrollments with advancing grades. The proportion of girls shrank only somewhat. In Muslim areas, on the other hand, not only the total population but also the proportion of girls shrank markedly with every grade after first.

Qinghai Province's ethnic minorities continue to have low educational achievement levels.[31] The Compulsory Education Law assigned to schools and teachers enrollment numbers, passing rates, and fines for noncompliance. Families were fined for nonenrollment. One source in a county seat town told us their school had to achieve an 80 percent passing rate or part of the teachers' monthly salary would be cut.[32] Some of the above-mentioned sociological studies concluded that girls' educational participation and attainment was negatively affected by both economic hardship and the fines levied on Tibetan households. Teachers in only one school appeared to fear these fines as a reality. A professor at Northwest Normal University

(NWNU) told us that compulsory enrollment sometimes leads to families "borrowing" a neighbor's child to send to school rather than sending their own.[33] In other schools, the enforcement aspect of compulsory education was not mentioned; instead, teachers showed a caring attitude toward children and helped them attend school.

Teachers in the schools reported unanimously that enrollments had been increasing due to the Compulsory Education Law and that nomadic Zang families had been progressively settling down in increasingly stable settlements near schools. They also reported that in Zang areas, boys and girls attended school in equal proportions.

Given the expansion of schooling under the Open the West policy of recent years and the national and local economic changes, I, on the other hand, argue that girls' enrollment and attainment has been increasing and will continue to do so more rapidly over the next few years.

Case Studies in a Zang Autonomous Prefecture

On-the-ground ethnographic evidence and narratives that I collected in the fall of 2004 compose a more holistic picture and, I argue, a more telling one regarding the situation for girls' schooling than the sociological macro data can. Complex relations emerged from this data that could not be captured in hypothesis-based sociological studies. Policy built on holistic, dynamic, and time-sensitive data promises to be targeted more accurately.

I describe the enrollment or attendance situation, some of the contextual background of schooling, and students' lives at a typical school in a county seat town and in a rural settlement in the same Zang autonomous county (*Zangzu zizhi xian*) in a Zang autonomous region (*Zangzu zizhi zhou*) in southwest Gansu. I draw on data from similar communities and only report what three or more sources revealed, unless otherwise noted. The majority of the data is given in the paraphrased words of individuals.

Zang County Seat Town School

The Zang bilingual primary school (*minzu xiaoxue*) is located in a well-maintained, historically important town, home to a famous Zang monastery and hence an international tourist center. There is another primary school in town, called the "regular" school by one teacher, which serves the mostly government-personnel Han Chinese population and the Muslim population engaged in commercial pursuits. According to the principal and corroborated by teachers, the Zang school is large, with 98 percent of its students ethnic Zang who fluently speak only Zang. It offers a Zang-language track

Table 4.1

Zang County Seat Primary School, Gansu

Grade	Enrollment total	Girls (%)	Overage (%)	Overage girls (%)
Kindergarten	125	NA	NA	NA
1	143	40	51	51
2	121	39	NA	25
3	100	NA	NA	NA
4	99	41	20	15
5	92	47	13	12
6	76	39	NA	36

Source: Observation on September 20, 2004, by Vilma Seeberg.

and a standard Chinese-language track.[34] The school was established in 1927, names important people among its alumni, and is relatively well resourced; for example, it had central heating, although it was not always operational. The associate principal stated that school costs including tuition of 89 yuan plus books and heat came to about 170 yuan per semester. The mother of one student told us the figure was more like 250 yuan per semester.[35]

The school was under pressure to perform from the county school bureau in town and posted official demographic and enrollment figures in the lobby. The charts showed that enrollments rose from 606 to 682 in the past ten years, due to increasing numbers of nomadic families settling in town. Among students, 47 percent were girls; 47 to 53 percent were registered poor. Classroom observations showed that the gender proportions were rather equal among the on-grade age group and the overage, but total enrollments declined rapidly after first grade (see Table 4.1).

Teachers and the two principals told us that 50 percent of students came from the grasslands and lived either temporarily in town with relatives or monks[36] or had parents who worked in the tourist services in summer and scraped by in winter. Zang educators insisted that "few" children in this county seat did not attend school, though at every promotion "some" dropped out because they did not make the minimum score. The bulletin board showed a 100 percent enrollment rate and a 100 percent promotion rate to junior secondary school. The principals admitted that the higher tuition and fees had caused some to quit. Abject poverty kept many out entirely. Under the compulsory attendance law, the central government does offer some scholarships to the poorest students. However, this was the only school that mentioned giving government financial aid to poor students, and only a handful at that.

Individual Stories

These stories were chosen to illustrate a diversity of student situations encountered in schools. They are not representative in number or situation. The stories are related as they were told to me, without further confirmation.

One fourth-grade boy in the Zang track was introduced to us as a "scholarship student." We visited his home in town, a plain, earthen, two-room shed off a courtyard, crowded with a cold stove, bed platform, two little wooden stools, and a table. Only his sixty-eight-year-old grandmother lived there with him. His mother was elsewhere working (*da gong*) but fatally ill, the father was divorced, and the grandfather had died three years earlier. They had moved to town from the grasslands fifteen years ago. Their only income came from grandmother's occasional sale of small items from her stool in the street. In the past, the boy said he had received the government maximum scholarship of 40 yuan toward the 178 yuan tuition per semester, but neither the school principal nor he knew whether he would get it the following year. The rest they borrowed, and sometimes an older sister helped. Of his three older siblings, he mentioned only an older sister who was in the Zang senior secondary school, where the tuition was 400 yuan a semester. Grandmother proudly stated, "She writes Chinese characters very well. She'll go to university." To pay for it, grandmother said she would sell the house. The boy said both he and his sister wanted to go to university to study medicine so they could help their sick mother.[37]

A female student in the sixth grade Zang track was an only child. Her mother was illiterate, and her father was a senior secondary graduate who worked as a government official (*ganbu*). Her paternal grandmother also lived with them. On weekends she was allowed to watch music videos on TV, and she had visited the capital of the province. She intended to go to the Zang upper secondary school and wanted to go on to university, although it would be difficult for the family to pay for it. In the long run, she wanted to return to work in town to be near her parents.[38]

A twelve-year-old girl in sixth grade in the Chinese track spoke of her fifty-year-old father, a government official, and her mother, who was "retired." She had a brother who had just graduated from the Zang senior secondary normal school and an older sister who was married and a housewife. Her parents wanted her to attend university, not the minority senior secondary normal school, to study medicine. She studied in the Chinese track in order to prepare for the university entrance examination and coursework.

These are but three stories that illustrate the overwhelming effect of income and employment status in the lives of urban Zang children. Apparently girls can persevere under difficult economic circumstances, but the likelihood that higher-status girls will be able to persevere is obviously greater.

Historical Changes, Teacher Perspectives

Teacher interviews give some insight into generational changes in the economic and cultural environment and the position of girls vis-à-vis schooling.

Teacher 2, one of the few ethnic Chinese teachers at this school, reported that the enrollment at the school had been growing.[39] The several reasons he gave were (a) more of the nomadic Zang had been building homes in the town "in order" to send their children to school, even though, out of pride, they kept their pastoral designation (*hukou*) status; (b) the lamas were telling families to send their children to school; (c) the school facilities were much better as was the teacher corps, because, due to the compulsory education law, the local leaders had started to pay more attention to schools and saw to better management. This had raised the status of the school and more people were attracted to the idea of sending their children to school.[40]

A young female fifth-grade head teacher of Zang ethnicity had graduated from Zang-language senior secondary normal school (*shaoshu minzu shefan xuexiao*) but had become a certified Chinese-language teacher at the Lanzhou Ethnic Studies Institute. Her own mother was illiterate but had labored in construction to pay for her schooling. "Ma was forward thinking. Girls didn't go to school when I did," she said. Her father was an official (*ganbu*), so she had grown up in this town and graduated from the Zang bilingual school. She was an only child. She said that in the past twenty years because of economic development and the success of population control, gender preference in schooling had disappeared, and parents, illiterate themselves, now wanted both girls and boys to go to university.[41]

It is plausible that in this fast-developing tourist town with many seasonal service and construction jobs, the climate for girls' schooling should have changed as dramatically as these personal anecdotes attest. The county government was reportedly responsive to educational needs and continued to enlarge the school. In 1992, the four-floor building was completed with central heat (though no plumbing), and plans for another building were still awaiting funding. With the availability of native-language schooling from kindergarten through senior high and senior technical-vocational schools, including teacher education and nursing, children could envision the possibility of obtaining a rewarding education. Given the confluence of these three factors, girls' schooling looked to be no more problematic than that of boys, the important factor being income and status of the parents.

Almost all university educators and teachers as well as students emphasized that students wanted to graduate from upper secondary school and higher, because they did not want to live lives that were as hard as their parents'. They wanted to be financially able to help their younger siblings go to school and pay back their parents for all their sacrifices. From only one university educator and teachers and family members in two of five Zang villages that practiced settled farming did I hear a divergent opinion. In the farm villages, the locals expressed contentment with their lives and expected their girl children in particular to stay at home to farm. This was corroborated by the young Zang teachers, who found it incomprehensible. An older teacher, however, felt it was natural that both his daughters "stayed at home" despite a junior secondary education.

In one of these two villages, which lay in remote mountains, teachers and families expected to build houses for their sons in the village; in a case where there was a fourth son, he had become a novice lama at age twelve. Teachers[42] did not expect girls to stay in school past fourth grade, at which time they would be big and strong enough to help in the house and field. Teachers said they themselves were expected to babysit the children of the village until they were needed to do the adult work.[43] Teachers, however, said the land was poor and the young men were beginning to leave the area to work (da gong).[44] They could only remember two girls who stood out, one had gone on to town for junior secondary school and the other had made it to senior secondary normal school. The primary school children themselves, when interviewed, articulated quite clearly that they wanted to go to university to become teachers or doctors.[45]

In the second village, which was located fifteen kilometers from the county seat, many of the young men were employed in a highly valued traditional religious handicraft, which brought in cash income. Girls and women did the farmwork and ran large family compounds, needing every healthy helper. A sizable temple in the village required families to contribute food and maintenance work, which could be a heavy burden. The temple also took in young boys as novice apprentice craftsmen. Interest in schooling was not high. A county education bureau staff member who accompanied us grew up in this village as one of seven children. He was the only one chosen to get an education. His father insisted that one of the children be educated and hence employable in a steady salaried job in order to tide the family over during hard times. Both farming and the traditional crafts have their dry periods.[46]

The examples from the settled farming villages show a slower development toward higher school participation for boys and girls and female participation in life outside the home than in the tourist town. Here traditional patriarchal culture and the farming economy combine to depress girls' schooling. As different from the high plateau nomadic areas, the settled farming communities were able to continue age-old practices and survive. Their relative backwardness as compared to the urbanized gold coast had not begun to drive out young talent and encourage youth to leave.

Division of Labor by Gender in Zang Culture

This topic is explored to elucidate this foundational cultural factor behind the social organization of Zang communities. As the gendered division of labor changes due to economic changes, so do Zang cultural factors that mediate gender roles and gendered schooling. The most striking observation we made in this area was of the absence of males of working age.

In Zang schools, both town and rural, we heard one family story after another wherein fathers were absent. Professor Wang of NWNU[47] had spent years working with Zang schools in the high plains and grasslands of Gansu. He spoke frankly about nomadic Zang culture and gender relations. The traditional lifestyle of Zang men was to follow the herds for months, even years. Life was dangerous, and not infrequently the men would never return home. Women would stay behind in settlements to raise children and do the subsistence agricultural work, for which many hands were always needed. They would rely on men when they were available and not necessarily on one man, hence not marriage, but childbirth, was the celebration of a lifetime. Motherhood was still highly revered in Zang culture in 2004; yet girls and women were thought to be inferior and subservient to men. Boys were raised into a separate male culture defined by a spirit of "machismo."[48] For men, there was no other worthy work outside of herding. Professor Lu of NWNU concurred that the pastoral Zang had always been and still were sheepherders and wanted to be nothing else. In modern times, Professor He at Qinghai Normal University added, when large-scale roaming of herds has been severely constrained and less and less productive, the traditionally rigid division of labor by gender had left the Zang male without much to do, without an identity. Zang men had come to be seen by their own people as lazy drunks and women as the stronghold of the family. Two polarized Zang male identities—the revered, intellectual monk and the Zang herdsman lost with nowhere to roam—peopled town and cityscapes in Zang areas. In a patriarchal society set on an exogenous patriarchal development path, the less than viable male gender identity had a harmful impact on family stability, income, children's development, and schooling.

It is expected that boys would suffer directly from this loss of identity, loss of direction, and loss of motivation and that girls would be impacted indirectly. Culturally, women were filling some of the vacuum left by disappearing males. New spaces for girls to redefine their identity had opened and enabled them to explore new roles and reconceptualize their potential. The context had shifted the meaning of educational attainment for girls and encouraged them to develop a new self-image that included being educated. For boys, the meaning of education had become more problematic in that it was not integral to the traditional Zang male identity. The rapidly changing economic circumstances created difficulties for adult male role models. For them it was difficult to reconcile Chinese-based public schooling with their traditional value orientation. The new Zang male found himself lacking a certain cultural niche and was indisposed toward making one within the larger Chinese culture. The loss of direction and motivation was evident in towns where Zang men clustered and in family stories about them.

At the micro level of Zang culture, another factor promoted girls' education. In primary schools, girls, boys, and teachers all described girls as the more conscientious students and boys as more "naughty" (*qiaopi*) and not on task.[49] This advantage bought girls leverage for staying in school. Many teachers told of their commitment to promoting girls because they were diligent and more worth the trouble than boys. This attribute is consistent with a traditional thought regarding gender traits wherein girls are seen as more disciplined though less creative than boys. Local educators seemed to look at girls' schooling in vocational rather than scholarly terms.[50] Girls' education was expected to bring financial rewards to the whole family. Family stories more often placed the expectation of caring for parents in their old age on daughters, whereas the future of boys was talked of in terms of further studies without much reference to returning home. This represents a departure from traditional patriarchal roles.[51] Though Zang parents, particularly those in the high plateau pastoral regions, may have wanted both boys and girls to be schooled and get a job, and may have seen boys' ultimate career achievement more positively, girls had gained an advantage by their studious behavior and by a changed filial pragmatism.

Zang Religion

In the two autonomous Zang county seat towns that were located around important lamaseries, the latter's influence was palpable. Saffron and burgundy-robed monks of all ages were visible everywhere. The monks and lamas were said by all to support public schooling for children. In Tibet, one of the heads of the lamasery told us that he had founded fifty schools in the area, which was independently corroborated by the county education bureau personnel. The director of the county education bureau was related through his wife to the high lama and worked closely with the leadership of the lamasery. The public and religious institutions seemed to be amicably intertwined and both were interested in increasing education among the population.

Lamaseries only accept boys as novices. In the fall of 2004, we saw and were told that when a family had too many sons, or was very observant, or had suffered hardships, they would see to it that a son join the lamasery. The

PRC government restricts the number of novices; however, due to the grow-ing number of lamaseries and temples in often-remote locations, it is no small number of boys that receive their schooling in the lamaseries rather than the public schools. Hence, some number of spaces in the public schools that might have been occupied by boys was available for others, including girls. Though this number did not strike me as significant, several educators brought it to our attention, and therefore it deserves mention.

In Zang Buddhism, the position of women in society is subordinate, and they are given no authority in the religious institutions. Women, it is said, are the most active in supporting their local temples, and they go on lengthy pil-grimages independently, as we witnessed in three lamaseries. This speaks to a kind of independence, determination, and courage that could lie at the foun-dation of the activities of girls who were insistent on staying in school, and the younger mothers who supported this. Harrell made a similar suggestion about Zang women of the Omdo branch in Sichuan. He saw them as more assertive, taking more leading roles in conversations than neighboring Nuoso women, for example, and speculated that this may translate into the observed gender equality in schooling.[52]

Zang County Remote Rural School in the Grasslands

In the rural Zang areas, distances between home and school are greater, par-ticularly in the high plateau regions, and enrollment rates, by all reports, are lower. Difficulties mentioned consistently by children, parents, and educa-tors were: distance, particularly for girls; poverty; family sickness; direct and in-kind school fees; harsh and unsafe living and sleeping conditions at school; lack of food and insufficient oversight in boarding schools; seasonal tending of animals; absence of men and boys while herding for months at a time; absence of one or both parents to find work in towns; early betrothal or pregnancy for girls; the endless chores associated with nomadic life, much of which is done by the women; parental illiteracy; and the burden of main-taining temples and monks in the village.

Our example of a remote rural school is a central (*zhong dian*) primary boarding school[53] lying at the edge of a high mountain grassland plateau. Although only thirty kilometers from the town school described above, it took us three hours by jeep to get there on a rutted dirt road, climbing over a mountain pass and crossing a vast grassland plateau. An official from the county education bureau who accompanied us had herself never been this far out. The school lies on the edge of a small settlement on a crossroad of paths leading over abruptly rising mountains to Qinghai Province.[54] The settle-ment consisted of a store, diner, medical clinic, gas and repair station, three or four adobe houses, and a few tied-up horses. The head teacher explained that of the 229 students, 167 lived on campus and 67 boarded in nearby villages. The students all came from seminomadic herding families (*mumin*) who had winter quarters within ten kilometers of the school. So that the children could be with their families, the school let out every twenty days for nine days. It closed during the coldest fifty days in winter and the hottest fifty days in summer.

Students slept twelve in a room by village of origin, gender-segregated, and were cared for on a rotating basis by older women from the villages. This was part of the in-kind cost to a whole village for sending children to school. Besides the 60 yuan in per-student semester fees, each family also had to pay cash for electricity and books; provide foodstuffs, soap, and so on; and donate two sacks of sheep dung to heat classrooms and for cooking in the dorm.[55] The dorm rooms were close to collapse, and the latrines were collapsing. One hand-drawn well served the entire school. The back one-third of each classroom and two schoolrooms were used for storage. Each classroom was crowded with desks and stools shared by two to three students each, a teacher desk, a stove, a small bookcase, and a blackened board on the wall. A donation of books constituting the library was locked up in one of the storerooms along with the teachers' motorcycles.[56] Teachers' living quarters occupied remaining rooms.

Enrollment

Since 2001, enrollment had been increasing, according to the head teacher. In 2003, total enrollment stood at 170 students. Huang[57] gave a total enrollment figure of 222, which probably includes enrollment at the attached teaching point (see note 27). The head teacher stated that 77 percent of the age group was enrolled in school and that, in 2003, 60 percent of primary school graduates were promoted to junior high in the county seat town.[58] In 2004, total enrollment stood at 234 students, including 67 at the feeder teaching point. The total enrollment increase from 2003 was around 5 percent.

Many girls, I was told, did not start school until age nine as was traditional here and had been so throughout China.[59] Girls constituted 40 percent of total enrollment. Forty-eight students received national compulsory education tuition scholarships; another 111 received tuition waivers, comprising 95 percent of students too poor to attend school without assistance.

In 2004, classroom observation showed that boys predominated but girls were well represented, and rather evenly in the lower grades. The overall high enrollment, particularly girls, in grades one and two (see Tables 4.2 and 4.3) supports the contention of many schoolteachers that the families use the

Table 4.2

Rural School 2003 Enrollment by Grade and by Gender

Grade	Enrollment total	Girls (no.)	Girls (%)
1	78	32	41
2	47	21	45
3	23	5	22
4	21	7	30
5	29	11	38
6	24	9	38
Total	222	85	38

Source: Observation on October 17, 2003, by Huang Weimei, "Action Research on Dormitory Management of Boarding Primary Schools in Nomadic Tibetan Areas: Exploration in G. Boarding Primary School," unpublished master's thesis, NWNU, 2004, p. 12.

Table 4.3

Rural School 2004 Enrollment by Grade, Overage, and Gender

Grade	Enrollment total	Girls (no.)	Girls (%)	Overage students (no.)	Overage girls (no.)
1	60	32	53	13	8
3	39	23	59	14	9
6	25	10	40	7	4

Source: Observation on September 22, 2004, by Vilma Seeberg.

schools as babysitters as long as the children are too small to be of substantial help around the homestead.

The overall enrollment held steady between 2003 and 2004. Again, grade-one enrollment required two classes, fell off immediately in grade two, and continued to decline to less than half of the first-grade enrollment. Girls' numbers and proportions of students were higher in the early grades in 2004 but also declined to a low in grade six, dropping from a high of nearly 60 percent to 40 percent (see Table 4.3).

Promotion to Junior High School

The school's principal and head teacher separately claimed a 60 percent promotion rate to junior high,[60] and the head teacher later said he thought most girls went on to junior high school.[61] I heard many reports in this region that girls would probably finish primary but not make the jump to junior high.

Because they would have to live in the county seat boarding school at a cost that was difficult even for town dwellers, it seems unlikely that many girls, or boys at that, would go on. Perhaps the figures represent those eligible rather than those actually attending. A negative factor for girls was early marriage. The head teacher, himself of Zang ethnicity and locally raised, noted that most girls were married at age fifteen and most men at age twenty.[62] Professor Lu of NWNU maintained that girls were often married as early as age twelve. In either case, because they did not usually start school until age nine, girls could not get in many years of schooling before getting married.[63] Considering the difficulties presented by the interaction of material with cultural factors, it seems unlikely that the promotion rate for girls could be as high as 60 percent. The popular phrase for promotion to junior high was "making it through the gate," and comments by many participants and observers long support doubts that girls went on to secondary school at the quoted promotion rate.

Individual Stories

A fifteen-year old girl in grade six told me that she was the oldest of three children.[64] Her younger sister also was in school in grade four, but her eleven-year-old brother was out herding the sheep.[65] Her brother wanted to go to school, so either she or her sister would have to drop out. She did not want to drop out because, she said, she was heading toward Beijing Central National Minority University. She was modeling her dream on the young lama in the Bang temple in her village who was studying for his master's degree at Beijing University and had come back last summer to urge the villagers to let their children get an education. She had started school late and dropped out in between, yet she held to her dream.

Another fifteen-year-old sixth-grade female student said she loves to study both Zangyu and Hanyu (mainstream Chinese). When I asked about her after-school studies, she explained that she did not often have homework and did not study in the afternoons. The teacher stated the children had to clean and do chores and had little energy beyond that due to poor nutrition and poor health. Her sleeping quarters had a lightbulb. She had to drop out in the spring semester but was getting financial help to study the next fall.

The families we visited in a nearby village were seminomadic, having both sheep to herd on the open grasslands and some grain farming. Water was scarce. The better-off family (see below) supported two sons in school, one of them in the county seat primary, and wanted them to grow up to be doctors. The poor family had one older son, who had left school to take their small herd of sheep on their trek, and a younger brother age thirteen in grade five. He had to drop out when there was no scholarship. They could not afford to even buy him pencils. It was difficult for their grandmother to talk about anything but her immediate survival needs, and questions about the boys' future seemed out of place, even hurtful. Professor Lu claimed that families negotiated with schools for scholarships and would not send their children without them.[66]

In this school, economic privation was the major problem, and it chose both boys and girls for its victims. Although boys outnumbered girls in enrollment, both boys and girls dropped out in great numbers. For many in this remote region, extreme poverty trumped gender as a determinant of who would get schooling.

Historical Changes

Educators in the area had not seen much change in the local economy except that more of the middle generation was leaving for longer periods. The school itself had changed the environment, however, and introduced cultural change. Professor Wang[67] told a story about the rural school that shows the depth of female inferiority in traditional Zang culture and how a school can impact and change patriarchy to empower girls by reorganizing its own structures. The school originally boarded all the children from one village in one room, boys and girls together. They required a few of the unmarried young girls from the villages to stay with the children as cooks and helpers. At that time, girls were dropping out of school in large numbers. One of Professor Wang's graduate students, Ms. Huang, was living at the school for a year of fieldwork. She observed that in the living quarters girls were being harassed and ill treated. The young women caretakers could not stand up to schoolboys who were successfully demanding all the food from the young cooks, leaving none for the girl students, or to male intruders from the surrounding area who could simply walk into the dorm rooms at night. Families withdrew their daughters and no one spoke up. Ms. Huang, however, did, and she convinced the principal to segregate the dorm rooms by sex and bring in older women with more authority as caretakers. The male abuses stopped, and female students returned to the school.[68] These are indeed historical changes promoting girls' schooling.

The Compulsory Education Law had made itself felt in the area, but slowly. Villages complied "with all deliberate speed" as they could. For example, in 1999 a village six kilometers from the rural central primary boarding school built a teaching point with four classrooms.[69]

In Qinghai's Huangnan Zang Autonomous Prefecture, schools are still being founded in the high plateau grasslands where the nomadic life predominates. One such boarding school, with an enrollment under 100, had been built by Save the Children–Hong Kong in 2000. Another school was rebuilt in a new location in 2000 because the old building was too inaccessible. The new school had to shut down for some months and reduce enrollment in the spring of 2004 after heavy floods washed out the roads and paths to it. The county education bureau reported that the central government would be building more schools over the next few years. The county and the county education bureau were collaborating on building a new junior high in the county seat town, seeking donations from outside philanthropic organizations.

Division of Labor in Zang Culture

Apparently, even in the high plains, the decline of the migrating herds and the nomadic lifestyle and the strict gender division of labor was beginning to change.[70] In general, boys from age five on helped in the herding; however, girls would also go out with the herd—I assume more in the vicinity of the settlement.[71] Girls were mainly expected to help plant and tend crops, do all the farmwork in the homestead, and process it to supply water, food, and shelter for family and animals.[72]

In the settlement near the school, we did not see one young or older man other than the teacher accompanying us. Women were present in all the homes, some with several generations. However, the middle-age range of mothers was underrepresented. They were off doing migrant labor elsewhere. The vacuum left by males was palpable.

Religion

There were many temples and lamaseries in the autonomous Zang county. The smaller lamaseries housed about 100 lamas. The large, ancient lamasery in the county seat town housed an estimated 3,100 novices and lamas engaged in various institutes, including higher learning in Zang medicine, Buddhist theology, and so on. About 20 percent of boys will be "lucky enough" to become novice monks.[73] In addition, there were many smaller temples, housing just a few lamas. The principal of the school, who was a primary school graduate, was related through his wife to a high lama at a local temple.

I was told by a young male teacher that one female student whom I was interviewing came from a nearby village that had retained its pre-Buddhist Zang religion called *Bang*.[74] This village, though very small, had its own temple, and the villagers had to repair and maintain it. Two lamas lived there, and this put a heavy burden on the village. The young lama on his summer break came back from Beijing where he was studying for his master's degree at prestigious Beida (Beijing University). Last summer he assembled the villagers and told them to send their kids to school, that the next generation needed to have an education and change their lives. He also convinced the old lama to volunteer to teach English at the teaching point. "The lamas love school," the teacher said.[75]

Dynamics Promoting Schooling for Zang Girls

With astounding unanimity, adults in all walks of life highlighted the following two themes as the most basic motivation for schooling: (a) Children have to "get out" because life is too hard here in the villages or on the grasslands; (b) to get a job, children need a senior secondary diploma and to go to a city. Otherwise, they will be condemned to hard work in poor conditions like their parents. Who would be able to make that transition, sons or daughters, was a complex decision composed of a network of personal relationships with material complications, family structure, illness, remoteness, ethnic narratives, identities and roles that were fading into nostalgia, and a culture undergoing deep changes.

The Siren Call of the Advanced Regions

Local farm- and land-based economic activity was described as poor everywhere in the Northwest, whether town or country. Compared to the cash economy—either seasonal or small-scale commercial activity elsewhere (*da gong*)—local economic activity did not bring in enough to feed every mouth in the family or buy an education. In the Yellow River valley in eastern Qinghai, in village after village, between 60 and 80 percent of the parent population was missing. The middle generation had left to find work elsewhere, and grandparents were left to tend the fields or let them lie fallow.[76] In the high plateau grasslands, pastures were overgrazed; sheep and yak herds were shrinking while the population continued to grow. Increased population pressure on the land was the cause of a sweeping national change: massive migrant labor flooded out from the Northwest and Southwest into the coastal regions exploding with export manufacturing. Many in Qinghai went to Lhasa, more than seven days' travel away.[77] These trends have reached a magnitude that American newspapers have picked up on.[78]

In the grasslands that we crossed, large-scale erosion was visible. University and urban educators as well as village leaders deplored the environmental degradation and the land use and farming practices that caused them. This was the pressure that caused grandparents, parents, educators, and children to declare that there is but one future for the children: to leave the land. Only in one Zang farming village did the elders speak of passing the land onto their sons, though the teachers doubted the viability of this.[79]

When fathers and brothers leave to pursue paying work elsewhere, boys are likely to follow in their footsteps, eager to earn money. Several, perhaps half, of the parents took sons with them for some or all of the time to take advantage of the better schools in the bigger towns. Patriarchal traditions promoted leaving girls behind more often than not. Girls turned to the only other route, education, to move out of poverty and to contribute to the future of the family.[80] Conceptually, boys and men leaving had given girls one choice and one advantage, the pursuit of an education. Several female primary school students told of their brothers who had gone away for good. They did not send money back to help the family—they were "a loss." In contrast, the girls wanted to stay in school and get a steady job to help the family. Schooling offered the girls a way to envision a different future and fashion a new role for themselves that was central to the well-being of their birth families.

To get a paying job in a town or city, it was commonly speculated, already required a senior secondary education. Parents who had gone off to work elsewhere were largely illiterate and got unstable or seasonal jobs of hard labor. Grandparents and educators hoped the children would do better than that, and that meant having a better education.

Mothers, grandmothers, and teachers who were fathers were not as vocal on their daughters' future as on their sons', which suggested vacillation to me. But the girls themselves were clear about their educational wishes, and they were clear that they would try to convince their parents to let them continue. However, all educators and parents or grandparents were unanimous that families were utterly committed to sending their children of either sex to school for as long as possible.

Parents and elder siblings did whatever they could to raise the money for the cost of schooling. They picked cotton in Xizang; sold trinkets on the streets of Lhasa; borrowed from family, friends, and neighbors; and begged, to "buy" one more semester of schooling. In an odd year, the men might get lucky and find the highly valued medicinal herbs and mushrooms that brought in incomparable earnings. The poor students and families we met did not know where the money would come from, especially in the lean spring months, yet they were desperate to keep their children in school.

The Compulsory Schooling Law assisted particularly girls' schooling. Families faced fines for keeping a child out. Some families would send girls and hide an older son. Some families paid other families to send a substitute, who was likely to be a girl. Families preferred to send girls to school, because they were not as strong as boys, who could better do the hard work, nor was it culturally appropriate to send girls out to the pastures for herding.

The utility cost of boys was higher, especially in families where the older men had left for cash jobs.[81]

In the Northwest, the combination of the Compulsory Education Law with the Open the West policy was serving as an important agent of school expansion and access for girls. The decline and relative backwardness of the local economy had laid the groundwork by draining males from the local economy, and the greater access to schools provided the vehicle for girls to become active in changing their lives. By taking on the educational prerogative traditionally reserved for some boys and taking on the central role in safeguarding the well-being of the elder generation, girls were realigning social relations in a fundamental way.

Once in school, girls proved themselves to be more able. Teachers uniformly praised girls as more dedicated and persistent students than boys. Some teachers complained that because the parents were gone and grandparents could not control them, the boys were hard to manage in school. Teachers expressed more sympathy for girls' difficulties and even helped them financially after leaving primary school so that they could attend junior secondary school in town.

The idea of new opportunities had not escaped the quiet female students. In the more remote rural schools, girls almost exclusively listed their career goals as becoming a teacher or doctor.[82] Upon gentle prodding, they admitted that they would have to and would like to go to university. Girls often mentioned that they wanted to stay near their parents.[83] In contrast, boys' career hopes were to be scientists, doctors, teachers, and officials, and several were clear that they wanted to live in a city.[84] Girls in more remote rural schools and some of the girls from poor families in town schools mentioned wanting to help and repay their parents and build them a house when they grew up, "because their life is too hard"; [85] some mentioned that they did not want to live like their parents.

In town and nearby rural schools, girls uniformly wanted to go university. They listed future careers such as TV host,[86] foreign language teacher,[87] boss, secretary, and teacher.[88]

In the answers of the rural girls, we can see the power of models. The girls knew women teachers and had heard of women doctors in nearby clinics.[89] The more urban female students had a wider horizon of models and could aim for goals that were more far-flung.

For Zang girls, schooling is their gateway to the world, as it has been to boys. This expands their vision and allows them to nurture hope for an unknown and better future. The attraction of schooling to girls can be easily understood in that schools, no matter how austere, involve them in activities that are entirely different from the back-breaking labor of house and farmwork. Studying, no matter how hard, was a new and preferable idea. They were attached to their teachers, some of whom were women, who modeled a different future than their families or villages provided.

Cautions and Caveats

Yet, in the remote high plateau grasslands, choices had to be made very close to the bone. Survival was the number-one issue for enough families to keep overall enrollment of boys and girls low. Though I argue that under some circumstances the relative economic backwardness promotes girls' schooling, at the absolute poverty limit, schooling must be abandoned.

As small-scale subsistence farming or herding fail to sustain a family, and the parental generation leaves to work in the cash economy, farming or herding as the main income of the family is neglected and even abandoned.[90] Families might move into urbanized areas, which raises the chances for both boys and girls to have access to schooling.

In the remote rural Zang villages on the grasslands, herding and farming was poor and declining, and many village parents had left. I observed few of the middle generation in any of the Zang and other ethnic group villages. The head teacher at the rural school said that typical income was around 400 yuan per year,[91] though this is probably inflated to keep up appearances. It was difficult to see the role of cash in the households we visited. The low income barely allowed for a life of subsistence. There was, however, significant disparity.

Due to the luck of birth, health, and offspring as well as personality characteristics, some families were more prosperous. One family, headed by the grandmother, had an older grandson who herded their 200 head of sheep and a second grandson who attended the Zang lower primary school in the county seat town thirty kilometers away. Grandmother was healthy and farmed enough grain to feed her family. Large stacks of grain were mounted in the courtyard, and several sheds were closed. At the time of our visit, the grandmother had just cooked and served a meal for several other women in the village, a commercial venture. This is one of the left-behind grandparents who felt she was leading a relatively good life with the income from the small business and remittances from her daughter and son-in-law working for cash somewhere in a city.

Their neighbors two courtyards away lived in a plain two-room adobe home, with no flooring and a simple clay stove. The grandmother, who was not in good health, said her daughter, the mother of two sons, unmarried, was sick in the hospital in town. Her first grandson was off with their herd of forty head of sheep. There was no grain in storage, and there was no money for school for the second grandson, age thirteen. He dropped out of school whenever he did not get a scholarship to cover everything, including pencils, as he had last spring semester. This grandmother was frail and bent, and it was clear that she needed help from her young grandson just to manage the household. How they would survive the winter was not clear. As Mark Bray commented, "the poorest of the poor simply do not have the resources to commit to long-term investments when pressed by the demands of basic daily survival."[92] Their long-term survival is also threatened.

Remoteness

In nomadic families with an alternative income, parents who were away to work probably had a good idea about the necessity of schooling for all their children, including daughters. In families where male labor power was critically needed, among the poorest of the poor, girls had an advantage for being sent to school—if they could get a scholarship, such as provided by Compulsory Schooling Law.[93]

Local incentives were hard to grasp. In the most remote locations, educational aspirations seemed almost out of place, at best vague. Rural schools, like the one sketched above, were immersed in a nonliterate environment; that is, literacy was not needed or evidenced in the living sphere. Even usable paper was scarce, except for a few minimal decorations.

Adult role models for education were absent in the remote grasslands, except in the schools. When asked about their heroes, students cited their teachers, the head teacher at the rural school, and the lama in the Bang village. Information from the "outside" was spotty. Only in the Zang farming village schools had students heard of the 2004 Olympics going on as we were there, or the successful launch of a Chinese astronaut earlier that spring. In the high plains remote rural school, students did not know what a train was or that roads have lanes, nor did they have toys or even balls.

Two of the educators, but not the parents, were cautious about the interests of nomadic and seminomadic Zang peoples in general in education. The high plains remote rural school's head teacher and Professor Lu in NWNU thought that parents would only allow their kids to go to school when the tuition was free. Because the heavy and never-ending house and farmwork of seminomadic families was done mostly by women, the help of children, especially stronger ones, was very much needed. Zang people, the local head teacher said, saw themselves as sheepherders and grassland people who did not want to go into business or leave their homelands: "they do not want to do anything but herd sheep."[94] The absence of the middle generation, however, seemed to contradict that statement, as did the poor state of farming and herding among seminomadic families.

In farming villages, the same kind of calculus applied as among nomadic families, because the impoverished economic conditions prevailed there as well, if not as extreme. Perhaps here too, culturally the Zang families might have preferred to carry on with their traditional way of life, but survival economics imposed another reality. The closer to urban centers (less than five kilometers), the more obvious became the need for an education. The closer to urban centers, the stronger was the draw on parents to find work for cash elsewhere and leave the children behind. In these villages, problems associated with family destabilization had become evident and harmful to children.

In urbanized or small-town families, the necessity for schooling was universally clear. Child labor markets were more underdeveloped than adult labor markets; therefore there was not much competition to schooling for young children. The utility cost did not greatly vary by gender. School enrollment was more gender neutral, and there was a lower dropout rate with age.

The Chinese government in 2004 made public its concerns with the effects of uneven development and its deterrence to the progress of compulsory basic education. At the National Seminar on Migrant Children in October 2004, Christian Voumard, the representative with the UNICEF office for China, said, "There are reports that say only a small fraction of migrant rural workers can afford to take their children with them to where they work. Problems related to the security, education, physical, and emotional care of these children who are normally in the care of their aging grandparents or relatives is becoming an increasing issue of concern." No investigation has been done about the exact number of these "left-behind" children so far. "Millions of left-behind children in China are facing various problems, they are vulnerable to outside threats and injuries without parents' timely protection; moreover, they themselves are likely to behave improperly, even breaking laws," said Yang Jin, an official with China's Ministry of Education.[95]

In sum, interviews with students, parents, teachers, and other educators raised the following material conditions as barriers to education, which were rather barriers to economic survival: (a) poor economic foundation due to environmental degradation, population pressure on the land, and decreased pasture land and fields in agricultural regions; (b) water scarcity, natural disasters, flooding, and drought; (c) poor infrastructure and roads, inaccessibility; (d) large sibling groups and boy preference; (e) absence of working-age parents, the burden on grandparents, and the need for children to help in subsistence food production.

The cultural context of expanding schooling and ties to parents off in a distant China and social transitions to keep up with the new economic realities were occurring at a tacit level, below the surface, and therefore not easily identified by those intimately involved. Yet, to the outsider, the changing role and presence of girls and women was as clear as the endless skies over the land.

The relative advantages of girls for schooling outlined above have their limits when it comes to extreme poverty. These limits apply to boys even more than to girls. In the poorest regions and among the poorest families, where the absent parental generation had to be replaced with youth in local food production, the gender advantage varied by who was available to see the family through on a daily basis. For these households, the long-term future had to be sacrificed for survival today.

Conclusion: Prevailing Against Patriarchy and Poverty, Creating Cultural Change, and Promoting Development

Zang cultural traditions and predispositions regarding gender roles and schooling assign women the heavy burden of farmwork as well as house-keeping and men the open sky and grasslands, riding with their herds. With dwindling herds and diminishing as well as deteriorating pasturelands, women's farmwork becomes central to the household. Yet the land does not provide. Households headed by women and absent adult males represented the overwhelming majority of the families we encountered.

The life narrative of the roaming sheepherder was receding into the past.[96] Zang men's essential roles were changing, and no local alternative was available. As the stronghold of the home, in the midst of family members dispersing, women were left with the young and the old to provide for. This task was so daunting that it is understandable that young girls might be strongly motivated to find another way, to avoid adopting the traditional role of their mothers.

The only alternative productive work was in the cash economy, most of it far away. Paying work accrued to boys rather than girls. However, both were faced with the task of defining new identities to match the new roles into which they had been thrust.

Because the pressure to marry is not as strong as in Han Chinese and especially Muslim families, Zang girls have more space to define new roles and identities. This is evident in the greater parity in school enrollment. Because Zang girls traditionally are expected to act as heads of households when the men were away, they may have a cultural advantage when redefining their roles. As Harrell noted in 1993, Zang women in Sichuan were more outgoing, "often taking leading roles in . . . conversations," which he theorized might translate into higher valuing of female education.[97] In the early part of the twenty-first century in relatively remote northwest China, among the seminomadic Zang, it must have seemed to the girls that adopting their mothers' role was fruitless, so they desperately sought new pursuits and new livelihoods. They chose education—there really was little choice. This answers my question as to the reason why some girls have acted so determinedly in the pursuit of schooling.

The connection between female-centric family structure,[98] traditional culture as a stronghold, religious influences promoting public education, women's role in rural and seminomadic households, the higher utility cost of boys' schooling for farm labor, new patterns of short- and long-term male migration for work, school availability due to the Compulsory Education Law and the Open the West policy, boarding school policies and practices, the attentiveness and studiousness of girls, the supportiveness of teachers, the example of female teachers, and the effectiveness of Zang language instruction and Chinese as a second language in secondary school form a cohesive net of factors promoting girls' schooling.

Thinking about these changes underneath the surface of life in the high plains and mountain regions, it becomes clear that the economic activity of the people cannot be understood separately from their culture. It is the cultural interpretation of their surroundings and their lives that influences choices the Zang make—in a declining pastoral economy in an absolutely and relatively underdeveloped, remote section of a country in the throws of rapid globalization—choosing new paths and life narratives. For girls there are expanding opportunities that can be grasped in and through schooling. Eager Zang girls were living the goal of EFA; they were struggling to get an education, thereby prevailing against patriarchy and poverty, creating cultural change, and, in the midterm, promoting development.

The policy implications that I draw from this scenario can be summed up simply: (a) vigorously expand girls' access to basic schooling followed by secondary schooling; and (b) vigorously expand scholarships to girls to cover not only tuition and fees but also living expenses. Because girls' roles are a stabilizing force in the family and the community, higher educational attainment will maximize their potential while at the same time benefiting the community. I am not advocating for hygiene and nutrition training but for comprehensive basic and secondary schooling in the home language followed by Han Chinese as a second language. Girls seek a thorough educational foundation because it resembles traditional Zang Buddhist notions of self-improvement and because it opens a window to the world, the world that has called so many of their older relatives. With this kind of education, girls will more fully understand the globalizing world into which their communities are tied and the effect this has on their lives, and, therefore, they will be able to make better decisions about the future of their families and communities. From the government's perspective, an investment in Zang girls' education is most efficient and will have the greatest multiplier effect through their position as heads of households.

I add a final caution that there is great variation in the ability of Zang households to participate in education. In the poorest families in the poorest counties, the utility cost of schooling alone may endanger survival. Where the cost is too high, schooling may have to be put off for a future generation. Local inputs and follow-up are essential in targeting and maintaining policy objectives.

In March 2005, PRC prime minister Wen Jiabao at the opening of the annual National People's Congress announced the abolition of primary school fees for fourteen million students in the officially designated poorest counties of China and subsequent expansion to include all rural students by 2007. Li Shi, a prominent sociologist, wrote in the official English-language newspaper, *China Daily,* that in 2002 the central government dedicated only 23 percent of its education budget to the countryside, where two-thirds of the population and an even higher proportion of its school-age children live.[99] Whereas the government long ago promised free compulsory nine-year education, funding had remained so low that most schools were forced to charge "fees." Yet, in 2005, action appears to follow on the directive. One journalist observed that in Ningxia in April of 2005, village schools had abolished those fees in the spring semester of 2005 and for the future.[100]

This study of high plains seminomadic and farming Zang villagers reveals how education is embedded in complex gendered relationships "constantly negotiated in . . . political-economic settings"[101] that are connected to vast global dynamics. Policy that is based on holistic, dynamic, and time-sensitive data promises to be targeted more accurately and have more desirable direct effects. Girls may indeed be the best allies EFA has, and they should be promoted through higher levels of education. The future of the region may depend on it.

Notes

The field research for this study was supported by the Kent State University Research Council, the Gerald Read Center for International Intercultural Education, the Kent State University Department of Educational Foundations and Special Services, and Save the Children–Hong Kong. I am grateful for the capable assistance provided by Ms. Hailing Gu of South China Normal University and the many individuals associated with Save the Children–Hong Kong projects in China, especially Professor Qiang Haiyan at South China Normal University, Dean He Bo at Qinghai Normal University, Mr. Zhu Yongzhong and his team at Sanchuan Development Association, Vice Provost Wang Jiayi at NWNU, and Ms. Zhao Lin at Shaanxi Normal University.

1. Jim Yardley, "Rural Exodus for Work Fractures Chinese Family," *New York Times,* December 21, 2004 (www.nytimes.com/2004/12/21/internatinal/asia/

21china.html?oref=login&oref=login); Bo Jin, "Giving Voice to the Voiceless," *China Daily,* (October 23, 2003). Retrieved on 10.23.2003 from www.chinadaily.com.cn/ en/doc/2003-10/23/content_274655.htm.feature; P. Haski (February 15, 2002) "La storia di Ma Yan," *Liberation* [The story of Ma Yan]. *Internazionale* 424. Permanently stored at www.internazionale.it/pagine/mayan/mayan_stampa.html.

2. Letter to Guanlan's mother from Shi Wen Go village. Cited in V. Seeberg, "Partner-ships with Girls in Rural Schools in China: A Case Study," paper delivered at the annual meeting of the Comparative International Education Society, Orlando, FL, May 22, 2000.

3. H. Ross, personal communication, March 2004.

4. N. Assie-Lumumba and M. Sutton, "Global Trends in Comparative Research on Gender and Education," *Comparative Education Review,* vol. 48 (2004), pp. 345–352.

5. Assie-Lumumba and Sutton, "Global Trends," p. 349.

6. Tibetan is translated to "Zang" in standard Chinese. I use "Zang." "Zangzu" refers to the ethnic or national group, and "Zangyu" refers to their language. The research took place in the Huangnan and Gannan autonomous prefectures of Qinghai and Gansu Provinces where Omdo (a.k.a. Amdo), one of three main Tibetan regional groups, reside. Since the guides were Chinese and the interviews of Tibetans were mostly conducted in Hanyu, the word Zang is used to reflect this.

7. *Ethnic minority* is the term used here for the Chinese term *shaoshu minzu,* which is sometimes translated as "national minority group." In some of the areas in Qinghai and Gansu, individual ethnic minority groups constitute the majority. Some of these areas, though not all, are autonomous regions to which apply special national regulations. Some of these areas, Linxia County in Gansu, for example, are combined ethnic group autonomous regions.

8. G. Zhang, "National Interest and Foreign Aid in China," unpublished disserta-tion, Kent State University, 2001, p. 31.

9. Deborah Davis, "Chinese Social Welfare: Policies and Outcomes," *China Quar-terly,* vol. 119 (1989), pp. 577–597, cited in Emily Hannum, "Poverty and Basic Edu-cation in Rural China: Villages, Households, and Girls' and Boys' Enrollment," *Com-parative Education Review,* vol. 47, no. 2 (2003), pp. 141–159; Keith Lewin and Yingjie Wang, *Implementing Basic Education in China: Progress and Prospects in Rich, Poor and National Minority Areas,* IIEP Research Report No. 101 (Paris: International Institute for Educational Planning, 1994), cited in Hannum, "Poverty and Basic Edu-cation"; E. Hannum, "Investigating Children's Schooling in the Interior: The Gansu Survey of Children and Families," *China Education Forum,* vol. 2, no. 1 (2001).

10. M. Bray, X. Ding, and H. Ping, *Reducing the Burden on the Poor: Household Costs of Basic Education in Gansu, China,* CERC Monograph Series, No. 2. (Compara-tive Education Research Centre, University of Hong Kong, 2004); World Bank, *China: Growth and Development in Gansu Province* (Washington, DC: World Bank, 1988).

11. The Ministry of Education in 2004 proposed a change in the Compulsory Edu-cation Law, which Yang Jin, deputy director for Basic Education, said would lead to a heavier input from central finance to underprivileged rural areas in western and cen-tral China in support of local education; *People's Daily Online* (November 8, 2004).

12. See note 10.

13. Hannum, "Poverty and Basic Education"; Hannum, "Investigating Children's Schooling."

14. Jan-Ingvar Löfstedt, *Human Resources in Chinese Development: Needs and Supply of Competencies,* IIEP Research Report No. 80 (Paris: International Institute for Educational Planning, 1990).

15. Diyu Xiao, "Investigation and Discussion on the Problem of Primary and Secondary School Dropouts in Poor Areas," *Chinese Education and Society,* vol. 33, no. 5 (2001), pp. 49–58.

16. W. Zhou, T. Zhang, W. Liu, Y. Ma, and J. Peng, "Research into Girls' Education in Four Western Provinces of China," *Chinese Education and Society,* vol. 34, no. 5 (2001), pp. 4–28. (The original article, "Wo guo xibei sixhangqu nuer jiaoyu yanjiu," appeared in *Jiaoyu yanjiu,* vol. 1 [1996], pp. 34–43.)

17. To better understand these seemingly contradictory forces, I set out to study the conditions from the girls' perspective, to provide rich description of the cultural and socioeconomic context and issues confronting rural girls and their interpretation of these circumstances as they relate to schooling, their future, and that of their families. For six weeks, I traveled with my family, including my Chinese-born daughter, to villages and towns in the mountainous, majority ethnic regions of Qinghai and Gansu Province, and the majority Han region in mountainous Shangzhou of Shaanxi Province. We conducted over 105 semi-structured interviews with educators, students, family members, and other villagers, accompanied by ethnographic observations at fifteen schools and their administrative agencies and many more towns and villages, conducted over forty background interviews at four universities, and kept multimedia records.

18. Tibetans are among the most populous three of the fifty-five ethnic minorities officially recognized by the Chinese government. In this region they belong to the Kham Tibetan group. They have had their autonomous prefecture status since prior to the establishment of the PRC. They called themselves Zang in Putonghua.

19. Most of the veteran teachers and school leaders spoke Chinese; therefore I needed no translation with them. The families, children, and younger teachers spoke only Zangyu (Tibetan), and the teachers or other school leaders translated into Chinese. A graduate student who spoke Chinese and some English assisted me. On a daily basis we compared and added to our notes. In taking notes, we recorded only the real names of university personnel, and we replaced place names with abbreviations.

20. For one of the most telling accounts of schooling in a minority region adjacent to the Tibetan areas written by two insider authors deeply embedded in these communities, see Zhu Yongzhong and Kevin Stuart, "Education Among the Minhe Monguor," in *China's National Minority Education: Culture, Schooling, and Development,* ed. Gerard A. Postiglione (New York: Falmer, 1999), pp. 341–384, particularly pp. 368–374.

21. UNESCO, *Education for All: The Year 2000 Assessment Final Country Report of China* (cited as EFA 2000 Country Report of China), Section 3.3.3 (www2 .unesco.org/wef/countryreports/china/contents.html).

22. According to the EFA 2000 Country Report of China, "In 1990 female illiterates account for 67.9 percent of total illiterate adults, and this figure increased to 71.4 percent, indicating an increase of 4.5 percentage points in five years" (Section 3.2.1). See also Su A. Wang, "Gender Analysis of Women's Illiteracy Elimination and Post-Illiteracy Elimination (IE) Teaching Materials," *Chinese Education and Society,* vol. 36, no. 3 (2003), p. 69; Xiao, "Investigation and Discussion"; Zhou, Zhang, Liu, Ma, and Peng, "Research into Girls' Education."

23. The same trends were found by D. Stephens, "Girls and Basic Education in Ghana: A Cultural Enquiry," *International Journal of Educational Development,* vol. 20, no. 1 (2000), pp. 29–47; C. Coclough, P. Rose, and M. Tembon, "Gender Inequalities in Primary Schooling: The Roles of Poverty and Adverse Cultural Prac-

tice," *International Journal of Educational Development*, vol. 20, no. 1 (2000), pp. 5–29; and by Kofi Annan, "Address to the World Education Forum: Building a Partnership for Girls' Education," *World Education Forum, Final Report* (Paris: UNESCO, 2000), pp. 40–43, www2.unesco.org/wef/en-docs/findings/rapport%20final%20e.pdf, accessed February 20, 2006.

24. EFA Country Report of China, 2004.

25. Lu, interview by author, Field Notes Journal no. 2 (2004), p. 8.

26. Ibid.

27. Qinghai teacher educators' focus group, interview by author, Field Notes Journal no. 1 (2004), pp. 1–10.

28. Northwest University interviews with Lu and Xu, Field Notes Journal no. 2 (2004).

29. It must be remembered that every higher level of schooling is located in evermore central and larger towns, with senior secondary schools being located exclusively in county seat towns. Hence, remoteness, distance, increased costs, and cost of living differentials constitute a significant part of the impassable "gate."

30. Harrell in 1993 observed that the Zang as well as other Buddhist ethnic groups had the best record of female education among the many ethnic groups in Sichuan.

31. Professor He Bo, interview by author, September 4, 2004, at Qinghai Normal University in Xining, Qinghai, PRC.

32. Interview no. 71 by author, Field Notes Journal No. 3 (2004), p. 9.

33. Ibid.

34. Many of those who choose the Han Chinese language track for their children are officials (*ganbu* or *guojia jiguan gongzuo*) and are aware of the value of this language track for college preparation.

35. To illustrate the real value of this amount, her son's tuition constituted 30 percent of her income at a state-owned shoe factory, where she earned between 80 and 170 yuan per month. On that income lived grandmother, mother, and two sons. For the older son she paid 500 yuan per semester at the senior high school in town. Interview no. 73 by author, Field Notes Journal no. 3, p. 9.

36. Lamas are highly revered religious personnel who tend to all matters of religion, including instruction. In Zang Buddhism they serve for life.

37. Interview no. 79 by author, Field Notes Journal no. 1, p. 165.

38. Interview no.78 by author, Field Notes Journal no. 1, p. 103.

39. Interview no. 75 by author, Field Notes Journal no. 1, pp. 101–103.

40. *Hukou* is translated as "household registration." It was the all-powerful connection of an individual to his or her place of birth under the prereform regimes and still held significance as a sort of domestic combined ration card–passport.

41. Interview no. 72 by author, Field Notes Journal no. 1, pp. 95–97.

42. Interview no. 11 by author, Field Notes Journal no. 1, p. 23; Interview no. 12 and Interview no. 13, p. 24.

43. Interviews by author, Field Notes Journal no. 1, pp. 22–28, and Field Notes Journal no. 3, p. 2.

44. Interview no. 11 by author, p. 23; Interview no. 12 by author; Interview no. 13 by author, p. 24.

45. Interviews by author, Field Notes Journal no. 1, pp. 18–23.

46. Interviews by the author with Education Bureau personnel and villagers, Field Notes Journal no. 3, p. 1.

47. Interviews by author, Field Notes Journal no. 1, pp. 114–117.

48. Direct quote by Professor Wang.

49. Interviews by author, Field Notes Journal no. 1, pp. 41–46; nos. 36–39, and others.

50. Interviews by author, Field Notes Journal no. 1, pp. 33–40; nos. 26–27, and nos. 70, 71, 72, 75, pp. 95–97, 101–103.

51. Fong, writing about ethnically Chinese urban singleton children, noted the gender shift in filial expectations as well. Both the younger and parental generation were more certain of girls' long-term care giving. See Vanessa L. Fong, *Only Hope: Coming of Age Under China's One-Child Policy* (Stanford, CA: Stanford University Press, 2004).

52. Steven Harrell and Erzi Ma, "Folk Theories of Success Where Han Aren't Always the Best," in G.A. Postiglione, ed., *China's National Minority Education*, p. 234.

53. Central primary schools (*zhongdian xiaoxue*) are schools located in either townships or more accessible central settlements that receive higher funding. They typically oversee staff development for approximately seven more remotely located primary schools and the teaching points associated with each of them. Primary schools (*xiaoxue*) are more accessibly located, complete five- or six-year schools. Teaching points (*xue dian*) are lower primary schools located in even more remote areas, usually higher in the mountains, and go through grades three or four. Their teachers are typically on temporary contracts, receive substantially lower pay (100 yuan per month compared to the 600 to 1,200 yuan primary school teachers' income), have lower qualifications, have high turnover rates, and are thought to be basically baby-sitters. In Gansu there are twice as many teaching points as primary schools (Journal no. 2, p. 9).

54. This same unpaved road is on a regular bus route from Gansu to Qinghai and apparently traveled by occasional tour buses to T. for its historic temples and artisans, though we saw only tractors and motorcycles in the course of one day. We were told that often tourists stopped by off the buses, helping local students to develop a broader worldview. We did not sense this in the avid response of the children to us outsiders, including our Chinese daughter.

55. In winter, from November through April, one bag of sheep dung heats one room for one day, which would require approximately 3,600 bags, but the student fee would bring only some 900 bags.

56. A philanthropic foreign professor had donated books. They were rarely used for fear they would be used up. Only half of the books were in Zang, and children, even in the highest grade, were unable to read Chinese-language books.

57. Huang Weimei, "Action Research on Dormitory Management of Boarding Primary Schools in Nomadic Tibetan Areas: Exploration in G Boarding Primary School," unpublished master's thesis, NWNU, 2004.

58. Interview no. 81 by author, Field Notes Journal no. 1, p. 112.

59. Interview no. 81 by author, Field Notes Journal no. 1, p. 108.

60. Interview no. 80 by author, Field Notes Journal no. 1, p. 108; Interview no. 81 by author, Field Notes Journal no. 1, p. 112.

61. Interview no. 81 by author, Field Notes Journal no. 1, p. 113.

62. Interview no. 81 by author, Field Notes Journal no. 1, p. 112.

63. Professor Lu had participated in teacher training at the school.

64. A local Zang teacher who had known the girl and her family for two years translated to Putonghua.

65. Interview no. 82 by author, Field Notes Journal no. 1, p. 109.

66. Interview no. 81 by author, Field Notes Journal no. 1, p. 112.

67. Personal communication, September 2004; Weimei, "Action Research on Dormitory Management," see Note 61.

68. Weimei, *Action Research on Dormitory Management.*

69. Interview no. 82 by author, Field Notes Journal no. 1, p. 110.

70. Professor He, Qinghai Normal University, Interview no. 2 by author, Field Notes Journal no. 1; Professor Lu, Northwest Normal University, Field Notes Journal no. 2.

71. Interview no. 81 by author, Field Notes Journal no. 1, p. 108.

72. Interview no. 82 by author, Field Notes Journal no. 1, p. 110.

73. Interview no. 81 by author, Field Notes Journal no. 1, p. 108.

74. The teacher had taught in the Bang village teaching point for two years.

75. Interview no. 82 by author, Field Notes Journal no. 1, p. 110.

76. Interview no. 25 by author, Field Notes Journal no. 1, pp. 33; Interview no. 26 by author, p. 37; Interview no. 33 by author, p. 38; Interview no. 36 by author, p. 41.

77. Many interviews by author, Field Notes Journal no. 1, pp. 33–57.

78. Yardley, "Rural Exodus for Work"; M.A. Lev, "From Field to Factory, by the Millions, Chinese Migrate for Better Lives," *Columbus Dispatch,* January 16, 2005.

79. A comparison can be made to the massive north migration of southern poor and tenant farmers, mostly ethnic African Americans, in the United States in the early twentieth century.

80. Interviews nos. 13 and 14 by author, Field Notes Journal no. 1, pp. 24–29.

81. Thirty interviews by author, Field Notes Journal no. 1.

82. Lu, interview by author.

83. Interviews nos. 18–23 by author, Field Notes Journal no. 1, p. 28.

84. Interviews with five girls by author, Field Notes Journal no. 1, p. 20.

85. Interviews with five boys by author, Field Notes Journal no. 1, p. 20.

86. Interview no. 42 by author, Field Notes Journal no. 1, p. 49.

87. Interview no. 30 by author, Field Notes Journal no. 1, p. 30.

88. Interview no. 37 by author, Field Notes Journal no. 1, p. 43.

89. Interview no. 42 by author, Field Notes Journal no. 1, p. 50.

90. At the macro level, a comparison can be made to the historical progress of African Americans on the move after slavery. Women who pursued an education in the late 1800s and early 1900s became the backbone of the African American teaching force in the United States. Seventy years later, African American women greatly outnumber men in university enrollment and many professions.

91. In 2004, the central Chinese government became concerned and mandated that head taxes on farm family members be lowered in order to reverse the trend of farm abandonment.

92. Interview no. 81 by author, Field Notes Journal no. 1, p. 113. The official per capita income for the county read 1,300 yuan per year, according to the teacher.

93. Bray, Ding, and Ping, *Reducing the Burden on the Poor,* p. 53.

94. Two financial incentives for enrolling children in school existed: the avoidance of a fine for nonenrollment and the reduction of the farm head tax when the child was away at junior and senior secondary school. It is unclear whether these fees and taxes were universally applied or what impact their nonpayment might have.

95. Interview no. 81 by author, Field Notes Journal no. 1, p. 112.

96. *People's Daily Online* (November 6, 2004). China's "left-behind" children need more care. The transition from nomadic to settled lifestyle and economics has repeated itself across the world. The romance of the free-roaming herder, whether on horse or camel, in Central Asia, the Americas, or Africa, lingers on in campfire songs

and Hollywood blockbuster movies. In real life, nostalgia does not replace the felt loss of a central productive role for the male of the culture. So it is in the high plains of Qinghai-Gansu as well.

97. Harrell and Ma, "Folk Theories of Success."

98. Nowhere did we see signs of or hear about polyandrous family structures. As mentioned repeatedly, rather, the absence of males was characteristic, with the exception of the one farming village. Here too we met grandparent-age couples and parental-age couples. However, we did not conduct a survey or meet sufficient numbers of families in this village to extend these comments beyond the several families we visited. Where we met men in the family surroundings was in farming villages, and they were teachers in the schools.

99. Jim Yardley "China Plans to Cut School Fees for Its Poorest Rural Students," *New York Times,* March 13, 2005 (www.nytimes.com/2005/03/13/international/asia/13china.html?oref=login&pagewanted=print&position=).

100. Pierre Haski, *La lettre des enfants du Ningxia—Mar.–Apr. 2005* [The children of Ningxia newsletter]. (Received April 20, 2005, from Pierre Haski.)

101. Dru Gladney, *Ethnic Identity in China; The Making of a Muslim Minority Nationality* (New York: Harcourt Brace, 1998) p. 109.

Part III

Rural Southwest

5

Rural Classroom Teaching and Nonfarm Jobs in Yunnan

Jin Xiao

Improving the quality of education in poor rural areas has been an important issue of education reform in the current "Go West" movement, which aims to better meet the demands of the new market economy. After interviews with rural firms that hire graduates from poor rural areas, this research focused on classroom teaching to find out if the traits judged by local rural firms as important, including the ability to relate theory to practice, open-mindedness, initiative, and a sense of responsibility, were being taught in schools. Five local primary schools were the focus of the fieldwork and interviews with teachers and students. The results show that classroom teaching, following the centralized and exam-oriented curriculum, is decoupled from the needs of the local firms that are supposed to lift graduates and the rural communities they serve out of poverty.

Schooling is an important component of socialist modernization in China. It is a key process for social upward mobility, and education credentials have been symbolic tickets for the rural population to enter urban and industrial sectors. Equality of educational opportunity refers to all citizens having an equal chance of achieving social status through education, regardless of their social background. However, inequality in schooling, inherent in China's urban-rural dual social structure, has been a long-standing issue as China enters into the twenty-first century.[1]

This urban-rural social structure began when China adopted rapid industrialization as a development strategy in the 1950s. It is the outcome of an

Reading aloud and learning together outside a classroom in rural Yunnan Province

unequal distribution of power and concentration of the country's resources for industrialization.[2] As a result, the population was divided then into urban and rural; the rural population was tied to the land, while the state guaranteed grain to the urban population.[3] This urban-rural structure eliminated competition from rural residents and also altered the social consequences of place of birth[4] and locked rural children to urban jobs.

Education then became a mechanism of control and selection in the dual social structure. Instead of seeing the problems of inequality in education as issues that can be fixed by policies, Li Shulei has argued it as a purposeful choice that the urban-rural dual schooling system is one that conforms to the urban or modern state.[5] Rural education bureaucracies representing the authority of the state in remote villages continue to indoctrinate the state's ideology. At the same time, the rural schooling and tests function as the selection of the most capable students for urban construction. Students are instilled with the ideology of serving the state and with the idea of getting themselves ready to be selected. Youngsters are willing to be selected because there are few jobs in the rural sector and because the rural population does not receive the same benefits that urban dwellers have, such as subsidized medical care and ready access to high-quality commercial goods. However, the selection for higher academic study, which would eventually lead to an urban job, was controlled by the ideological criteria of being "red," or loyal to the state.

In the 1990s, the emerging nonstate economic sector claimed an expanding share of the labor market. The state relaxed its control over the population, and rural migrants to urban areas have become a major force of cheap labor. The "Go West" economic project in the later 1990s further reinforced the idea of expanding economic opportunities to poorer western regions and made poverty-reduction efforts effective.[6] Compulsory education in rural areas, therefore, assumes an important role in preparing rural youth with the knowledge, skills, and values to take advantage of the new job opportunities.

In regard to education and market needs, Western scholars have different views. Human capital theory expects that education would improve the quality of the population by imparting useful knowledge and skills and thus raise the productivity of workers in jobs.[7] It also expects the market's invisible hand will help education respond to the labor market and adjust demand and supply. Bowels and Gintis, with their neo-Marxistist viewpoint, elaborated on the function of schooling as equipping students with the attitudes that serve employers' needs, thus reproducing the inequality of the market economy.[8]

The purpose of this study is to examine whether the revised curriculum mandated by the state helps poor rural schools to respond to the labor needs of the new market economy as rural-to-urban or agricultural-to-industrial migration accelerates. The research took place at schools in Mile County, a mountainous county in Yunnan, a province in southwest China, with only 6 percent of its land as flat areas. The region has a population of 490,000, 40 percent of which is ethnic minority Yi and Hani people. The study was conducted from 2000 to 2002 on classroom teaching in five rural primary school classrooms. In order to determine if rural schooling prepares students to enter the emerging labor market, interviews were first conducted in 2000 at three firms located in the same communities as the schools.

Firms' Perspective on Qualities Required of Workers

Developing certain qualities in the prospective workforce is an important issue when industrial jobs become available to the rural population. Out of a survey study of thirty-four sampled firms in Mile County, Yunnan, three industrial firms were selected for focused interviews in 2000. The first is a tobacco firm, which was set up in 1985. It is state-owned but self-responsible in management. The second is a sugar cane firm, which was removed from the control of the state in 1997 and became self-responsible in management. The third is a private vineyard firm set up in 1997. All of these firms use agricultural products as raw materials and process them respectively into cigarettes, a variety of food sugars, or wine for urban markets. They are all located next to agricultural fields.

Each contributes substantially to local tax revenues: the tobacco firm, 22 percent; the cane sugar firm, 6.6 percent; and the wine firm, 7.4 percent.[9] Employees of these firms consist of the local population, people from neighboring counties, and a few from urban areas. The tobacco firm has about 1,600 employees, the cane sugar firm about 1,074, and the vineyard 180.

In each firm, three types of employees were interviewed: managerial staff, professional and technical staff, and frontline workers. A total of twelve people were interviewed to define competence in job skills or to determine what qualities these firms seek in their employees. Although occupying different positions, managerial staff, professionals, and frontline workers perceived that four major attributes are important.[10]

The first is the ability to relate theory to practice. Our interviewees often defined knowledge and skill in terms of the context of their jobs and daily routines. For instance, when talking about work on the factory floor, they frequently used the Chinese term *lilun lianxi shiji*, meaning translating book knowledge for real-world practical use. The first dimension deals with routines in the "real world." To government officials, development means increased gross domestic product. But for firms and their employees, profits and income come from quality control. "Good" employees make sure that their routines are up to standards by drawing on their previous learning and experience to improve the work at hand. In educational terms, the ability to relate information from different sources and to foresee the consequences of one's immediate work requires a cognitive capacity for induction or deduction. Quality work not only requires attentiveness to technical details but also requires an understanding of the relationship between each detail and other production processes.

The second dimension of quality is open-mindedness and comprehensiveness of learning (*yanjiekuan, siluguang*). In additional to understanding the firm's own production processes and technology, all three firms require employees to have some knowledge of the entire product chain, from suppliers to the end product. At the supply end is knowledge of agriculture and farming technology. At the other end is knowledge of market, competitors, and competition based on quality and innovation. These are critical to train peasants to grow high-quality crops and to the design of the product's processing/manufacturing technology. Open-mindedness is coupled with a holistic understanding of the production process and its socioeconomic context. Employees need the ability to make working life a process of learning.

The third dimension, willingness to find ideas and conceive creative solutions and to take the initiative, refers to making efforts and taking an innovative, active approach to improving one's work. The floor workers in the sugar cane firm learned by "making efforts, being humble and learning and observing every detail of production" (*jinli, xuxin quexue, guancha xijie*).[11] Such effort is often demonstrated when an employee raises questions and talks with peers and supervisors about problems. One floor worker, through his efforts and continuous learning, rose to a supervisory role and became able to solve complex equipment problems. However, trying out new methods can result in numerous failures. Innovative approaches can also initially appear "strange" to established values and convention. Both the firm and the employees need courage to face the challenges of potential failures. It takes more than just words, but pursuing efforts.

The managerial staff have found that "there is always uncertainty over what firms are going to deal with; the market brings risk with possibilities, and demands creativity." For example, the cane sugar firm almost went bankrupt until it increased the range of products from only food sugar to a variety of sugar ingredients for big soft drink firms including Pepsi, Coca-Cola, Wa-Ha-Ha, and so on. These firms have all developed different products for different markets. They find that allowing innovations and new technological ideas enhances the sustainability of the firm.

The fourth dimension, a sense of responsibility, refers to the quality that employees hold themselves accountable for the assignments they have assumed. For them, assignments are not only the tasks established by superiors or supervisors, but something they take pride in. Good employees find a niche for their position in the firm, which is interrelated to other positions and to the larger picture. For instance, making wine is like "taking care of a baby." The sense of responsibility is more an internal locus that expresses the idea "I want to do it well; if my part is done well, it will enable other parts to carry on. . . . I want my peers and my firm to perform well." It is the willingness to give attention and care. Employees with such a quality require minimal supervision; they do not work only to please their superiors, nor do they shy away from problems. They want to see their contribution as part of the greater accomplishment of the firm.

Five Schools in Yunnan

In the mountainous county where the study was carried out, there are 54,679 school-age children and 639 elementary schools, out of which 162 have first through sixth grades, 115 have first through third grades, and still another 362 are one-teacher teaching stations. Forty percent of the students are from the Yi ethnic group or other minorities. At remote rural teaching points (*jiaoxuedian*), one teacher usually teaches two to three grades of a dozen students each. In Mile County, there are only twelve lower secondary (middle) schools and six complete secondary schools with both lower and upper secondary (middle and high) schools. This research includes five primary schools, in different locations and with varying enrollments. The first school is TB Primary School, with only three classrooms in a small village, one for each grade, first through third. The school is located in the center of the village with one principal and three teachers to run it, serving about seventy students. Many students walk long distances along mountain trails every day to reach the school. The second school is PLZ School, a complete primary school with six grades, eighteen classes, and 400 students. On average, there are about thirty students or fewer in each class. The school is located in the center of a large village with about 400 to 500 households and over 2,000 residents. Five neighboring villages, within a distance ranging from three to six kilometers, share this school. Many children must begin walking to school at six-thirty A.M. or earlier in the dark to arrive at school shortly before seven-thirty A.M. for the morning reading sessions.

The third school, HJZ School, is located at the center of a township that contains only three small streets. The small township is made up of 20,000 rural residents in twenty-three villages. This township elementary school serves about six villages within a distance of five kilometers. Roads within the township are paved with cement; however, once outside the township, mud or coal ash roads dominate. Some students ride bicycles to school because the township is located at the center of a small, flat basin. The school is a dilapidated building made of red bricks and mud. All the children of the first three schools are sons and daughters of peasants and dress in mismatched clothes that have not been washed in days or weeks.

After visiting the village school, the center school, and the township school, I visited Mile County School, a key primary school. It is located in the middle of the town, near the county government building. Its two buildings resemble an ordinary four-story urban school. The school facilities include a standard staff room, music room, library, simple labs, and a large playground. Outside school there are busy streets and shops. Students are town residents and have uniforms.

Finally, I visited NY School, a private elite school in the next county, which admits children from the neighboring prefecture and provinces. The school is located on a hill and consists of a kindergarten, elementary section, and a secondary school section with both lower and upper levels. The total student body is 1,800 pupils. School buildings, facilities, and dorms are palatial and among the best found in rural China, similar to elite schools established in urban areas of China. The classrooms are bright and spacious, equipped with audio-visual technology. There are science labs and an observatory. In addition to a standard sports ground and swimming pools, there are indoor sport facilities and private music rooms. The dorms have eight students housed in each room with residential assistants to care for the students. The campus, with trimmed plants and colorful flowers, resembles a large garden. Students come from both rural and urban regions of southwest China. These children usually have examination scores just below the cut-off point to enter the best provincial schools. Parents can afford the 17,000 yuan to 20,000 yuan annual fee and hope that this private school will help their children get accepted into good universities.

Teachers at the three rural schools and the county school received nine to twelve years of education and then obtained a teaching credential. Teachers in Mile County School received teacher training from the prefecture Normal School. Teachers at NY School received a university-level education, and their school principal was hired from Shanghai. Principals from the other rural schools were usually promoted from teaching positions within the school.

In spring 2000, about two classrooms in each grade were randomly chosen from a larger school sample and were visited. Their teachers were interviewed. In early April 2001, one classroom in grade three of each of the five schools[12] was videotaped for both a Chinese-language class and a mathematics class. Before the videotaping, the schools were visited a number of times to reduce the level of excitement among the teachers and students. After each class was observed, the teachers and select students were re-interviewed.

What Does Classroom Teaching Develop in Students?

The five schools differ in facilities and enrollment but are all the same in one respect. Hanging on the walls of the corridors and classrooms are posters with four different slogans, designed by the Ministry of Education. The first group consists of pictures of revolutionary leaders such as Mao Zedong, Zhou Enlai, Zhu De, Deng Xiaoping, and Jiang Zemin, with quotations from them encouraging students to study well and follow the course of socialist construction. The second group consists of pictures of the nation's heroes, such as Lei Feng and Nai Ning.[13] They are models because their deeds were consistent with Party ideology and in the interest of the country and the people. That is, one should regard the interests of the Party, the country, and the people as lifetime priorities. The third group consists of pictures of famous scientists such as Einstein and Newton, who made great contributions to knowledge. Their exploratory spirit of working hard is believed to be the key to scientific and technological developments that will lead the nation to the frontier of development. Finally, the fourth group of posters consists of behavioral regulations and rules for primary school students to obey in and out of school. The classrooms in all five schools are decorated with these posters.

This section analyzes those qualities that teachers stress in class. The work described below is based on videotapes of classroom teaching in the five schools. Instead of finding that the schools foster the four qualities as demanded by the local firms, the study illustrates four major issues of classroom teaching that align learning toward the state-controlled curriculum and drill students for examinations.

Alienating Students from Everyday Life

An important quality mentioned by employers is the ability to relate previous learning or theory to daily work and to improve the quality of the work. Everyday work is full of routines and tedious details. This is even true in innovative projects that require employees to attend to many details so as to perfect operations. Capable employees are those who relate previous learning to these tedious details in their everyday work. As discussed in the previous section, this ability is the "acquisition of the meaning of those tedious details . . . what they are doing in everyday life, and the ability to understand."[14] Accordingly, I hypothesize that school teaching can develop such cognitive abilities in students. That is, if students are trained to take information from books and reflect on events in their community, they would eventually develop the habit of connecting information or "theory" to their future work and life around them; such an ability would facilitate their acceptance of challenges to improve their work and life situations.

At grade three, two texts are required for intensive study. One is titled "Jinhua Twin Dragon Caves" ("Jinhua shuanglongdong") and the other "When the Plums Are Ripe" ("Yangmei shu liao"). The former is an essay about a calcareous sandstone cave (Shihui longdong) in Jinhua County, Zhejiang Province. The latter is an essay in which the author describes his observations of the plum trees and fruits in his hometown. The theme of both texts, according to the teaching guide, is a patriotic one: the author's love of the motherland expressed through descriptions of the beauty of the natural wonders and the plum trees.

These texts are taught in much the same way in all of the five primary schools—the TB teaching station, PLZ School, HJZ School, Mile County School, and NY School. The teaching guidelines are standardized and the teachers have to prepare teaching notes. The teachers compare their notes, and the notes are checked by a head teacher.[15] All of the Chinese-language classes at the five primary schools visited were taught by women. The female teachers were dressed in clean blouses and skirts, pantyhose, and black leather shoes, or in a suit. They were all well prepared for each class. They enthusiastically stood at the podium like army generals and spoke in good

Mandarin without much of an accent. In sharp contrast to the shabbily dressed children, who live in dust-covered walls and muddy houses, these teachers represent a symbol of authority and modernization. The teachers at the rural teaching station/school were hardly distinguishable from the teachers at the CLM County School, located in the county seat. Teachers at NY wear a teacher's uniform.

The teachers used very precise and vivid language to introduce their students to the contents of the text. It was almost as if they were together with the author at the Twin Caves or tasting the purple, juicy plums themselves. Their teaching was carried out in logical steps. In teaching "Jinhua Twin Dragon Caves," the teacher took the students along with her (or the author) figuratively, walking from the outer cave into the inner cave in zigzag paths, observing the beauty of strangely shaped stalactites along the way. In teaching "When the Plums Are Ripe," the teacher helped the students imagine how the plums turn from light pink to black purple, at which point the fruits became sweet, juicy, and mouth-watering. By the end of a teaching unit, all of the teachers had concluded their lessons in the same way. They wrote the major themes of the texts on the blackboard, such as "This text describes (1) the author's experience of visiting Jinhua's Twin Caves and his detailed observations of the beauty of the twin caves; and then (2) through his writing of the beauty of the landscape, the author expresses his love for our great motherland." Or "through his observation of how the plums turn ripe, the author expresses the beauty of the plums in his hometown, and the essay reflects his love of our motherland." As a teacher explained in one class: "If the author did not love his hometown, part of our motherland, he would not have given such a detailed and vivid description of what he saw." The teacher tried to convince the students of this point, stressing the word *our* frequently.

From the texts, it could be seen that the teachers were right about the first point—that the writings focus on describing what the authors experienced and express their feelings about what they saw. However, to deduce from the authors' personal experiences of traveling and loving plum trees that they embraced the major theme of loving the motherland seemed groundless. The lofty themes of patriotism come from a teaching guide, a subjective goal of the centralized curriculum authorities. That we must love the Great Country and that we must serve it define the meaning of the texts and signify the symbolic devotion that the next generation should have for the country.

During my interviews, all these teachers told me almost the same thing, that "these writings reflect the beauty of our motherland and the authors' love of it. We have to nurture such love while the students are young." As the texts were beautifully written, the teachers did not want to "waste time" on things other than "let the student know the best example of writing and shape their love of the motherland" at the same time. The standardized state examination system certainly motivated the teachers to teach that on which students will be tested and that on which their teaching will be assessed for promotion. They literally have no time to listen to the students talk about their lives, even though captivating scenes can be beheld right outside the school building.

When asked if they could understand the two texts, the common answer from students was "The description is beautiful and vivid . . . it shows that our motherland is very beautiful." When asked if they could write about a cave near their hometown and/or about the fruit that their families grow, the students replied shyly, "No, only authors can write." When asked if they thought their hometown was beautiful and our motherland great, the students had a puzzled look, and they stared at me, trying to think of an answer. Obviously, they had never thought about observing fruits growing in their own orchards and writing about them. They had never thought that those beautiful words in the text could also describe the details of their hometown and everyday lives.

Outside the school window, this highland is full of beautiful details, rice waving in the paddy fields among irrigation ditches and abundant orchards. Mile County is famous for growing sugar cane, tobacco, and grapes, as well as pears, oranges, and lotus for the fruit markets. These are the major sources of income for the households. Children herd sheep, water buffaloes, and horses after school and play in the lotus ponds. What is more, there is one stalactite cave named White Dragon Cave in Mile County and another one in the next county that have become main tourist sites in recent years. However, such description of the local beauty is never reflected in teaching or in the students' writings.

The teaching does not help relate students' learning to their lives in the village. Instead, it is very simple for the teachers merely to follow the teaching guide. The teaching paradigm of cramming continues to emphasize rote memorization for tests and instill symbolic ideology conception as ascribed by the centralized curriculum. These alienate the students from their own immediate surroundings.

Molding Young Minds with a Centralized Curriculum

Nowadays, it is commonly believed that education is a major agent through which students acquire knowledge and skills, thus preparing them for the market economy. One important quality of cognitive ability recognized by employees and employers is open-mindedness and comprehensiveness of learning. Being open-minded is coupled with having a high level of reading comprehension and ample knowledge resources. Accordingly, it is hypothesized that the learning experience should direct students to a variety of learning resources in order to nurture open-mindedness. The observations focused on two aspects: resources for teaching and learning, and references that teachers use to guide the students' understanding.

It was noted that the teachers prepared detailed teaching notes for each class and the teaching proceeded in logical steps. The teachers first gave the students a rough idea of the core themes. The class would then read the text aloud together, familiarizing the students with the text. Most of the time would then be spent going over every sentence, giving definitions, and interpreting the underlying meanings. After the teachers had gone over every word, they would write a summary of each paragraph on the blackboard, followed by an overall summary. During class, the students' priority is to take notes, copying down religiously whatever the teachers puts on the blackboard. At the end of a teaching unit, the students are tested, much the same as they are tested in the entrance examinations for secondary school and university. In order to prepare students for the tests, the teachers thoroughly cover every detail in their teaching guide.

Teachers seldom refer students to other sources of learning, other authors, other works, or other pieces of writing or books. Due to financial constraints, none of the rural schools could afford to open a library. Mile County School has a reading room with a few volumes available only to the teachers. NY School has a small library with some books available to children after they complete their homework, perhaps about once a week. The singular focus of teaching and learning is the assigned text.

In addition to the content of the learning, the interactions between the teachers and the students were also observed. During class, teachers would draw students' attention to major points by asking pointed questions. For instance, one teacher at the TB teaching station asked, "How do you describe plums?" A student replied, "They are full of tiny sharp points." Then the teacher asked in firm manner, "Then what is its shape? Liu Ying, please answer!" "Round," Liu Ying answered. The teacher was not satisfied and pursued. "Yes, it is round. But how does the text describe it?"

No one raised a hand to reply. They were discouraged and intimidated. They did not understand what the teacher expected. All of the students looked down, avoiding the teacher's eyes. Seeing that no one volunteered, the teacher answered the question herself: "It is round and it is as big as a longyan.[16] You can see from the picture that it is full of sharp points on its body."

Another student was asked the same question again. The student then read the text to reply: "It is round and it is as big as a longyan. It is full of sharp points. When plums are ripe, the sharp points become flat and the plum sweet." The teacher was pleased this time and said, "You are right.

Please sit down." Obviously, the teacher expected the students to adhere strictly to the original text.

One difference among these schools is whether the teachers will allow the students to read the text in class when answering. It is almost impossible for a rural student to preview the texts at home. Farm chores such as tending to livestock take up most of their afternoon and evenings. Their families are not rich enough to keep the lights on for many hours after dark. So the teachers will ask the students to read the text to find the answer to the question. At the Mile County School and NY School, the teachers will mark a student lazy if he or she cannot come up with an answer quickly. Most often, the teacher's immediate retort is "Please read the text well at home next time. Sit down!" To students and parents, the textbooks edited by the People's Education Press are the only source of learning. Assignments are strictly based on the texts.

Denying Access to Wonderland

Taking the initiative in economic activities is stressed in the workplace. The education reform movement asserts that initiative is important in order to carry on research in science to creativity in high-tech industries.[17] Schools are supposed to nurture this quality. However, it is a pity to see that the teacher-led classroom suffocates any student's attempt at taking initiative.

As illustrated by Table 5.1, in class, the teachers mainly use questions to direct the students' learning. The questions are mostly factual, which only require the student to give terse replies or to read from the text. The following episode illustrates one teacher helping students understand a description of a scene in "When the Plums Are Ripe."

> Teacher: Who would like to read this paragraph? Wang Jiansheng, please read aloud.
> Student 1 (Wang Jianhua): (Reads a paragraph.)
> Teacher: Okay, let us discuss this paragraph. The author writes: "It rains like thin silk." In what season does it rain like that?
> Student 2: These are the spring rains.
> Teacher: Then what does it mean by "it rains like silk"? How does it rain? What does it mean?
> Student 2: Very thin.
> Teacher: Yes. It means that the rain in spring is very thin. But how thin is it?
> Student 2: Like silk.
> Teacher: You are right! It is as thin as silk. In spring, it rains; the rain is very thin, as thin as silk. So as the idiom goes like: Thin rains are like silk [*xiyu ruxi*]. Another idiom says: Spring rain is as valuable as oil [*chunyu gui ru you*]. In spring, every growing plant needs rain. So spring rain is like a treasure. The

Table 5.1

Teachers' Questions and Students' Responses

	School and teaching sessions					
	TB Math	TB Chinese	HJZ Chinese	Mile County Chinese	NY Math	NY Chinese
Teachers' questions (N)	23	109	23	22	40	26
Factual/close- ended (%)	87	83	74	59	93	58
Directing (%)	13	14	13	14	8	23
Open-ended (%)	0	0	0	0	0	0
Correction(%)	0	1	4	14	0	0
Denial (%)	0	0	9	9	0	0
Encouraging (%)	0	2	0	5	8	4
Explanation	0	0	0	0	0	15
Students' responses (%)	21	87	16	26	30	19
Matching-up (%)	84	89	94	85	78	100
Not matched (%)	16	6	6	12	22	0
Expressing ideas (%)	0	0	0	3	0	0
Silent (%)	0	5	0	0	0	0

Source: Videotape of teaching sessions in these schools.

author used silk to describe the rain. . . . (The teacher then starts to read and suddenly asks a question) . . . "Plum trees greedily suck dew." How else does the author describe the rain?

Student 3: As dew.

Teacher: Yes. What is dew?

Student 3: It is a metaphor, a beautiful description.

Teacher: Please sit down. How do the plum trees grow in spring? Please think and answer my question (the teacher points to a student).

Student 4: (Stands up, but buries her head in the text for thirty seconds and still cannot find the answer.)

Teacher: Please sit down. (The teacher raises her voice and speaks to the whole class.) Which paragraph were we talking about? The second! But she is not there. Her mind has been wandering.

Figure 5.1 **Snowflake**

剪雪花

下午四堂开始这课剪活动，剪纸课。约有15了学生，在8至口发之间。

学们围坐了桌子，静静地看一位年轻的女教师，(二十生头)教他们

All five schools teach in this rigid fashion. In fact, the teachers use this strategy to determine whether the students are following the teacher. Students who do not follow the teacher are caught very quickly and their unsatisfactory learning behavior is criticized and corrected immediately. There is very little opportunity for the students to express their own understanding or to comment about the author. Discussions that require student initiative and critical thinking do not exist.

The classroom environment, and everything that goes on, is monopolized by the teacher. Once, a student described the colors of plums as "green, yellow, pink, and very red." With a stern face, the teacher asked her to reread the text aloud to the class. The text read that plums are "light pink, and then turn dark red and, finally, almost black." The student's tentative effort at bringing in her own imagination of the colors was quickly suppressed by the unyielding adherence to the text and the teaching guide.

The timetable of the five schools is the same. The teaching hours each week per subject required by the Ministry of Education are ten for Chinese, twelve for math, four for social science, and six for science. Students sit in class all day long much the same way as described above. The only difference in the curriculum is that the private school provides extracurricular activities for children after class in the later afternoon. The other three rural schools and Mile County School do not have the resources to do this. An extracurricular class at NY School was observed in the hope that outside the authority-controlled curriculum the students had some room to exercise their imagination.

A Chinese paper-cutting activity illustrated a typical episode of an extracurricular activity. About fifteen students were participating, with five sitting around each table. A young female teacher in her early twenties first carried out a demonstration. She asked the students to be quiet and sit up straight and to watch how she folded and cut a piece of paper into a snowflake. Afterward, she gave each student pieces of paper about the size of a palm and of different colors. The students then were asked to fold and cut, following the teacher step by step. At the end, each student submitted his or her snowflake to the teacher. The teacher looked at all of the flakes then picked up one, which was objectively beautiful to the author (see Figure 5.1). However, the teacher commented, "What a pity that this corner is shorter than the others. It would have been a beautiful star if it had six corners. Now, we cannot exhibit it because it is not perfect. Zhang Ling [name of the student], you did not pay attention when I was telling how to fold. So, your snowflake has only five corners. That is why we teachers always ask students to pay attention to our teaching. Otherwise, you will miss some information that you need to learn."

The extracurricular class, which was to be designed to suit students' own interests, turned into formal instruction. The teaching of math that I observed was even more rigid because the teachers stress logic, and there is only one right answer. The students must memorize standard equations to learn the problems. In the long run, the classroom teaching became a process of taming the young minds into submission. There is no wonderland for these youngsters to imagine. In sum, instead of nurturing inquiring minds, such schooling suppresses critical consciousness.

Motivation from External Control

According to interviews of employees and employers, taking the responsibility to complete assignments and being accountable are important because they affect the quality of the product, which is essential for the firm's survival. The workplace belief stresses consciousness, with the locus of control coming from within the employee him or herself. Chinese schools give students a plethora of assignments. As discussed in the previous sections, students' learning is rote memorization based. The teachers' questions in class are designed to check whether the students have completed their memorization. However, it seems that the homework does not serve to develop a self-consciousness of one's responsibility.

When interviewed, those students who did not give the right answers in class replied with spontaneous self-criticisms: "I did not do the homework well. I am irresponsible to the state, to my parents, and to teacher." "They want us to study well and to be able to serve the nation. If I do not do my assignments well, I will not serve the nation well in future." One student did not conduct a self-criticism, but confessed that "I did not have time; I had to herd sheep . . . well, the teacher will teach in class."

The teachers' viewpoints on the issue of the students taking responsibility for doing their work are similar to those of the students: "Our responsibility is to let them know that they have to study well at school so that they will contribute to the construction of socialist modernization when they grow up." "There are models of great scientists who contributed to the world for them to follow. Certainly, if one cannot be great, those heroes show them what kind of person one should be." "At least our students should complete the lower-secondary level. We expect them to complete upper-secondary school and go to university and then become capable professionals for our nation's modernization movement."

Both students and teachers put the nation's political goal of strengthening the country through economic modernization as the ultimate aim for which they are responsible. The second responsibility is to their parents, who are raising them and paying for their tuition. Teachers in schools become the representatives of the state and of the parents, and they help in the eventual realization of these goals. Their demands are legitimate as far as consistency with the ultimate aim, and the students are responsible for fulfilling them. The role of teachers as a reminder to students of their duty toward the state and their parents is well illustrated by the comment "We will teach them and they [the students] have to understand that we teachers are teaching them how to become qualified capable personnel. So they have to listen." At the private school, the teachers stressed that "Their parents put them into our hands. . . . We will turn their children into capable professionals."[18]

While closely monitoring the students' behavior every day, teachers seldom encourage the students to comprehend why they should take responsibility for the state and their parents; students are simply told to do so. At the same time, stimulation mostly comes from outside, through external control and remote images of the state or the abstract concept of modernization.

This is different from the views in the workplace that "[We] want to do our task well. I feel satisfied because I can do it and have the ability to do it." In explaining why he wants to do the task well, one employee said: "Details are important. If I do my part well, my peers can carry on better . . . we can make things together." "This [responsibility] makes our life meaningful . . .

we create from all minor details and quality products come from them . . . the state is too far away."[19]

As described above, on the walls of the classrooms and in the corridors there are colorful and eye-catching posters of the great leaders and their instructions, world-class scientists, heroes, and regulations for student behavior. These are everyday reminders to the students of their future. The students in these schools, and probably in many other schools as well, are held responsible for completing their homework as required. They also behave decently in and out of school. However, the students were not observed being treated as autonomous beings with their own space in the process of learning.

Responses from Education Officials, Teachers, and Parents

The "backstage" of the teachers' preparation and curriculum as well as the textbooks are of great interest in studying the performance of teachers in the classroom. Education officials, the director of the county teachers' school, and the teachers whose teaching was observed were interviewed.

It was observed that all of the schools used the same textbooks published by the People's Education Press in Beijing. In remarking about it, the provincial official told me that by 2001, there were 24,000 primary schools in Yunnan. Of them, 21,000 were teaching stations with only one or two teachers.[20] There are twenty-six minority nationalities in Yunnan, comprising up to one-third of the province's population. Most of them had no written language before 1949. In the 1980s and 1990s, when central controls had relaxed somewhat, some ethnic groups began to create their own written languages from spoken languages, but not very successfully. In the first three years of primary education, teachers use both local dialects as well as Putonghua to teach. However, when science is introduced in the fourth year, and when it becomes necessary to teach math at a more sophisticated level, teachers find it difficult to use ethnic dialects to teach:

> Translating [textbooks] into local dialects costs so much that we could not afford it. In addition, there are no equivalent words for modern technical terminology. Local dialects are not adequate enough to allow them [ethnic groups] to communicate with the external world. Many teachers have not been to a county town. They do not understand many modern devices. . . . [For example,] a teacher told the students that a train is a moving house because people can eat and sleep in it.[21]

Speaking about educational achievements, a provincial education head official told me that by 2000, out of 128 counties in Yunnan, 88 had popularized nine years of education. Compared with the nation's overall rate of enrollment in post-secondary education at 9.1 percent for the cohort in 1990, Yunnan had a rate of 3.8 percent in 1990 and 4.9 percent in 2000. He fretted that "By the year 2010, the overall rate in China will reach 15 percent; Yunnan is only ahead of Tibet or Qinghai." To government officials, for striving to expand education and to include the entire rural and ethnic populations, the use of Putonghua and standardized textbooks is an obvious and significant solution, although there is a dilemma between maintaining the local ethnic culture and introducing modern knowledge and skills.

I found two localized textbooks, one about how to grow fruits in Honghe Prefecture where I conducted the study and one on ethnic cultures in Yunnan. Both were published by Yunnan Education Press. I visited Mile County Teacher Training School a few times and showed the principal these books. He did not show any interest in these two books. Neither was he happy about the education in the schools. He told me that quality education (*sushi jiaoyu*) has been talked about for some time, but he hardly saw any scope to take a different approach or to use alternative books:

> "Quality" is still linked with the higher education entrance examination. We use the unified curriculum and textbooks by the People's Education Press. You do not dare to use alternative materials [for the teacher training program], do you?[22]

With his ten years of efforts in building private schools across China, the former president of NY School Grouping criticized China's education system when recalling his experience of running NY schools:

> The system becomes a gigantic bureaucracy which uses the national uniform higher education entrance examination as a convenient tool to control schools over China and to grasp power in its hand. The examination directs all teaching and tests in high schools and middle schools and primary schools. It suffocates any creativity of teachers and their self-esteem and independent thinking and then teachers do the same to children's. I have no way to motivate teachers and students. Students also know that lying or empty statements [*jiahua*] makes one a high score.[23]

The principal, in addition, described another problem, the difficulty of getting rural teachers to come for retraining. He remarked,

> The Provincial Bureau of Education requires that 5 percent of the rural schoolteachers go through a short retraining course and that each year 2 percent of them get one year of training. All rural teachers try to find a position in a township school, then in a county school, and then to urban schools. So we are short of teachers for the rural schools and the teachers are overloaded with teaching. No rural schools could afford to send their teachers for retraining. If one teacher

is sent here, the teaching of several courses has to stop because there are only one or two teachers in each teaching station. What is more, after training, good teachers will leave the rural areas. At the same time, our county schools are crowded with too many teachers who received retraining again and again.[24]

Retraining is supposed to give teachers some new ideas about improving teaching. In responding to my questions about retraining, the village school teachers showed mixed feelings. One in PLZ School thought of her experience as a relaxing time for both herself and for her students. However, she had to push her students to catch up with their counterparts in other schools when she returned because the teaching was scheduled by the county bureau.[25] Another teacher in HLZ School felt that the messages conveyed about retraining were not clear:

> Quality of education is stressed a lot and new methods have been talked about to motivate students. . . . Teachers can ask questions to motivate students to think and answer, but it was clear we could not move too far away . . . every school has to report the students' test scores. . . . Knowing the contents of the test well is important. At retraining, we teachers shared a great deal about what to emphasize in teaching.[26]

In order to understand what parents see as education for their children, a few dozen households were interviewed.[27] In one Yi ethnic family, I met a woman in her seventies. She told me that the Yi ethnic people love to sing and dance to the strumming of three-stringed guitars after field work. When speaking of this matter, the old women became very excited:

> Just after the Liberation I loved to dance, and my son loved to dance . . . but now we only dance once a year, or twice at most. . . . Last year, on March 8th [International Women's Day], the cadres organized us to dance and it was all the fifty-, sixty-, and seventy-year-olds who could dance . . . before, there used to be wrestling and dancing, and all the young people would have a go, but now they don't know how . . . children study in school and dancing cuts into their school work time.[28]

In a high mountain village, I interviewed a Yi girl at her home after school. She was with her grandmother, mother, aunts, and uncles. The whole family was busy braiding tobacco leaves onto a bamboo pole and getting them ready for drying.

> I asked, "Did your teacher teach about one ruler, one cup of milk, one slice of bread?"(Each noun in Chinese has a specific "measure word" associated with it, which must be used when referring to it in quantities, e.g. *bei* for cup of milk, *pian* for bread, *ba* for ruler. These must be memorized.)[29]

The girl proudly told me: "Yes!"

"Did your teacher teach you about one house, one horse, one mule, or one hoe?"

The girl was puzzled at my question and answered "No."

"Did your teacher teach you how to take care of your chicks, your pigs . . . ?"

The girl was even more puzzled and did not say anything. She was ready to take my "test," but it did not seem to her like what would be discussed in a schoolbook.

"Did your teachers teach you about 'Look to your left before crossing the road'?"

The girl looked pleased and hastened to answer "Yes," obviously trying to make up for the last two questions.[30]

The girl's home is in high mountains at an altitude of 2,200 meters; there are no significant roads around her area. Her family uses a mule to carry tobacco leaves from the fields back to their home. She had never been to the county town, which was about a two-hour drive away. Her grandmother had five sons and two daughters. Two of the sons completed nine years of education at secondary school. Three sons and two daughters received only an elementary-school education. In talking about keeping them at school, the grandmother said, "Even if they are accepted [to a university], we could not afford to send them." Her youngest son, twenty-nine years old, cut in with questions:

Do you mean peasants going to university? Upon graduation, one cannot get an assignment for a job. So, the money is wasted. My neighbor went to the Prefecture Teachers' College, but he did not get a teaching job. He has been at home for over a year now.[31] . . . Going to school requires money. If it [the state] does not give money, who would want to go to school? It takes us 400 yuan a term to send my daughter to primary school.[32]

The peasants were confused about the new educational policy. They felt cheated because while the government required them to pay to educate their children, it did not give a job assignment in the city. They wanted their children to become capable persons (*you chuxi*) and to go out in the world to earn more money.

"What is a capable person?" I asked the teachers in the schools and the county education officials. The typical reply was as follows:

[They] are those who finally go to university and find other jobs. They get jobs in Shanghai and Shenzhen, for instance. There is one person with a Ph.D., an engineer, and some who hold positions in the Party or leading positions in the government administration.[33]

This remark is consistent with the following report in the school yearbook: "Upper-secondary graduates who advance to the next higher level of educational institution are referred to as contributions to the state [*shucong rencai*]."[34]

Concluding Discussion

In the current economic tide to "Go West," China is proceeding with another major effort to reform education by consolidating compulsory education in rural areas.[35] There is no doubt that the market economy has bought opportunities to rural populations, who can now work in urban areas and in the industrial sector. Classroom teaching has a direct influence on preparation of the rural young for their future. This study examines the issue of whether schools improve equality by preparing rural children for the forthcoming economic opportunities that the "Go West" development project will offer. However, this comparative study shows that China's policy of educational expansion is not helping or put into context for rural western China. Education, as a government-controlled institution, is not responding to the growing economic sector.

The above discussion shows that the teaching occurring in the classroom may be teaching children how to read and write but does not at all reflect the generic conceptions of ability and knowledge that firms value. Schools and local firms have different agendas. Firms are building the capacity to compete and have to deal with uncertainties in the market. Survival is their bottom line. In western China, the industries are mostly marginal, as compared to those in the metropolitan and provincial capitals or in eastern China. They are facing ever greater challenges because of the poor infrastructure at the county level. Many more are cooperative townships or small private businesses. They are still learning how to stand up on their own and thus are often very vulnerable to market forces. Therefore, the firms see human resources as crucial to survival. In hiring, the firms want find people who understand the meaning of everyday routines, who have an open mind, who can take initiative to improve, and who want to take responsibility and do things well in the workplace. The difference between what the workplace demands from its employees and what skills the schools are imparting to the students reveal a widening chasm between educational policy and the demands of the human capital market.

Schools are supposed to be the suppliers of human resources but are fully controlled by central policies. They still aim high to serve the state's lofty goals of modernizing the nation, which, paradoxically, bears little meaning to local and rural everyday life. The priority within the classroom is to maintain a steady following of the state-approved curriculum. School tests ultimately lead to the dreaded higher education entrance examination, which decides eligibility for university education and, in due course, access to urban, white-collar jobs. For rural children, failure means falling back to scratch. For schools, a high rate of students advancing to the next rung on the academic ladder is a sign of the quality of education being offered at that school. To government officials, it represents the achievement of educational expansion for a province, a prefecture, or a county. Therefore, giving children drills to help them achieve high marks becomes the nucleus of classroom life.

Although inclusive education is reinforced in every village, the teaching of information relevant to localities and to the new, growing social groups is not taking place. Scholars have also noted that inequalities in education have been aggravated by an increased disparity in school enrollments and attainments between those from rural and urban areas, and between regions.[36] It is important to understand the paradox of the tremendous expansion in education and, at the same time, growing inequality.

The education system in rural areas reflects the aim of selecting personnel for modernization in the urban state, a development scheme followed by Chinese leaders since the late 1950s. As noted by this study, the uniform curriculum is still designed by the state to instill lofty notions that are removed from daily rural life and actual occupational opportunities open to rural people. Grassroots schools continue to take as their only mission the selecting of potentially capable students from county schools to enter provincial schools and metropolitan universities.

With schools teaching the same state curriculum, students at the NY School or at Mile County School may eventually have access to urban jobs through their parents' social connections. But only a small percentage of rural children can pass all the tests and examinations to enter universities. Eventually, the rural population sacrifices the local tradition and culture to send their children to school: Their children lose indigenous knowledge and the desire to dance, sing, and wrestle in the traditional manner. They think highly of "modern" clothing. They become alienated from their own heritage but are not able to take advantage of good job opportunities. Even if they manage to land an urban job, it is usually a menial one.

Teachers implement the state curriculum on a daily basis. By doing so, they institutionalize the state's ideology, and school remains a state apparatus. The teachers have not acquired any knowledge about what the local/township industry needs or about what the peasants need to know to improve productivity. Our teacher informants remarked, "Farming does not need what we teach; our students can learn that from their parents." After the Cultural Revolution, none of the teachers ever bothered to work with the peasants in the fields or to visit local industries. Monitoring the students' learning is enough to satisfy the duties required of a teacher.

Teachers are also in a very vulnerable position, because their livelihoods depend on the government. To be promoted from people-run status (*minbai jiaoshi*) to publicly run status (*gongbai jiaoshi*) signifies leaving one's rural status behind. In the transition, individual teachers gain urban citizenship by imitating the clothing of urban people as well as believing the dominant ideology. Consequently, the teachers' own existential reality blocks them from the reality of their origin, the rural populace. They have no reason to create values that are different from the urban-biased ideology. Although they are from the local area, they have little sense of the value of the local cultures, which have long been ignored in the curriculum and in their education. There is little expectation that the current education system will create a new role for teachers or that teachers themselves will do so.

It is commonly expected that education will improve the quality of the population as well as the equality of the population through extending educational opportunities to include all children. But this study illustrates that education and the market do not match as expected. Due to the government's tight grip on curriculum, the local schools are not freed or given autonomy to respond to the challenges of matching supply with demand. On the other side, the firms have not yet developed to the point of being able to negotiate with the state-controlled schools or the state over its demands with regard to human resources. Therefore, we will continue to see the urban-biased curriculum condemn most rural children to the bottom of the job queue in the labor market. More time will be required before greater social equality is attained through education.

As illustrated in the analysis, although teachers stress the beauty of the great motherland, they themselves have seldom laid eyes on the beautiful red soil of the highlands outside the classroom. One can find among the students' surroundings the upper reaches of the Pearl River, mountains full of natural wonders, a variety of crops and fruits, and many ethnic cultures. The urban-biased education has blinded the teachers and, thus, their students and parents to finding their own values in local development. It is a paradox that while economic opportunities are emerging with the "Go West" tide, the rural children of the western rural regions do not have the capacity to meet these opportunities and still harbor the desire to "go out to the outside world" on the east coast to become cheap labor for the urban population.

Notes

The study described in this chapter is part of a research project, "Education and Work: The Efficacy of Schooling in Human Resource Development in Three Regions in China" (CUHK 4379/00H), which was supported by the Research Grant Council of Hong Kong. The author is the principal investigator. It was presented at the Forty-eighth Annual Conference of the Comparative and International Education Society (February 9–12, 2004) in Salt Lake City, Utah.

1. Li Chunling, "Pinkun diqu jiaoyu" (Education in poor regions), in *Zhongguo nongcun ru ershi yi shiji* (Rural China entering the twenty-first century), ed. Xiong Jingmin (Beijing: Guangming ribao publications, 2000), pp. 228–237; Zhang Yulin, "Fenji banxue zhiduxiade jiaoyu ziyuan fenpei yu chengxiang jiaoyu chaju: Guanyu jiaoyu jihui jundeng wenti de zhengzhi jingjixue tantao" (The allocation of educational resources under the school classification system and the gap in countryside education: Concerning the exploration of the political economic study of the problem of equal educational opportunities) November 10, 2002, *Zhongguo nongcun yanjiuwang* (China rural research network), www.ccrs.org.cn.

2. Hu Angang, Wang Shaoguang, and Kang Xiaoguang, *Zhongguo diqu chaju baogao* (China's regional disparity) (Shenyang: Liaoning People's Press, 1995), pp. 173–245.

3. Dorothy. J. Solinger, *Contesting Citizenship in Urban China: Peasant Migrants, the State, and the Logic of the Market* (Berkeley: University of California Press, 1999), pp. 27–55.

4. Deborah S. Davis, "Social Class Transformation in Urban China: Training Hiring, and Promoting Urban Professionals and Managers after 1949," *Modern China* vol. 26, no. 3 (2000), pp. 259–261, 268.

5. Li Shulei, *Cunluo zhongdo guojia: Wenhua bianqian zhongde xiangcun xuexiao* (Village China: Countryside schools in cultural transformation) (Hangzhou: Zhejiang People's Press, 1999), pp. 118–144, 152–171.

6. "Honghezhou renmin zhengfu, jiakuai nongye changyehua de fazhan" (Honghe prefecture people's government, speed up the development of agricultural industrialization), *Zai 2002 nian quansheng nongye chanyehua jingying gongzuohuiyi de zhengfu baogao, Honghe zhou, Yunnan prefecture* (Yunnan: Provincial Agricultural Industrial Development Management Work Meeting Report for 2002, Honghe Prefecture, 2002), pp. 12–23.

7. See G.S. Becker, *Human Capital* (New York: Columbia University Press, 1964); J. Mincer, *Schooling, Experience, and Earning* (New York: Columbia University Press, 1974).

8. S. Bowles and H. Gintis, *Schooling in Capitalist American Educational Reform and the Contradictions of Economic Life* (London: RKP, 1976), Chapter 5.

9. See Su Jin, "Zhongguo xibu liangxian jingji ziyuan de chouji yu fenpei anli yanjiu: cengjia jiaoyu touru de kunjing ji chouzi jianshe" (Research on the collection of funds in two counties of western China and the allocation plan: The dilemma of increasing educational costs and building resource funds) Academy of Social Science: *Caimao jingji* (Finance and trade economics), no. 3 (2004), pp. 18–27. The paper describes in detail the livelihood and social environment in this remote county.

10. The work described in this section is from interviews with the three firms.

11. From interview note ML_Firmfieldnote4, p. 3.

12. Other grades were also visited. The final decision for grade three as an observation subject was based on two reasons. First, there were limited resources for a larger study. Second, in the first two years, much of a teacher's attention is directed to classroom management and orienting the students on the track of learning. By grade three, the students have become used to regulations and teachers can handle teaching with ease.

13. Lei Feng was a People's Liberation Army soldier who became a model for serving the people. Nai Ning was a youth who died while trying to put out fires in mountains, protecting the public property.

14. From interview note ML_Firmfieldnote1, p. 3.

15. The head teacher has to make sure that students are taught what will be tested. In addition, teaching notes are used for purposes of assessment and promotion.

16. A *longyan* is a kind of fruit grown in south China. It is about the size of a Chinese plum but is covered with a yellowish shell.

17. Jiaoyubu (Ministry of Education), *Mianxiang 21 shiji jiaoyu zhenxing xingdong jihua* (The action plan for facing the twenty-first century education) (Beijing: Ministry of Education of the People's Republic of China, 1998).

18. From interview note ML_Schoolfieldnote6.2, p. 16.

19. From interview note ML_Firmfiedlnote4b, p. 2.

20. From interview note ML_Officialfieldnote1, p. 30a.

21. From interview note ML_Officialfiedlnote1, p. 33a.

22. From interview note ML_Teacherschoolfieldnote1, p. 41b.

23. Ren Jinxi, *Jiaoyu lianyu shinian* (Ten years of educational purgatory) (Unpublished manuscript, 2004), pp. 4, 7, 21, 23. This unpublished manuscript is a self-reflection of Mr. Ren's ten years' experience of establishing Nan Yang private school groupings in China.

24. From interview note ML_Teachershoolfieldnote1, p. 43b.

25. From interview note ML_PLZfieldnote1, p. 94a-b.

26. From interview note ML_HLZfieldnote1, p. 95b.

27. I visited a dozen households. For other issues on rural development please see Su Jin, "Xiandaihua jinbu zhong yanzhong zhihou de cunluo: xibu nongcun de shehui huanjing" (The seriously sluggish village within the modernization progress: Western China's social environment). *Zhanlue yu guanli* (Strategy and management), vol. 63 (2004), pp. 21–31.

28. From interview note ML_VillageWS5.2_pp. 9–11.

29. April 10, 2001, I videotaped her class for a math teaching session, which covered nouns and their associated measure words. Her math teacher gave examples on the blackboard from textbook. From videotaping ML_Sch0016, 2_p2b.

30. From interview note ML_VillageDS5.1, p. 44a.

31. From interview note ML_VillageDS5.1, p. 40.

32. From interview note ML_VillageDS5.1, p. 41a.

33. From interview note ML_Officialfieldnote2, p. 30a.

34. *Mile County Yearbook (1993–1997)* (Kunming: Yunnan Ethnic Press, 1999), p. 306.

35. See Note 18.

36. See Note 2.

6

Education in Rural Tibet

Development, Problems, and Adaptations

Gerard A. Postiglione, Ben Jiao, and Sonam Gyatso

Like other aspects of Tibet's development, rural education gives conflicting impressions. China assures the world that great gains have been made in literacy and basic education, while the Western media is fueled by the image of nomads forced into schools that deprive them of their culture. Despite interventions of several international nongovernment organizations, there has been little effort to gather systematic data on rural education in Tibet. Descriptive literature and policy justifications can be found in several academic journals, some of which are more tightly coupled to the official state line than others.[1] Books focus on a number of topics, including traditional Tibetan culture and values, monastery education, historical accounts of the development of state education, and modernization of education. While most are within the framework of the State's views, there is by no means a consensus on all topics.[2] Among the many contested educational topics, for example, is bilingual education. Political sensitivity makes it difficult to run bilingual education experiments with a high degree of objectivity because proponents risk being labeled as extremists. Though a viable system of bilingual education is indispensable to national development, one scholar points out that China's minority languages, including Tibetan, are not easily engineered to promote the national developmental aims.[3] Another researcher of Tibetan education argues that despite the Western rhetoric, Tibetan language textbooks contain a fair amount of materials relevant to Tibetan cultural life, though not as much as Tibetans crave, and that some "forceful lessons about Tibetan culture can be taught to students through lessons that derive from works that are culturally and historically distinct."[4] These points are in keep-

A young rural Tibetan family with their daughter who they want to attend school.

ing with Bass, who provides a comprehensive overview of educational reform in Tibet since 1950, noting that the basis of educational policy in the Tibetan Autonomous Region (TAR) are measures designed to improve school access for ethnic minorities in China.[5] Case-study data and analysis of specific rural communities can further increase understanding of the situation.[6] Are rural Tibetans attending school or dropping out, and why? How effective are Tibet's educational policies? Does the situation differ a great deal from education in other rural areas of China?

Region, Field Site, and Data

This research aims to identify the factors associated with school attendance and discontinuance, including specific educational policies and practices. Two counties, Penam and Lhundrup, were studied. The focus was on the villages of the *xiang* (township) in each of the two counties. The counties differ on the basis of their remoteness from the major centers of economic activity. More important, however, the *xiang* and the villages within them differ greatly for the same reason. A brief background sketch of each county is provided here.

Penam County is on the southern banks of the Yarlong River, about 290 kilometers from Lhasa. It encompasses about 2,460 square kilometres and its 40,000 Tibetans account for 99.82 percent of the population, spread over 11 *xiang* (two of which are herding *xiang*) and 113 villages. It sits high astride a mountainous area ranging from 3,850 to 5,300 meters and is surrounded by three mountains above 5,700 meters. Tibetans here produce barley, wheat, potato, peas, and rapeseed; the local economy also depends heavily on livestock (yak, oxen, horses, donkeys, mountain goats, sheep, and pigs).[7] The *xiang* that was the focus of the fieldwork is located in the middle of a deep twenty-four-kilometer-long ravine that hugs the Nianchu River. Roads are poor, there is virtually no electricity, water is drawn from a common well, and economic development is below the TAR average.[8]

The second county, Lhundrup, is located in central Tibet on the Lhasa River, about sixty-five kilometers from Lhasa. It encompasses an area of over 4,000 square kilometers and is comprised of cultivated land, grasslands, and forests.[9] Though surrounded by breathtaking mountains, it has a vast area of fairly level, cultivated land. The county is in the Yarlong River belt, and its boundaries are formed by the two mountain ranges.[10] The northern part, bordering the Lhasa River, averages over 4,000 meters in altitude whereas the southern part averages 3,850 meters.[11] Despite droughts, mudslides, severe hail, and blizzards, the local residents manage to produce barley, wheat, and some marketable vegetables. They also depend upon yak, oxen, sheep, and mountain goats and produce some traditional handicrafts.[12]

Penam County's Mag *xiang* and Lhundrup County's Khartse *xiang* were the field sites for this research. These are typical subsistence *xiang* within Tibet. However, Mag is more remote from the county seat than Khartse, and this was reflected in their levels of economic development. Mag had 185 households and Khartse about 199. The Mag *xiang* data came from 153 households in four villages: Sokang, Makang, Gokhang, and Goetoe. The Khartse *xiang* data came from 150 households in four villages: Thongmon, Chashi, Bhongdrong, and Ghangkha. Data were also collected from schoolchildren (101 from Mag and 109 from Khartse *xiang*). Finally, 305 teachers across three counties—59 in Penam, 173 in Lhundrup, and 73 in Gongga—were surveyed.

Field visits began in December 1998 and took place once or twice per year thereafter.[13] Most lasted one to three weeks. Meetings were conducted with county education department officials before proceeding to the *xiang* and village levels. Upon arriving in the *xiang*, residence was often arranged in a village school and interviews were conducted with the *xiang* head and central school principal. There was little interference, and we could move around as we liked. The days were spent visiting homes and schools and interviewing families, their children, village heads, and school personnel. At the village level, interviews were conducted with families, school personnel, and students at school. The main survey instruments were three questionnaires for parents, children, and teachers. Their design was based on an initial visit to the project villages, background documents and interviews, and experience with similar studies in other ethnic minority regions. The household interviews focused on the family profile, education and work experience, perspectives toward the school, school participation, contact with teachers, school fees, educational relevance, household labor, and economy. The interviews were used to gain an understanding of the factors that support or block school participation. After being translated into Tibetan, the survey instrument was piloted and revised. The survey was administered by five to six Tibetan research assistants who were teachers from Tibet University and other schools and colleges in the TAR. After training, their interviews were monitored at random in different household settings. Completed questionnaires were photocopied, with originals sent to Hong Kong in packages of twenty, and the data were entered according to a coding scheme. The open-ended responses in Tibetan were translated with the English printed alongside and sent with the questionnaires.

Schools

Village schooling has to be seen in regional- and countywide context. According to the TAR Vice Director of Education, the enrollment rate was 60 percent in 1991, when most villages had only popularized two to three years of education and less than 20 percent of Tibetans had a primary education.[14] At the turn of the century, only 6 percent of the counties had achieved nine-year compulsory education, 70 percent had achieved six-year compulsory education, and 22 percent had achieved or nearly achieved three-year compulsory education. By 2001, the official enrollment rate was 83.4 percent; illiteracy and semiliteracy stood slightly above 50 percent.[15] Three-quarters of all schools were village-level teaching points (*jiaoxuedian*).[16] The rate of qualified teachers at the primary schools was only 67 percent.[17] At the county level, Penam was typical with sixty-eight schools, including one primary and one junior secondary school in the county seat. There were eleven *xiang*, each having one central primary school surrounded by village-level feeder schools, fifty-five in all. The schools had 344 staff, 285 of whom were teachers, serving 7,305 students (450 at the secondary school). Of the 6,855 primary school students, 3,648 were at central primary schools (county and *xiang* levels) and 3,207 were at other primary schools (village schools and teaching points). Thus, 19 percent of the county population was at school, and the official enrollment rate was 90.2 percent, though fieldwork led to viewing this figure as inflated.[18]

The school levels in Tibet conform to the system in other parts of remote rural China, in which the villages are responsible for early primary education, with small schools of one to three rooms handling primary grades one to three. The *xiang* has a central school with grades four to six that draws graduates from the surrounding villages and boards many of those children. Graduates of the *xiang* central school may go on to attend junior secondary school in the county seat or designated secondary schools for Tibetans in Chinese cities across the country.

Education at the village and *xiang* levels typically has gone through several historical stages of development. For example, the first period of Mag *xiang*'s school development under the People's Republic of China (PRC) government was from 1960 to 1966, when there were six *minban* (locally established and supported) schools and one central school. The second period, from 1967 to 1980, was the communal period, when the *xiang* was divided into production brigades, each having a school, thereby increasing the number to ten. By the end of the period, the enrollment rate had reached 79 percent. The third period was the land reform period, 1981 to 1992, when the rural production responsibility system began, and children were desperately needed for household production work. School access and equity were a major challenge during the land reform period following the Cultural Revolution. From the household point of view, there was less of an incentive to send children to school, and there was little systematic organization of either the management of schools or the work of teachers. Therefore, even though the population increased by almost 20 percent, school enrollment dropped to 35 percent and only 11 percent of the girls attended.[19]

Those families with four children usually sent one to school. The view of the *xiang* head was that some children had to care for the old while others had to work hard at home. He explained that parents have an ideological problem (*sixiang wenti*) because they do not see the value of schooling. In 1998, Khartse *xiang* had the lowest enrollment rate of all *xiang* in Lhundrup County. There were 396 students of school age, of which 318 were said to be enrolled in school.[20] The central primary school had 163 students (out of an eligible 196) in seven classes (two grade fours). During the first visit, grade five had five students; the following year that number dropped to three.[21] Meetings were held in each village on several occasions to explain the importance of sending children to school. Parents were told that their children should learn scientific knowledge to improve farming, as well as to become literate for agricultural and business purposes.

Three schools were consolidated during the period, leaving Mag *xiang* with seven schools across its eleven villages, serving 589 households and 4,556 people (2,277 males and 2,279 females).[22] In 1984, the county used

6,969 yuan (about U.S.$870 today) to build the Sukang Xiang Primary School. Most other educational costs had to be covered by the local people. If the county government provided building materials, it was often the village people who did the construction work and maintenance and helped out in other respects. Beginning in 1985, the county government began to expand *minban* education, and in 1989, the *xiang* government set up a system of school rules and regulations (*guizhang zhidu*). Despite the compulsory school law, the imposition of fines was ineffective at addressing the rapidly rising school dropout rate. As one official put it, "People did as they pleased and there was not even a party organization (*xiaoxiandui*), a book of primary student rules and regulations, or a work and rest system."[23] School matters were formerly under the *xiang* party secretary but later came under the authority of the principal of the *xiang* school.

In 1992, a 100-square-meter school with two rooms was built. By that time, Sukang School had 260 students, with eight teachers in nine rooms, thirty-two sets of desks and chairs, ten blackboards, and three tape recorders. Funds generally went to teacher salaries. There were no ink, pens, paper, or maps. The school had a tiny area of land that was used to plant barley and, on June 1 (Children's Day), the barley was sold. Lhundrup County allocated funds directly to village schools. The *xiang* provided some funds to the school at the Children's Day festival each year.

Before the end of the century, the *xiang* village schools and their central school were much like their counterparts in the rest of rural Tibet. Village schools were small, run-down buildings without lights or electricity. Of the seven schools in Mag *xiang*, for example, five were the poorest buildings in the villages. In two of the village schools (Zemai and Puxi), the classrooms had only three walls, so teachers conducted class in the yard. The lucky schools had chairs, desks, and blackboards. As the research progressed, it became apparent that all children had desks and chairs. Chalk, pens, papers, and dictionaries were another matter, and these were often difficult to acquire.

Khartse *xiang* had one complete primary school and three village schools. One village school opened during the commune period and was re-established in 1992. At that time, there was one *minban* teacher, and because it was located near a monastery, a literate monk taught at the school. At first, families did not send children to the school, though enrollment eventually reached twenty-one and then leveled off at twenty-nine despite pleas by the school principal. Another village school took in children from four villages and had two teachers for primary grades one through three. In the past, each village had its own school, but the poor conditions led to consolidation. The third village school catered to two villages. Built in 1995, it was enlarged in 1998.

The major cost for schools was the recurrent expense of teacher salaries.

While the rest of rural China had phased out the locally paid *minban* teachers (and *minban* schools), rural Tibet still had many of these at the end of the century. Teachers were usually locally educated, recruited, and paid, with low levels of education, perhaps a year or more higher in primary school than the grade they were teaching, and no training as a teacher. Few could speak Chinese.

In the early PRC period, there were three types of teachers at the village *minban* schools in Tibet: lamas and monks that resumed secular life (*huansu*), former housekeepers or domestic servants of landlords, and those in the old society who had it quite well and had attended some kind of private schooling. According to a local agricultural specialist, these teachers had good Tibetan language skills, but their mathematical ability was very poor. There were no teaching materials, so they often read scriptures, told stories, and read legends. Most were older with little or no teacher training. After 1965, the *minban* teachers were recruited from the graduates of these primary schools, so they were younger and had some formal schooling. It was not until near the end of the century that there was the beginning of a steady stream of young Tibetan teachers from outside the *xiang* who were graduates of teacher training colleges.

Minban teachers were sent to the county to hear the *gugan* "backbone teachers" share their experience of teaching and were paid according to three salary levels. At the top was the 182 yuan per month category, followed by the 117 and 127 yuan rate levels, the latter being about average. It was explained that salaries were previously based on attendance, as is still the case in Penam County, but that this was discontinued in Lhundrup County because it led to abuses of the system.

A typical teacher organizes instruction for a non-age-graded one-room schoolhouse.

> After I teach the first class, I teach the second one while the first one does review. This is an interruption to the teaching, but most of the teacher's energy has to be put on the year-two students, because this is related to the teacher's salary. In general, the teacher can send a year-two student to go and teach the year-one students and all the teacher has to do is to go and take a look once in a while.

In fact, a certain portion of the salary was withheld by the Penam County education authorities each year and was awarded back to teachers based on attendance rates and students' passing of examinations for promotion to the upper primary *xiang* central school.

It was also not unusual to see a student standing at the front of the room for a good part of the day, chanting the lines on the blackboard, with the class following in unison. Because most of the teachers were locally recruited and had similar household economic pressures, teachers sometimes did not appear at the village school and children would spend most of the morning on the school ground, singing couplet songs, playing on the dirt field, or climbing to the un-netted basketball hoop.

The TAR government was taking steps to upgrade and convert *minban* teachers and train and place young graduates of teacher training colleges in *xiang* schools throughout Tibet. At the end of the century, the Khartse *xiang* school had nine teachers, including three from Lhasa (one the principal), one from Hefei, one converted *minban* teacher (*minzhuangong*), plus four *minban* teachers. Sometimes converted teachers still had *minban* teacher salaries. Teachers who had training usually received it from Lhasa City Normal School or the Hefei Normal School. There were also a few graduates of the *neidiban* (inland) schools recruited to the *xiang* central school to teach grades five and six. Their years spent attending school in Chinese cities meant that their Chinese was better than that of the other teachers, though the reverse was true of their ability to speak Tibetan.[24]

Given the lack of resources and highly trained teachers, schooling itself was boring and monotonous, though the children seemed to survive by their own wits. Classrooms were cold, dark, and unheated in winter except for a stove in some part of the classroom. The schedule was irregular, depending on the weather and time of year. Few students attended during the harvest, when they were needed at home. The school day began at ten o'clock with six class hours to follow, including two hours for eating and resting. Each class session lasted about forty-five minutes. Primary school children were taught Tibetan with some Chinese in the morning, followed by mathematics in the afternoon. Most children had school books in Tibetan script, except for the subject of Chinese language. The village schools teach Tibetan, Chinese, and mathematics, but never get through the first volume of the Chinese reader. Before Tibet began to produce its own teaching materials, the schools began to use the "Five Province/Region Tibetan Teaching Materials" (*wushengqu jiaocai*) national standard school textbooks across a range of subjects that were translated from Chinese into Tibetan language. Not surprisingly, much of the curriculum is divorced from daily life. Yet, the TAR primary school texts do have pictures of yaks, agricultural tools, and names familiar to local people. The Tibetan epic Gesar is also taught in school. The *xiang* central school and some of the primary schools have wall hangings, similar to those found in classrooms throughout China, including Marx, Engels, Lenin, and Stalin. Chinese leaders, including Mao, Deng, and Jiang are also represented, as well as Chinese historical figures, especially scientists, and Western figures such as Einstein, Mozart, and others. No pictures of Tibetans grace the school or classroom walls.

Constraints exist on religious activities in school, yet religion penetrates most aspects of village daily life. Religious symbols, prayers, offerings, donations, and rituals are evident everywhere. Nevertheless, religious scripture cannot be brought into the school, and, unlike virtually every home in every village in Tibet, there are no prayer flags on the school. When literate teachers were scarce after the Cultural Revolution, some monks were invited to teach at schools, and later some who were expelled from monasteries for nationalist activities found work as village teachers. In neither case was religious symbolism, in form or content, permitted in the schools. Children who want to become monks must now wait until they are at least eighteen years of age, though this is not strictly enforced in some cases. In Mag *xiang,* where four of the county's twenty monasteries are located, 10 percent of the graduates eventually become monks/lamas or nuns.[25]

Aside from the policy restricting children from monastic study until after they have completed basic schooling, there are a number of other measures that have been implemented to increase attendance. Until nearly the end of the last century, the "one child kept policy" permitted parents to keep one child at home to support the household economy. For example, if a family had four children, three were to be sent to school. That policy is no longer recognized. In September 2002, we watched as about 100 village families were interviewed, one by one, in the *xiang* central school by county and *xiang* officials about why they still kept one child home from school.[26]

Other educational policies are derived from national policies for minority regions, including bilingual education and boarding schools. Because of the sparseness of the population in rural and nomadic areas, boarding schools are a central part of the educational system. For example, in Khartse, there were forty-two children with their teachers living in the *xiang* primary school. There are educational policies that apply specifically to rural Tibet, the most well known of which is the *sanbao* policy, which is designed to relieve families of costs associated with schooling.[27] It provides *baochi* (food), tea for children who live beyond two kilometers from school during the daytime, and *tsampa* (ground barley meal) for those who board at school. It also provides *baochuan* (schoolwear and/or a blanket) for boarding school children and *baozhu* (living accommodations) for boarding rural school children.[28]

Despite the policy, rural children bring their own food to school, which can be a heavy burden for poor rural households to bear, though children are provided with tea three times a day.[29] School officials and parents repeatedly emphasize that no fees need be paid for school. However, by the end of the century, 20 percent of the textbook fee (less for the lower grades) was collected from parents (although on our last visit to Mag in 2002, this practice had been discontinued).

Households

Most households we visited were three- or four-room structures, separated into two floors, the lower occupied by animals and the upper containing a kitchen, a sleeping room, a storeroom, and sometimes a prayer room. Within the household compound, prayer flags fluttered at each corner of the roof, and homes were surrounded by a mud brick wall with a wooden door under an archway. Some families had a common sitting area open to the outside light where guests could be received in warmer seasons.

Village life revolves around the growing seasons. Therefore, interviews were mostly done in winter, mid-summer, or just before or after the harvest. Herding was done all year round, but the pace was less urgent than in agriculture. School-age children contributed significantly to herding, which often required little more than watching over and moving a small number of livestock from one place to another. Households would work together during harvest season, when children seemed to play an even more essential role. During the interviews, we were able to move from the village school, where we lived to the households, spending a morning or an afternoon at each household.

Xiang Household Profile

Though the surveys were carried out by trained researchers, they are used here only to reflect the general household situation, attitudes, and issues that relate to the schooling of children. Percentages are reported when they seem meaningful in the context of investigation.

The average number of people in each household was 6.47, and the average number of schoolchildren per household was 1.51. The family structure across the two *xiang* varied but averaged 17 percent polyandrous and 3 percent polygamous. Over 60 percent of families viewed themselves in the middle-income range, and, with the exception of two, the rest saw themselves as poor. There was a government initiative for nomadic and poor rural households that remained poor after the land reform. They would be moved to new areas (*kaifadi*), and some of these *xiang* families were affected by this policy. At least half of the families had one adult engaging in nonfarm labor. This usually means they have migrated to a more prosperous area for work, including the cities.

Almost half of the village family members had no skills outside of those related to basic farming and animal husbandry. About 30 percent of Khartse *xiang* households, who lived closer to Lhasa, had members with carpentry or weaving skills, with about 10 percent having masonry skills and 3 percent having skills to paint simple Tibetan art. Those who had these skills had better possibilities of finding work in nonfarm settings. However, they still had to compete with outside migrants who were often advantaged over the rural Tibetans by their Chinese language skills and networking with large infrastructural projects. The demands of the household economy made it necessary for many families to borrow money, and about one-third had done so. Usually the loans came from relatives or from the monastery, though a small proportion, about 5 percent, were given by banks. Despite the *sanbao* policy, families with children in school were more likely to borrow money. Between 36 and 47 percent had loans ranging from 20 to several thousand yuan, the average being about 1,500 yuan.

Prosperity depended on owning land and livestock. The amount of land per household in both *xiang* ranged from two to forty-eight *mu*, with the average being around ten *mu*. About 90 percent of the families owned sheep, goats, cows, and or *dzo*.[30] A much smaller proportion owned an ox or yak. Horses were found only in a third of households, usually one per family for transportation. Others had donkeys and pigs, and many had a few chickens. The difference between the two *xiang* was mainly in the number who had oxen (70 percent in Khartse) and chickens (59 percent in Mag).[31] Almost 40 percent of households had battery-powered tape recorders used for playing music and about a quarter of households had a hand- or foot-powered sewing machine. Loans affected the ability to pay school fees, whereas the number of animals affected children's contribution to household labor and the lack of household machinery, such as tractors and sewing machines, provided less opportunity for schools to capitalize on vocational training. One *xiang's* proximity to Lhasa gave it an advantage in acquiring information.

Household Youths' Access to School

Parents were asked about their oldest school-age child because there was no particular preference expressed as to which child was sent to school. Larger families would tend to educate a younger child before an older one. However, patterns varied depending on the age of the parents, the timing of the village's push into popularizing primary schooling, the form of marriage, and the gender of the children. Sometimes we would come upon a household with most members out working or at school, and either a grandmother whose children were already grown or a daughter or son, yet without children, would be interviewed.

Most parents agreed that the school's teaching of basic reading, writing, and mathematics skills could be of some benefit to the household. From their perspective, however, these skills could be acquired in one to three years. Though households had few if any reading materials, some said that the storing of barley for transport and sale could be improved if one could read labels and calculate costs. Parents were requested to provide one or more reasons why they sent a child to school. About a third associated schooling with attaining a better life, something they were told at meetings with the village and *xiang* leaders. In general, this meant that, with education, children could become better off than their parents. About a fifth of the parents in one *xiang* and a third in another indicated that having their child in school provided him or her with a path to becoming a local government official. Three reasons for sending children to school—becoming literate in Tibetan and mathematics, having a better life, and becoming a local official —were most often cited in the interviews as reasons to attend school. Few associated schooling with learning a manual skill. In both *xiang*, even fewer associated school with their being a good parent or with helping their child develop good morals, become a good citizen, or serve the public. Such notions are difficult to make sense of in communities where schooling is not only a relatively new phenomenon but also one that is culturally removed from traditional monastery education. Finally, only about 10 percent of *xiang* households responded that sending a child to school had to do with increasing the possibility to earn more income, revealing a significant difference between official and popular perspectives. In fact, between 10 and 20 percent indicated that sending their child to school was a way to avoid being fined by the authorities. Regardless of the financial penalties for not going to school, there were also household opportunity costs associated with school, in particular, the loss of household labor. For this reason parents usually ignored the penalties, because the other penalties were more costly. As one parent put it,

> The child is useful because if a cow goes into another household's fields and eats or tramples crops, we will be fined for this and it can cause much hard feeling between families.[32]

This view was expressed by more than one parent. In one case, a parent pointed out that a child can actually save the family money by staying home from school to keep the cows from grazing on another household's fields. Another family who had recently borrowed money for building a new home in the village was very concerned about paying off the loan. When asked whether having their son attend university someday would be a guarantee to a better family income, the mother replied

> Our son can never attend university because we have no connections and no money. But, we have to send him to some schooling because many of the villagers close by here are starting to send their children for education. We hope he can learn a skill like carpentry.

Attendance and Discontinuation

It was easy enough to acquire the basic county-level statistics for school attendance. These were supplied by the Education Department, and on the first field visit, the enrollment figures were between 70 and 80 percent. However, it was more difficult to learn of the statistics for individual *xiang* and villages. Village schools sometimes had attendance figures for the village posted on a blackboard. As there was an incentive to report higher rates, these figures were not always reliable. In fact, the figures did not always correspond to the number of children at school that day. One of the ways to circumvent this problem was to examine the profile data gathered from the household interviews. Because each household filled out a profile sheet that contained the names, ages, and school enrollment status of each school-age child, it was easy to check these against official data. In fact, the household data indicated that the official data were not greatly exaggerated, even though the true figures were lower. This was probably due to the fact that the villages we were examining were not as well off as the average county villages. The problems with attendance figures in rural education in China are well known and are not be discussed here. Suffice it to say that official figures are more often inflated than attendance figures.

Xiang *School Enrollments*

Of the 153 families surveyed in Mag *xiang,* there were 103 with children of school age (between six and fifteen; see Table 6.1). Of the 150 families surveyed in Khartse *xiang*, there were 103 with children of school age (see Table 6.2).

There are a few points of note. First, the proportion of girls to boys in the population is much higher than in other parts of rural China, something probably due to less population control resulting in less infanticide. Second, the proportion of girls to boys in school is not far from the national average. Third, little more than half of school-age children were in school, a rate below official county-level figures. Fourth, there was little difference in the attendance rates across family structures, whether monogamous, polygamous, or polyandrous.[33]

Although compulsory schooling in China begins at six years of age, most village children in rural Tibet do not begin school until about two years later. Attendance increases after that. In the case of these two *xiang*, it reached full attendance for boys and not quite full attendance for girls (86 percent). In one *xiang*, for example, attendance peaked for boys at about age nine to ten and for girls at age eight to nine. Most children of school age begin at age eight

Table 6.1

Mag *Xiang* Enrollment of School-Age (Six to Fifteen) Children

No. of school-age children in family	No. of such families	No. of school-age children in family			No. of children at school			No. of children not at school		
		Total	Boys	Girls	Total	Boys	Girls	Total	Boys	Girls
0	50	0	0	0	0	0	0	0	0	0
1	26	26	12	14	12	6	6	14	6	8
2	32	64	33	31	38	20	18	26	13	13
3	27	81	36	45	47	27	20	34	9	25
4	13	52	27	25	29	18	11	23	9	14
5	5	25	13	12	12	6	6	13	7	6
Total	153	248	121	127	138	77	61	110	44	66

Table 6.2

Khartse *Xiang* Enrollment of School-Age (Six to Fifteen) Children

No. of school-age children in family	No. of such families	No. of school-age children in family			No. of children at school			No. of children not at school		
		Total	Boys	Girls	Total	Boys	Girls	Total	Boys	Girls
0	47	0	0	0	0	0	0	0	0	0
1	36	36	18	18	22	11	11	14	7	7
2	41	82	44	38	57	31	26	25	13	12
3	18	54	20	34	28	10	18	26	10	16
4	6	24	15	9	14	7	7	10	8	2
5	2	10	5	5	4	3	1	6	2	4
Total	150	206	102	104	125	62	63	81	40	41

Table 6.3

Percentage of Girls and Boys in Two *Xiang* Attending School and Percentage at Which Attendance Peaks

	School-age children at school (%)	Attendance peaks (%)	
		Boys	Girls
Mag *xiang*	56	100	80
Khartse *xiang*	60	100	86

Table 6.4

Percentage of Children in Two *Xiang* Attending School Before and at Eight Years of Age

	Children attending school before age eight (%)	Children attending school at age eight (%)	
		Boys	Girls
Mag *xiang*	<40	90	
Khartse *xiang*	<15	71	80

and most have stopped attending by age fourteen. By age fifteen, only about a third of boys are attending, which is more than the figure for girls (see Tables 6.3 and 6.4).

Family Perspectives on Attendance and Discontinuation

Household Labor

The major reason children failed to attend school was their role in farming and livestock tasks. Families with school-age children were asked about household labor's effect on school attendance, and slightly more than half said their children never miss school for that reason. Yet, a little less than half said it sometimes, rather than frequently or always, affected their children's attendance. Nevertheless, it was very common to hear from teachers and officials that household labor responsibilities greatly contributed to school discontinuation (see Table 6.5).

As for the kind of work that children were doing at home that might interfere with school attendance, there was agreement between parents of the two counties about children tending livestock. Given the seminomadic nature of the household economy in the region, this was one of the most sensitive issues between the educational authorities and households. Livestock is a

Table 6.5

Parents' Replies Regarding Their School-Age Child's Housework and Homework (%)

	Mag xiang	Khartse xiang
Believe their children never miss school because of family labor	54	51
Believe family labor affects their child's school attendance	42	44
Believe their child spends less than one hour on homework assignments	59	61
Parents check child's school assignment some or most of the time	69	73
Parents do not understand their child's homework some or most of the time	68	56
Parents understand their child's homework assignment most of the time	21	32
Believe their child liked studying Tibetan most	66	75
Believe their child liked studying mathematics most	13	12
Believe their child liked studying Chinese most	18	28
Believe that Tibetan is the most useful subject	63	81

central element in the rural economy, and young children can be more help-ful in this respect than in agricultural work. This was slightly more the case in one *xiang*, where about four in ten parents indicated their children were assigned such tasks. In fact, when interviewed separately, children reported much higher percentages than their parents. About three out of four students said they had to tend livestock. Thus, parents were more aware of the sensi-tivity of this issue than children and answered more conservatively. Observa-tions bore out children's responses. Because every household had livestock of various sorts, parents were not able to tend to both agricultural and hus-bandry work simultaneously.

There were also important differences between the two *xiang* in some cases. For example, more than half in one *xiang* said their children had to ship goods by cart, whereas only 1 or 2 percent in the other so indicated. It was common to see school-age children sitting on a horse-drawn cart in the poorer *xiang*, whereas the other *xiang* had a few motorized tractors that a school-age child could not handle. These small tractors, though not owned by most families, could be shared to handle goods transportation for several families.

Finally, fetching well water was also a task that villagers indicated their children needed to do from time to time, though not as often as tending livestock. Again, parents' indications were conservative when compared with their children's. We noted that girls and young women were generally entrusted with this task, since this related closely to cooking tasks.

The issue of household labor continues to be part of an ongoing issue among the village leaders, school principals, and household heads. A system was devised in which a group of households would pool their herding resources by rotating to a different family each day so as to free up children to attend school. Although this practice was used by some families, it did not become widely institutionalized, partly due to its being seen as out of step with the new household responsibility system.

Homework and Housework

Fewer than 10 percent of the children interviewed reported they had no chores to do, half of the rest said they had chores to do before going to school, and more than half reported they had chores to do on arriving home from school. The figures increased dramatically for nonschool days, with nearly all having to do household chores. Yet most parents did not think household chores interfered much with teacher-assigned homework, and children had a similar view.

Most children reported doing less than an hour of household chores on school days and that this did not interfere with class assignments, which they generally completed on time. They did not think these assignments took too much time or were burdensome. Most reported finishing their homework assignments on time. In fact, most parents said their child did less than an hour of homework a night, and, in separate interviews, students agreed. Thus, whereas 80 to 90 percent of *xiang* students reported getting assigned homework regularly by their teachers, more than half said they did less than an hour of homework a day and most of the rest said they did between one and two hours.

It appears that village teachers do act in concert in terms of assigning work to students and that schools adjust the days of class to the growing seasons and harvesting duties where necessary. Yet, although homework was not a problem insofar as it was jeopardized by home chores, attendance at school was. In fact, homework was largely symbolic in many ways. Village teachers' time after school was also spent on agriculture or animal husbandry tasks, though this was less the case for the new teachers assigned from outside the region.

A high proportion of parents, roughly 70 percent, said they checked on their children's homework most or some of the time. Nearly as many parents did not understand the homework some or all of the time, with only a fifth to a third saying they understood it most of the time. In this sense, the parental support was more a ritual act rather than hands-on coaching.

School Subject Preferences

As for the content of the schooling offered, the ethnic culture of the region was reflected in parents' responses. Two-thirds to three-quarters of parents said their children liked studying Tibetan the most, followed by mathematics. Regarding whether their children liked studying Chinese the most, a smaller percentage agreed. Two-thirds to four-fifths believed that Tibetan was the most useful subject, much more than for mathematics and two to three times more than for Chinese.

Culture and Economy in Rural Education

The research indicates that rural Tibetans are now beginning to attend schools in greater numbers. Enrollment rates have been rising and will continue to do so. However, the data show that dropout rates are also rising along with the attendance rates and that they are rising faster than in other parts of rural China.[34] The reasons include the fact that household labor is especially critical in the harsh climate of Tibet, but, more importantly, there are serious doubts about the benefits of schooling, in particular as it related to attaining jobs in the increasingly nonfarm wage-labor sector.[35] School attendance is in some ways a ritual performed at the request of the authorities who themselves are pressured to get the abysmally low attendance rate figures to rise in order to satisfy Beijing's need to present its attendance rates at international meetings. There are also indications that more and more of the graduates of the inland Tibet schools are not finding urban jobs and are appearing in rural *xiang*-level schools as teachers, most without teacher training.[36] Moreover, it is likely that before long, the wave of migrant labor that has entered Lhasa and other cities of Tibet will begin to spill over into the county seats and other rural townships, making local inhabitants compete even more for their livelihood in nonfarm occupations. In short, post-Mao reforms have freed Tibetan villagers to migrate to the cities; however, the ineffectiveness of their education restricts their ability to find jobs there.

Education in rural Tibet could hardly exist without the *sanbao* and other policies that help households afford school fees and opportunity costs. Yet, the *sanbao* policy is less of a special preferential treatment policy for rural

Tibetans now that it was extended in 2003 by the State Council to poor rural areas throughout China. Like other autonomous areas in China, established to provide for the special situation of economy and culture of China's national minorities, Tibet needs special consideration in the area of education. Unless educational policies show how rural schools make Tibetans suitable competitors with outside migrants, they risk losing some of their legitimacy. The blame cannot be placed on Tibetans and their culture just because educational policies, including school subsidies, bilingual instruction, and boarding schools do not address the special situation of rural Tibet. To rural Tibetans, the school is a place that promises progress. Yet, there is little sense that the schools have become key institutions for helping Tibetans integrate into the market economy.

Schools are supported by the government with no fee burden to rural households. Moreover, points earned for attendance in some places may even bring money back into the household. Yet the opportunity cost is still steep for many families in terms of the labor it draws away from the largely poor rural household economy. Many families would like to keep at least one child at home to support the household economy consisting of both agricultural and herding tasks. Most important, it is less apparent to families that schooling represents a path to a better life through jobs acquired. This can be discouraging, as the schools are also the only place in the village without any religious symbols.

Thus, schools faces an uphill battle for the hearts and minds of a people who are struggling to pull themselves out of poverty while seeing migrants from elsewhere moving in to take advantage of infrastructural projects and other jobs for which they are poor competitors. Otherwise, attendance rates would be higher and dropout rates lower. Some families are aware that their children's attending school could lead to a position in the local county government or the *neidiban* (inland Tibet secondary schools). However, there were few apparent examples in the villages where this research took place. While families are coming to realize they have to make schooling part of their strategy for a better life, it is not easy for the average household to see the connection between a commitment to it and the rigors of daily life. The official ideology about the value of schooling makes its way to families through the village leaders, who struggle to convince parents to keep their children in school, using fines as a last resort.

Thus, it is left up to Tibetan schoolteachers to link state schooling to cultural values that support improved standards of living, community development, and jobs. Unfortunately, their training hardly prepares them for this role, and it is difficult to attract good teachers without more funding. As the graduates of the *neidiban* schools return and find urban positions much harder to come by, they will increasingly be found teaching at rural township boarding schools. This could have a positive effect on the quality of rural education. However, graduates of teacher training colleges within the TAR may have advantages in terms of training received in teaching methods and Tibetan language skills.

Although the rural schools do provide a learning environment, there are significant gaps between the quality of teaching at the village, township, and county levels, with many villages still relying on *minban* teachers. Children who live in villages closer to the township school are advantaged, and children in households remote from village schools attend less frequently. Though the schools accord opportunities across gender, attitudes in school and home affect attendance rates, which drop off faster for girls than boys as they move up the school-grade ladder. Families are aware of equity issues and are concerned about the possibility of having to pay school fees in the future.

Although there is no doubt that poverty directly affects attendance and dropout rates, cultural factors cannot be totally discounted, especially because much of the content of school curriculum is divorced from community life. In short, rural Tibetans would probably give more support to state schooling, even accepting some of the acculturation sacrifices involved, if they could see a more direct economic return in the form of helping them attain good jobs that make them competitive with outsiders.

Of course, this might also hinder the possibilities for Tibetans to master the mainstream knowledge required to earn high university entrance examination scores. This is not to say that Tibetan cultural capital has lost its market value within the economic life of the TAR. As Tibetan educational levels rise and Tibetans improve in competing with migrants from other parts of China in the marketplace and government, there may very well be a renaissance of Tibetan culture that resituates itself within the larger cultural environment of China and improves access to social networks attached to job allocation. In the meantime, educational policies and practices that emphasize Han cultural capital will be a central part of the education system. Unless Tibetans begin to achieve higher levels of success in education, they may continue in their tendency to believe that schooling does not outweigh the sacrifice of their indigenous cultural capital.

Notes

This research was supported by a grant from the Hong Kong Research Grants Council. The authors also acknowledge the support of the Wah Ching Centre for Research on Education in China of the University of Hong Kong. This article is reprinted with permission from *China: An International Journal*, vol. 3, no. 1 (2005), pp. 1–23.

1. This is more the case for *Education in Tibet,* published by the Education

Commission of the Tibetan Autonomous Region (TAR), while *National Minority Educational Studies* is published by a national university, under the Ethnic Affairs Commission.

2. Badeng Nima, *Wenming de kunhuo: Zangzu jiaoyu zhilu* (Civilization's puzzle: The road for Tibetan education) (Chengdu: Sichuan minzu chubanshe [Sichuan Nationality Publishers], 2000).

3. Regie Stites, "Writing Cultural Boundaries: National Minority Language Policy, Literacy Planning and Bilingual Education," in *China's National Minority Education*, ed. Gerard Postiglione (New York: Falmer Press, 1999), pp. 95–130.

4. Janet Upton, "The Development of Modern School Based Tibetan Language Education in the PRC," in *China's National Minority Education*, pp. 281–340.

5. Catriona Bass, *Education in Tibet: Policy and Practice Since 1950* (London: Zed Books, 1998). The educational policies adopted for ethnic minorities are carried out by the Department of Ethnic Minority Education under the State Ministry of Education (which became the State Education Commission in 1985 until 1998), with corresponding organizations and appointments made at the provincial *(minzu jiaoyu chu)*, prefecture *(minzu jiaoyu ke)*, and county levels *(minzu jiaoyu gu)*.

6. See Melvyn C. Goldstein, Ben Jiao, Cynthia M. Beall, and Phuntsog Tsering, "Development and Change in Rural Tibet: Problems and Adaptations," *Asian Survey*, vol. 43, no 5 (2003), pp. 758–779.

7. Fish are also plentiful, and forest resources support traditional family-produced handicrafts and grain oil products. Other locally produced goods include boots, mattresses, perfume, and fertilizer.

8. Xizang zizhichu cehuiju (Survey and Mapping Bureau of the Tibet Autonomous Region), *Xizang zizhiqu dituce* (Handbook of regional maps of the Tibetan Autonomous Region) (Beijing: China Map Publishing House, 1995), p. 137.

9. An area of 4,517 square kilometers, with 180,000 *mu* of cultivated land, 37,180,000 *mu* of grassland, and 1,320,000 *mu* of forests. The population is 52,000, and there are 19 *xiang* and 169 villages.

10. The Nianqingtanggula and Zhiyongkala mountain ranges.

11. It belongs to the Pengbo River area. The entire county averages 3,900 meters above sea level. With 3,000 hours of sunshine a year and only 120 days without snow, it has a rainy summer and 491 millimeters annual rainfall. Lhundrup County, known in Tibetan as a naturally formed place, was established in 1857. In 1959, it was combined with Banduo to form Lhundrup County.

12. Xizang zizhichu cehuiju, *Xizang zizhiqu dituce*, p. 22.

13. On a field visit in September 2002, over 100 families from four villages of Mag *xiang* were called to the school to explain to visiting county education officials why at least one of their children was not being sent to school. Officials contend that because households do not have to pay school fees, all children should attend.

14. Wu Degang, *Zhongguo xizang jiaoyu gaige yu fazhan de lilun yanjiu* (A study of educational reform and development in Tibet) (Kunming: Yunnan Press, 1995), p. 354.

15. See Jianxin Wang and Furong Qiu, "Xizang qubu jianle xiandai minzu jiaoyu tixi" (Tibet takes steps to establish a modern ethnic education system), *Zhongguo jiaoyu bao* (China education daily), May 30, 2001 (www.jyb.com.cn/gb/2001/05/30/zhxw/jyzx/3.htm).

16. There were about 4,000 schools, 820 primary and secondary schools, 3,033 teaching points, 110 regular and vocational secondary schools, and 4 institutions of

higher education. There are 360,000 TAR students in all forms and levels of education and 19,000 teachers.

17. By 1998, the percentages of qualified teachers at different levels were: 63 percent in upper secondary, 72 percent in lower secondary, and 59 percent in primary school. In the meantime, 1,377 *minban* teachers would receive training, and some were converted to *gongban* (regular public teachers). A limit of 2,000 *daike* (substitute teachers) was set in 2000. There were plans to improve the teaching force so that between 1995 and 2003, 10,000 teachers would be trained. This included 559 in higher education, 400 in middle-level specialized schools, 750 in senior secondary schools, 2,600 in junior secondary schools, and 5,700 in primary schools. "Xizang zizhiqu minzu jiaoyu 50 nian" (50 years of ethnic education in the Tibetan Autonomous Region) in Xia Zhu, Ha Jinxiong, and Abadu Wushouer, *Zhongguo minzu jiaoyu 50 nian* (Fifty years of ethnic education in China) (Beijing: Hongqi chubanshe [Red Flag Press], 1999). The rate of qualified teachers at the primary, middle, and upper secondary schools was 67 percent, 77 percent, and 75 percent, respectively.

18. Field notes from interviews of county officials.

19. "Education Is the Wing of the Economy—An Investigation into the Rural Education," Suolan Jiacuo, unpublished manuscript, 1995.

20. Only 359 if those with disabilities were not counted. Many children with only slight disabilities were kept out of school.

21. The principal said he was twenty-seven years old and had attended the Lhasa Number 1 Middle School.

22. The *sanbao* policy was canceled in 1997 and then reinstated in 2002.

23. Field notes. Only one person out of the 1990 population of 4,136 had a senior secondary school level specialized education. Eight had a junior secondary education, and 463 had some primary schooling.

24. Interviews, September 2002.

25. Sukang School was the night school for adult literacy classes. Staffed by *minban* teachers, it was supported by the Xiang Women's Federation and the Village Committee. Newspaper reading was the primary method used. A fine of 5 *mao* was levied for homework not done. This money was used to keep the school open. In 1985, there were penalties of 15 yuan for missing the first semester of Primary One and 20 yuan for missing the second semester.

26. Primary school age is usually six to twelve in China. However, children in rural Tibet started later, and a graduate of primary school could be as old as seventeen years of age.

27. Initiated by Xizang zizhiqu renmin zhengfu yinfa (The People's Government of the Tibetan Autonomous Region), *Guanyu woqu zhongxiaoxuesheng xiangshou "sanbao" he zhuxuejing de zanxing guiding de tongzhi–zangzhengfa* (Approved regulations concerning our region's primary and secondray school students receiving the three guarantees and scholarships), Document no. 30, 1994.

28. The other major policy with significant implications for rural education in the TAR is the *neidi Xizang ban* (inland Tibet secondary school), which provides for sending primary school graduates to inland secondary schools across China. The TAR government selects and recommends primary school graduates of ten to twelve years old for these inland schools. The majority of the students attend segregated classes in urban secondary schools. However, at least eighteen of the schools are only for Tibetan students. Reports say 1,300 primary graduates from the seven TAR prefectures were sent to sixteen classes or schools in inland cities in September of

1985. Ten times as many are sent now. These figures do not include all TAR students enrolled outside the TAR.

29. In the four *xiang* schools, a total of 2,610 yuan was collected.

30. *Dzo* is a yak-cow cross.

31. Oxen amounted to 70 percent in Khartse *xiang* and 32 percent in Mag *xiang*. Chicken amounted to 17 percent in Khartse *xiang* and 59 percent in Mag *xiang*.

32. Field notes from June 11, 1999.

33. Ben Jiao, "Socio-economic and Cultural Factors Underlying the Contemporary Revival of Fraternal Polyandry in Tibet," unpublished Ph.D. dissertation, Case Western Reserve University, 2001.

34. Gerard Postiglione, "National Minority Regions: Studying School Discontinuation," in *The Ethnographic Eye: Ethnographic Research on Education in China*, ed. J. Liu (New York: Falmer Press, 2000), pp. 51–71. See also G. Postiglione, with X. Teng and Y. Ai, "Basic Education and School Discontinuation in National Minority Border Areas of China," in *Social Change and Educational Development: China, Taiwan and Hong Kong Mainland,* ed. G. Postiglione and W.O. Lee (Hong Kong: Centre of Asian Studies Press, 1995), pp. 186–206.

35. Goldstein et al., "Development and Change in Rural Tibet: Problems and Adaptations," pp. 758–779.

36. See Gerard Postiglione, Zhu Zhiyong, and Ben Jiao, "From Ethnic Segregation to Impact Integration: State Schooling and Identity Construction for Rural Tibetans," *Asian Ethnicity*, vol. 5, no. 2 (June 2004), pp. 195–217.

Part IV

Urban Divisions: Migrants and the Middle Class

7

The Integration of Migrant Children in Beijing Schools

Julia Kwong

With the introduction of market socialism, Chinese society has become more heterogeneous. Moreover, diverse sectors of the population are more likely to express their differences compared with the previous period. Some aspects of this diversity, such as ethnic and regional differences as pointed out by Gerard Postiglione, have always existed. Yet, differences in religious, political, and sexual orientations have become more pronounced and visible in the increasingly more tolerant political climate. Still other differences, like the polarization of wealth and the resultant variations in lifestyle, have emerged only as a result of the economic policies implemented in the new era. Jing Lin, in the next chapter, points to the emergence of the middle class in the once largely egalitarian Chinese society. This new phenomenon of growing differences and their articulation raises issues of diversity and integration and prompts me to take a new look at the integrative role of the schools—the most organized and structured socialization agents in a society still very much concerned with preserving homogeneity and uniformity.

This chapter examines how the social experiences of rural migrants as a minority group in the cities result from the intersection of their two characteristics—geographic origin and social class—and the role the educational system has played in diluting, perpetuating, or accentuating their differences. Rural migrants to the cities stand apart from the urban population in their adopted place of domicile. Because they lack economic and political power, they belong to the lowest social stratum and are looked down upon by

Migrant children waiting for their turn on the lunch line

the majority or dominant group. Unlike ethnic minorities, their differences from the urban populations are not visible because of their skin color or physiological characteristics. They did not choose their places of birth, but their geographic origin and upbringing have brought about observable acquired differences in their mannerisms and behavior that set them apart from the urban population. However, unlike Chinese ethnic minorities, rural migrants in the city do not enjoy any special safeguards of their rights or affirmative treatment in education, employment, or family planning. On the contrary, official arrangements discriminate against this group, depriving them of entitlements available to other citizens. They suffer both informal and formal discrimination in their new places of domicile.

In the following pages, I look at how the combination of formal and informal discrimination in education keeps the present generation of rural migrants apart from the larger population. In particular, I examine how official educational policies extend this marginalization to the next generation, relegating them to the lowest social stratum. The government educational system excludes migrant children from attending public schools and discriminates against even those enrolled in them. Finally, I examine the alternate schools provided within the migrant communities and evaluate the extent to which they succeed in integrating these children into the urban environment. Examples in the following analysis are taken mainly from Beijing and Shanghai, where large numbers of such migrants congregate; their experiences in these two metropolitan areas provide a glimpse of the situation of similar groups in other large cities.

Rural Migrants as a Minority Group

As in many other societies, Chinese urban dwellers consider themselves more educated, informed, sophisticated, and cultured than their rural compatriots. The latter are considered country bumpkins: dirty, rude, uncouth, and uneducated. Furthermore, many urban residents blame rural migrants for every conceivable urban social problem from traffic congestion to crime. However, high crime rates attributed to the migrants may be as much a result of the zealous prosecution of migrants in the criminal justice system as of their propensity to commit crimes. Whatever the reality, some urban residents see migrants as the scum of society and a threat to public security. More interestingly, they accuse rural migrants of taking away their jobs when in truth the migrants, for the most part, take jobs urban workers do not want.[1]

Until 1976 the *hukou*, or household registration system, established in 1958 as a means of regulating the movement of population, prevented the rural population from moving into the cities. Under this regulation, those born and registered in a particular place could move to another locality only with official permission, and authorization to transfer was hard to obtain. Beginning in the 1950s, some rural residents worked as contract laborers in the cities, but they had to return home when their contracts expired; few could change their official registrations from rural to urban. During the Cultural Revolution, Chinese youths were encouraged by the government to work in the countryside, but this population movement flowed one way, with few rural youth going in the other direction.[2] Aside from these brief exceptions, rural and urban populations have remained distinct and apart.

With the introduction of liberal economic policies in the late 1970s, the Chinese government no longer strictly enforced the *hukou* policies even though the regulation has remained in force on paper. This change of official attitude toward enforcing the *hukou* system, together with growing wealth, more employment opportunities, and better amenities in the cities, provided incentive for rural residents to defy the legislation and venture into the cities. By 2002, it was estimated that there were three million migrants in Beijing and four million in Shanghai, making up about 10 percent of the migrant population across the country.[3] Unlike popular migration patterns in many countries where migrants settle in their new destinations once they arrive, these Chinese rural migrants behave more like the illegal international migrant workers, moving from place to place following job opportunities. They are labeled the "floating population."

Like migrants around the world, these migrants are young and adventurous. Over 70 percent of them are less than forty years old, and men make up over 55 percent of the migrant population. The majority receive only junior high education; their average educational level may be higher than their rural counterparts, but it is below that of the urban population.[4] Over 70 percent in the migrant community are single, but even those who are married come to the city alone, leaving their spouses and children behind until they are financially more secure. It was not until the mid-1990s, when more families were reunited, that children constituted a significant sector of the community. By 2002, there were about 100,000 school-age migrant children between the ages of six and fourteen in Beijing and 240,000 in Shanghai.[5]

The relaxed enforcement of the *hukou* system has provided rural workers with opportunities to start new lives in the city, but its continued existence segregates them from urban residents and deprives them of the basic entitlements and amenities available to the latter. Rural migrants are looked down upon by urban residents for their attire, mannerisms, living habits, and accents in speaking Putonghua, as well as for their low educational level, low-status employment, and poverty. True, their lack of education prevents them from getting good jobs, but the *hukou* system to a certain extent has contributed to their low social status. Because they lack urban residence registration, local legislation has excluded them from taking government employment or other high-status jobs even when they are qualified. In Beijing, they are restricted to 200 job categories that include the lowliest and dirtiest blue-collar jobs; similar measures have been taken in Shanghai. As a result of these personal and artificial limitations, about 57 percent of the Anhui migrants in Beijing are construction workers doing carpentry, bricklaying, cement work, painting, electrical installation, and cleaning; the rest work in restaurants or as domestic helpers.[6] Their wages are low, they work long hours, and they have no job security. Even when they hold the same jobs as urban residents, they often receive lower pay than their urban colleagues. As a result of such discrimination and their lack of education, the average income in the Beijing migrant community by 2000 was 900 yuan a month when the city average was 2,000 yuan; in Shanghai, their average monthly income was 680 yuan, about two-thirds that of the average income in the city.[7]

Not only are rural migrants not socially accepted by many urbanites, they are not considered members of the urban community. Over two-thirds of the Beijing, Shanghai, and Wuhan migrant respondents in a 1994 survey felt that they were discriminated against by the city people and did not want any contact with them.[8] Rural migrants form a community living geographically and socially apart from the urban society and even separate from migrants who come from outside their home regions. Many migrants have followed friends, relatives, or family members who have come to the city before them; a survey carried out in eight provinces at about the same time found that over 54 percent of the rural migrants came through social networks. As a result, they do the same work and live in the same neighborhoods as their predecessors and form not one but numerous migrant communities identified by home regions.[9]

Because migrants do not have urban household registration, some government officials consider them illegal residents in their own country. Like international migrants without the proper residence documentation, they can be prosecuted or sent back to their places of origin should the local officials choose to do so. Their vulnerability often leads to extortion or other forms of abuse from officials. Many migrants have complained that they have been stopped by public security and peremptorily extradited to their home regions without their family members in the city being notified.[10] Since 1997, those with secure jobs or assets can apply for temporary residence or a blue card, but they are not completely free from occasional harassment.[11] These "legal" newcomers, like their "illegal" counterparts, do not enjoy the rights of urban citizens and are not entitled to education, health, housing, or other social benefits that come with registered residence. Moreover, they do not have political representation or channels through which to voice their opinions.[12] Those who choose to live in the migrant communities are more likely to be subject to harassment. Local officials sometimes level the migrants' walled "cities" only to have them return to rebuild their communities when the storm blows over. Zhejiang Cun, the walled settlement in Beijing of migrants from Zhejiang, was razed in 1995 and 18,000 people evicted;[13] but they soon returned to rebuild their city. In short, rural migrants in the cities have remained a distinct pariah group socially isolated from the larger urban population.

Education and the Integration of Migrants

Besides the migrants' ethnicity, age, skills, length of stay, and other personal characteristics, education is perhaps the most often cited and the most salient factor affecting their integration and absorption. Those with higher levels of education integrate more easily into their newly adopted place of domicile than do the less educated ones. Even though the educational system in each country has its own characteristics, there are enough commonalities in structure and overlaps in educational content to allow the educated in different

countries to engage in a common dialogue. The educated migrant can usually speak the language of the adopted place of domicile, qualify for employment, and socialize easily with host members.[14]

These benefits of education that help newcomers to cope in a new environment in a foreign country should be even more pronounced in the case
of internal migration. The educational or work experiences of international
migrants may not always be recognized in the adopted country, which generates frustration among the educated migrants, but internal migrants exposed to the same accredited educational system as that of their new place
of domicile do not face such hurdles. Their educational credentials can
facilitate their getting work. Because they speak the language and are con-
versant with the society's values and norms, they have little difficulty integrating with host members. This is also true among the rural migrants in
Chinese cities; Xu found that rural migrants with higher levels of education are more economically integrated, have more opportunities to mix with
the local people, have more friends among the locals, and are more satisfied with their new environment.[15]

Official Educational Policies and the Exclusion of Migrant Children

Despite the above observations on the importance of education, the Chinese
rural migrants are busy with work, and few make use of the educational
facilities in the city.[16] But if the second generation of rural migrants who
grow up in the city are to establish themselves there, they should strive to get
an education. More than any other agent of socialization, schools inculcate
the values and skills that underpin the existing economic, social, and political arrangement; open opportunities of mobility; and make the incumbents
and especially those left behind receptive and content with their status quo.
For this and other reasons, governments are willing to provide compulsory
public education to the young. The socialization experience provided by
schools can overcome the different or conflicting values sometimes offered
by the families and transform the next generation into a relatively homogeneous group. Most parents are willing to send their children to school to give
them a chance in life.

The *hukou* system, however, has prevented the young rural migrants from
sharing this educational experience with their age cohort in the city. In 1986,
the Chinese government introduced compulsory nine years of education for
children six to fourteen years old, making local governments responsible for
providing such facilities to children in their jurisdiction; however, the legislation did not anticipate the population movement of the 1990s. Local gov-

ernments are held responsible only for the education of children with local residential registration. Migrant children are considered rural, not locally registered urban residents. Even those born in the city are regarded as rural residents, inheriting the *hukou* of their mothers. Consequently, no rural migrant child is automatically entitled to receive public education.[17]

In Beijing, only migrants with temporary resident permits who have met the government family planning policy requirement can apply for the admission of their children into public schools; in Shanghai, they have to show their birth certificates and work permits as well. In both cities, in addition to the tuition and miscellaneous fees that the regular students pay, they have to pay an educational rental fee (*jiedu fei*). In the early 1990s, the educational rental fee was about 480 yuan per term at the primary level and 700 yuan at the junior high school level in Beijing; in 2002, the fees were reduced to 300 yuan and 500 yuan, respectively. The rate in Shanghai is generally lower at 200 yuan a term. In practice, the amount collected is much higher. Furthermore, parents are required to pay a school selection fee (*zexiao fei*), sometimes known as an education compensation fee (*jiaoyu buchang fei*), as well. Rates for the school selection fee depend on the prestige of the school; some can be as high as 230,000 yuan.[18] In fact, despite the 1996 central directive delineating the qualifications of those to be admitted, public schools do not restrict access to registered temporary residents; they open their doors to any student ready and able to pay. In the era of decentralized financial management when schools can make money and keep it, any contributions that augment their operating budget are welcome. Few migrants qualify for temporary residence. A 1999 study carried out in Beijing's Fengtai district found that only 18 percent of the working migrants had temporary work permits—an essential requirement for temporary residence.[19]

True, some migrants can afford to send their children to private schools that charge much higher fees than public schools and are beyond the reach of the average urban resident. They are the successful business entrepreneurs who made their fortunes in the city. But parents with such financial resources are few and far between. Those who can afford the high rates charged by the public schools are also limited. So even if public schools are effective institutions to integrate migrant children into the local community, many migrant children do not have the opportunity to receive this experience.

Reports on the percentage of migrant children in school fluctuate wildly. In 2001, the China News Agency reported that only 12.5 percent of migrant children in Beijing were in school, but a year later the Xinhua News Agency reported that 800,000—almost 80 percent of these children—were attending public schools. The same report estimated that more than 100,000 of the 240,000 migrant children in Shanghai were in public school, when a survey carried out by Shanghai Academy of Social Sciences estimated that only 60 percent of the migrant children were receiving some form of education.[20] Although it is difficult to estimate the percentage of rural migrant children who are in school, it is not realistic to share the optimism of the Xinhua News Agency report. Given the fact that attending public or private schools can take up a third if not more of migrant parents' incomes and the larger-than-average number of children in migrant families, it is highly unlikely that rural migrants send many of their children to public schools, and only the occasional one can send their child to a private school.[21]

Even when rural migrant children are enrolled in the public system, they are not treated as integral members of the school. Because they are not legal residents, local departments of education do not count them as bona fide members of the student body. They cannot join in extracurricular activities and cannot become Young Pioneers. Teachers in China are evaluated on their students' progress, but not on the performance of the migrant children in their classes. Consequently, some teachers ignore these children and do not give them the help they are supposed to get. Many are left behind, which only reinforces the stereotype that rural children are stupid. Outstanding migrant children also do not get the credit they deserve. They cannot be nominated as "three-good students" (good in academic work, character, and physical ability), a coveted honor for Chinese students. Some may even be good enough to represent their schools in local competitions, but because they are not bona fide students, they have to compete using the names of other local students, and thus they do not even get the honor they deserve. When they graduate, migrant children are awarded the Rental Education Graduation Diploma, not the high school diploma given to other students.[22]

There is also a class difference between the rural and urban children enrolled in the public school. Urban parents are generally more educated and better off financially than the rural ones. Their children live in better homes, have more educational toys, and are better prepared for school. In the materialistic contemporary society, the urban children, like their parents, look down on their poorer fellow students from the countryside and consider themselves superior. They see migrant children as rude and without manners. They see them as dirty with unkempt hair and ragged clothes and as slow in their studies; they will not play with them.[23] The migrant children reciprocate these negative feelings toward the local group. They dislike the local children because they are arrogant and bully people. Some despise local children for their lack of life experience and independence, and find them weak and spoiled.[24] Schools are supposed to be places where bonding occurs and friendships are made for life. Instead, in this prejudicial school climate close proximity between the two groups only reinforces the stereotypes; the divide between these urban and rural children is as pronounced as in the adult world. Such experiences only make the migrant children more acutely aware of the unfairness of the situation, and they feel like second-class citizens in their own country. Being familiar with the urban children in school, they will find it harder than their parents to accept their subordinate status. When these children finish school without a recognized diploma, they will still have difficulties either furthering their education or finding work, and with their negative experiences in school, they will likely follow their parents' footsteps and retreat into their migrant enclave instead of venturing into the larger urban society.

Migrant Children's Schools and the Isolation of Migrant Children

Some Chinese officials have accused the migrant parents of ignoring the educational interests of their children when they move to the city, but such accusations are not completely true. Migrant parents place the education of their children only second to their own security.[25] They see education as something inherently good and valuable and a way to allow their children to climb the social ladder and leave the migrant community. They may also have an immediate and practical reason—schools are good baby-sitters. Parents work and want someone to look after their children and keep them off the streets. Sending their children to school is better than leaving them at home.

In the new market economy, when there is a demand there is supply. In the beginning, parents requested the educated among them to teach their children literacy and numeration. Sometimes the home governments of the migrants have organized schools for the children in the city, but these facilities are no better than the migrant children's schools discussed in this section because the home governments are poor with few resources. Soon the more entrepreneurial in the migrant community saw they could make a living or even a profit from educational activities. By the late 1990s, migrant children's schools sprang up and multiplied in areas with high concentrations of migrant children. For example, in Shanghai's Baoshan District, there were only 8 migrant children's schools in 1995, but the number increased to 18 in 1996, 36 in 1997, 72 in 1998, and 105 in 2000. In 2002 there were more than 500 migrant children's schools in Shanghai and 300 in Beijing.[26]

These schools are set up by migrants for migrants. Because of the limited resources within the community and the weak buying power of the clientele, migrant children's schools are makeshift schools with poor facilities. Many are located in abandoned buildings, warehouses, and homes of peasants, and some are simply sheds put up on empty plots close to where the parents work. Some schools buy used tables and chairs for the students, but their furniture is often not enough and several students have to share one desk. Lighting is inadequate and the ventilation bad. There are not enough toilets, let alone playgrounds. More important, the schools do not have adequate numbers of teachers. School proprietors often hire their friends as teachers, and there is a high turnover rate, in some cases as high as over 40 percent. The teachers often are not trained or qualified. A study found over 65 percent of them with no previous teaching experience—some have been vendors, nannies, or construction contractors before taking up the new position. The schools are supposed to follow the national curriculum, but many have only instruction in basic language and mathematics; courses in social sciences, music, physical education, or art are not offered, and the children learn by rote.[27]

Despite the schools' inferior quality and lack of accreditation, migrant parents send their children to these schools because getting some education is better than none, and the price is right. They pay about 800 yuan tuition an academic year compared to the minimum 2,000 yuan in the public school. Unlike public school practice, migrant children's schools refund the unused portion of tuition if the parents move away. In 2000, it was estimated that about 40 percent of the migrant children in Beijing and more than half of the migrant children population in Shanghai were enrolled in these schools.[28] In general, the standards in these schools are not as high as the public ones. The principal of Xingzhi Migrant Children School, the best among these schools in Beijing, admitted that their students do not perform as well as public school children in the same grade. However, Liu and Zhang's study using students' essays to examine their orientation show that some do have good language skills. Furthermore, they are highly motivated and mature. They embrace the mainstream value of achieving mobility through education. They appreciate the sacrifices their parents have made and want to get a good education, find a job, make money, and look after their parents in return. The children are learning, and some parents are quite satisfied, especially when they compare these schools to those in their hometowns.[29]

These schools, however, do little to socially integrate the migrant children into the urban community, even though in the more amicable climate of the migrant children's schools, sharing the same school experience instills a sense of camaraderie among members of the same cohort and often creates a bond lasting through life. Except for the few local children rejected by the public schools, it is mainly migrant children who attend migrant schools. They do not have an opportunity to mix with local children; about 3 percent of these migrant children in Beijing have never even come into contact with a local child. They never learn the subtleties of urban culture or share an identity with the urban children. Instead they develop a sense of identity with other migrant children of different ethnicities from all over the country, and their reference group boundary expands beyond their home regions. Students in Xingzhi Migrant Children School play with Han, Manchu, Mongol, Uighur, Miao, and other ethnic minorities coming from twenty-four provinces, including Anhui, Henan, Hebei, and Hunan. They learn each other's dialects, customs, and habits, but their circle is still confined to the migrant community, and they still see themselves as a pariah group apart from other urban children.

Because of the low quality of the teaching staff and the poor facilities, local departments of education do not recognize these schools and occasionally even close them down for violations of fire or health regulations, thus interrupting whatever education these children may be getting. For example, Fengtai district government in Beijing closed thirty-three of the fifty migrant children's schools under their jurisdiction in the latter half of 2001, and Changnin government of Shanghai shut down all such schools in their district about the same time.[30] Not only are these migrant students doing less well than urban students in public schools, but even if they do well and graduate, their diplomas will not be recognized by employers. They will have even more difficulties than migrant children from public schools in finding work in the larger society, let alone having the opportunity for moving upward to escape the migrant community.

An Assessment and Perspective on the Future

The educational system in China not only does little to bridge the differences between the rural and urban population living in the cities but actually perpetuates their differences. This is not to suggest that public schools have failed as effective socialization agents in introducing the young to mainstream culture, creating a sense of identity among the different cohorts passing through the system, or preparing the young for the work world, but they have failed to integrate the rural migrant children into the urban community for the simple reason that migrant children are excluded from and discriminated against in the public schools.

Instead of introducing them to the mainstream culture and providing them with the opportunity for making friends with local children of their own age through state-sponsored educational activities, the existing educational arrangement excludes the majority of migrant children from attending school and sets them apart from their age cohort, thus separating them from their urban counterparts. As in most societies, education in China is the equalizer that provides opportunities for those less fortunate to prove themselves and move up in society. Schools are the channel of social mobility. Yet the *hukou* system together with the 1986 education law requiring nine years of education have served to deprive migrant children of these opportunities. This ensures their continued marginalization in the lowest stratum in the city.

Limited efforts in the public schools to remedy the situation have not been adequate. Not many migrant children have been able to take advantage of the few accommodations made in the educational system. Migrant children going into the public schools are a minority. Even those fortunate enough to enroll in them face prejudicial treatment by their fellow students and systematic discrimination from the school administration. They pay higher fees than the local students but get less help from the teachers. They are not adequately rewarded for their achievement, and their diploma is considered inferior to that of the regular students. Such negative experiences as second-class students can only perpetuate, if not accentuate, their sense of distinctiveness, isolation from, and mistrust of the urban population.

Nor can the schools within their communities fully compensate for the lack of opportunities and other inadequacies in the provision of public education. Although large numbers of migrant children may be attending migrant children's schools, not all do so. Pedagogy in these schools is substandard and does not provide adequate or accredited training for teachers to prepare the children to play an active role in the urban community. Furthermore, mainly migrant children attend these schools, and their interactions with migrants from different parts of the country only enhance their identity as integral members of this outcast group, again distinguishing them further from the local urban residents.

Having been brought up in the city, this generation of migrant children knows little about the countryside and probably calls the city "home." In Han's study, 10 percent of migrant children considered themselves "Beijing people."[31] Even those who have not gone through the public school system are exposed to the same larger environment of the city as the local children, share their urban values, and want to live like them. Those attending public schools are even more attuned to the nuances of the mainstream urban values. They embrace and entertain the desire for upward mobility; they want to move upward and live like the rest of the urban population. Yet they are denied even the initial step of getting an accredited education to attain this goal. Their channel to fulfilling their ambition is blocked and their ambitions thwarted. Such thwarted ambition can only lead to growing frustration. Unlike their parents, who accept the urban discrimination by rationalizing that they are the outsiders, this generation sees its exclusion from public education as unfair. As a result, dissatisfaction and hostility among rural migrant children increases.

The Chinese government has not intentionally discriminated against migrant children, and to find a solution to integrate the migrant children in the city is not easy. The situation is largely the fallout from the lag between educational legislation and the unanticipated nature and pace of social changes introduced by the market economy and the more liberal official stand on population and other social policies. In education, the problem is both cultural and structural, and the responsibility does not lie within the educational system alone. Prejudice toward the rural migrants is embedded in society; what goes on within the schools reflects what occurs in society. Eliminating prejudice and changing attitudes toward the rural population takes time. Discrimination in education to a large extent can be traced to the *hukou* system. Even though the *hukou* system has been undermined since the 1980s, the government is unlikely to abolish it given the broad ramifications this measure may bring in the state delivery of not only education but medical care, employment, housing, and other social services. However, something has to be done if the social gap between the rural migrant children and their urban counterparts is to be bridged and hostility to be avoided.

In recent years, the central government has taken some action in this direction by passing temporary regulations on the education of migrant children in 1996 and exhorting local governments to use various means to provide for their education. As a result, Shanghai passed its temporary regulation patterned after the central regulation on the education of migrant children in 1998, and Beijing did the same in 2002.[32] However, introducing these special regulations only shows that migrant children are not treated like the local children. These regulations exhort local governments where migrant children reside to take up the responsibility of educating them, but local governments are reluctant to pick up the cost. Migrants congregate in cities where the economy is good and employment opportunities are available, and they contribute to the growth of these local economies. Often it is the local government's lack of will and not resources that prompts it not to take action. The temporary regulations also propose home governments from where the migrants came, private organizations, and individuals to run schools for these children. Such provisions in the regulations only create a gray area in the distribution of responsibilities in which local governments can hide their inaction. These temporary regulations are clearly not adequate in resolving the issue.

If the Chinese government sees basic education as a public good and is determined to enforce nine-year compulsory education nationwide, local interests have to give way to national ones. Stronger legislation, with a clear definition of local responsibility in the provision of education for all children living in the geographic region, is needed. As when food coupons in the city were abolished in 1992 so that the rural population could get food while they worked in the city, the central government could take the pragmatic and feasible step of amending the 1986 educational legislation to include all school-age children regardless of their residence registration. In so doing, the central government does not touch the *hukou* system, and the legislation will force local governments to provide education to migrant children. Bringing rural migrant children into the public schools and treating them like local students will give these children the opportunity to share the dream of the urban children, to mix with the locals socially, and to be prepared to participate later in the urban labor force. Such interactions on an equal basis between the two groups will help the urban children to see the "rural" children as equals, become friends with them, and overcome their prejudice toward them. Thus, this change in educational policy could bring migrant children immediate benefits, change the attitudes of the urban children, and ultimately lead to the integration of migrant children into the urban community.

Notes

This research acknowledges the support of the Social Sciences and Humanities Council of Canada.

1. Shi Bainian, "Chengshi liudong ertong xiaonian jiuxue wenti zhengce fenxi" (A strategic analysis of school attendance for the mobile juvenile students in the city), *Zhongguo qingnian zhengzhi xueyuan xuebao* (Journal of China youth college for political sciences), vol. 21, no. 1 (2002), pp. 31–35; Li Qiang, *Zhuanxin shiqi de Zhongguo shehui fenzheng jiegou* (Social stratification in China's transitional society) (Harbin: Heilongjiang Renmin Chubanshe, 2001), p. 146; Xu Demin, *Shanghai shequ wailai renkou sixiang gongzuo yanjiu* (A study of attitudes of the Shanghai migrant population) (Shanghai: Shanghai Renmin Chubanshe, 2003), p. 67.

2. Li Qiang, *Zhuanxin shiqi de Zhongguo shehui fenzheng jiegou*, pp. 360–361.

3. www.cinfo.org.cn/dtgj/liudongrenkuo/035.htm2002/9/1; www.dt.gov.cn/jjxx/sjzw/ffd8.htm2002/9/2; Liu Yingjia, *Zhongguo chengxiang guanxi yu Zhongguo nongmin gongren* (City-rural relationship and Chinese peasant workers) (Beijing: Chinese Academy of Social Sciences, 2000), p. 157.

4. Li Peilin, ed., *Nongmin gong: Zhongguo chengzhen nongmin gong de jingji shehui fenxi* (Rural worker—A socioeconomic analysis of peasants in the city) (Beijing: Social Sciences Documentation Publishing House, 2003), pp. 140, 263; Li Qiang, *Zhuanxin shiqi de Zhongguo shehui fenzheng jiegou*, p. 127; Xu Demin, *Shanghai shequ wailai renkou sixiang gongzuo yanjiu*, p. 40.

5. Shi Bainian, "Chengshi liudong ertong xiaonian jiuxue wenti zhengce fenxi," pp. 31–35; Li Qiang, *Zhuanxin shiqi de Zhongguo shehui fenzheng jiegou*, p. 341. The estimates vary widely. Some estimates are as high as over 160,000 school-age children in Beijing.

6. www.cinfo.org.cn/dtgj/liudongrenkuo/016.ttm2002/9/1; Li Qiang, *Zhuanxin shiqi de Zhongguo shehui fenzheng jiegou*, p. 139; Liu Yingjia, *Zhongguo chengxiang guanxi yu Zhongguo nongmin gongren*, p. 169.

7. www.cinfo.org.cn/dtgj/liudongrenkou/1drk-025.htm2002/9/02; Li Qiang, *Zhuanxin shiqi de Zhongguo shehui fenzheng jiegou*, p. 124; Dorothy Solinger, *Contesting Citizenship in Urban China* (Berkeley: University of California Press, 1999).

8. Li Qiang, *Zhuanxin shiqi de Zhongguo shehui fenzheng jiegou*, pp. 364–374.

9. Ibid., p. 131; Zhu Hongjia, *Zhongguo liudong renkoushengtai diacha* (An investigation into the life of the migrant population in China) (Jinan: Shandong Friendship Publishing Company, 2001), pp. 109–132; Li Peilin, *Nongmin gong*, pp. 96–115; Li Zhang, *Strangers in the City* (Stanford, CA: Stanford University Press, 2001).

10. Li Peilin, *Nongmin gong*, p. 261.

11. Li Qiang, *Zhuanxin shiqi de Zhongguo shehui fenzheng jiegou*, p. 123.

12. Ibid., p. 130.

13. Zhu Hongjia, *Zhongguo liudong renkoushengtai diacha*, pp. 109–132.

14. Alejandro Portes, ed., *The Economics Sociology of Immigration: Essays on Networks, Ethnicity and Entrepreneurship* (New York: Russell Sage Foundation, 1995); Alejandro Portes, *The New Second Generation* (New York: Russell Sage Foundation 1996); Alejandro Portes and Ruben G. Rumbaut, *Legacies: The Story of the Immigrant Second Generation* (Berkeley: University of California Press, 2001); Anthony Richmond, *Global Apartheid: Refugees, Racism, and the New World Order* (Toronto: Oxford University Press, 1994); Ruben G. Rumbaut and Alejandro Portes, *Ethnicities: Children of Immigrants in America* (Berkeley: University of California Press 2001); Xu Demin, *Shanghai shequ wailai renkou sixiang gongzuo yanjiu*, pp. 55–58.

15. Richmond, *Global Apartheid*; Rumbaut and Portes, *Ethnicities*; Xu Demin, *Shanghai shequ wailai renkou sixiang gongzuo yanjiu*, pp. 55–58.

16. Li Peilin, *Nongmin gong*, p. 140.

17. www.cinfo.org.cn/dtgj/liudongrenkou/017/htm2002/9/2; *Jinghua shibao* August 16, 2002, p. A04 (www.people.com.cn/GB/kejiao/39/ . . . /801520.htm2002/9/1; www.cinfo.org.cn/dtgj/liudongrenkou/1drk-025.htm2002/9/02); Han Jialing, "Beijingxi liudong ertong yiwu jiaoyu zhuangkuang diaocha baogao" (Report on the education of migrant children in Beijing), *Qingnian Yanjiu* (Youth research), no. 9 (2001), pp. 10–18.

18. www.cinfo.org.cn/dtgj/liudongrenkou/017/htm2002/9/2; Zhang Yongqian, "Liudong de shengwo, daiban de tizhi–Beijingshi liudong renyuan zinu jiuxue tanxi" (Flexible life, ossified structures—Study of Beijing migrant children), *Renmin fayuan bao* (People's court news), June 3, 2000, p. 2; *Jinghua shibao*, August 16, 2002, p. A04.

19. Li Qiang, *Zhuanxin shiqi de Zhongguo shehui fenzheng jiegou*, p. 134.

20. Xinhua News Agency, June 15, 2001 (www.people.com.cn/GB/kejiao/230/5650/5651/20010615/490085.html2002/9/1); Xinhua News Agency, April 11, 2002 (www.china.org.cn/chinese/difang/131033.htm2002/9/1).

21. Xu Demin, *Shanghai shequ wailai renkou sixiang gongzuo yanjiu*, p. 41; Han Jialing, "Beijingxi liudong ertong yiwu jiaoyu zhuangkuang diaocha baogao," pp. 10–18.

22. *Zhongguo qingnianbao* (China youth daily), June 15, 2001; *Beijing qingnianbao* (Beijing youth daily), August 6, 2001.

23. Liu Yingjia, *Zhongguo chengxiang guanxi yu Zhongguo nongmin gongren*, p. 169.

24. www.cinfo.org.cn/dtgj/liudongrenkou/1drk-025.htm2002/9/02; Han Jialing, "Beijingxi liudong ertong yiwu jiaoyu zhuangkuang diaocha baogao," pp. 10–18; Fan Guorui, "Chengzhang zai dushi bianyuan" (Growing up on the margin of the cty), *Minban jiaoyu dongtai* (Trends in private education), February 2002, pp. 5–9.

25. Duan Chengrong and Zhou Hao, "Beijingshi liudodng ertong xiaonian zhuanchang fenxi (An analysis of Beijing migrant children), *Renkou yu jingji* (Population and economy), no. 1 (2001), pp. 5–10; Peilin, *Nongmin gong*, pp. 206–226; Liu Cuilian et al., "Jiaoyu buke weiwang de yikuai–Shanghai mingong zidi xuexiao diaocha baogao" (A sector of education that should not be forgotten—Report on the Shanghai peasant-workers' children schools), *Shanghai gaojiao yanjiu* (Shanghai higher education research), no. 5 (1998), pp. 7–11 (www.cinfo.org.cn/dtgj/liudongrenkou/017/htm2002/9/2).

26. Liu Cuilian et al., "Jiaoyu buke weiwang de yikuai."

27. Xinhua News Agency, June 15, 2001 (www.people.com.cn/GB/kejiao/230/5650/5651/20010615/490085.html2002/9/1); Han Jialing, "Beijingxi liudong ertong yiwu jiaoyu zhuangkuang diaocha baogao," pp. 10–18; *Beijing chenbao* (Beijing morning news), September 6, 2001; September 10, 2001; Xu Demin, *Shanghai shequ wailai renkou sixiang gongzuo yanjiu*, pp. 117–129.

28. *Beijing chenbao* (Beijing morning news), September 6, 2001 (www.people.com.cn/GB/kejiao/230/5650/5651/20010906/553077.html2002/9/1); Xu Demin, *Shanghai shequ wailai renkou sixiang gongzuo yanjiu*, p. 120; www.cinfo.org.cn/dtgj/liudongrenkou/017/htm2002/9/2; *Liberation Daily*, September 10, 2001 (www.people.com.cn/GB/guandian/182/6549/20010910/556303.html2002/9/1); Han Jialing, "Beijingxi liudong ertong yiwu jiaoyu zhuangkuang diaocha baogao," pp. 10–18; *Beijing qingnianbao* (Beijing youth daily), May 10, 2002; Du Wenpin, "Liudong renkou zinu jiaozhiguan cunzai de wenti zi jiaoyu ganyu" (Problems existing in the values of the migrant children and the intervention of education), *Jiaoyu yanjiu* (Education science research), no. 11 (2002), pp. 51–52; Lu Shaoqing and Zhang Shouli, "Chengxiang chabie xia de liudong ertong jiaoyu" (Urban-rural disparity in the education of migrant children), *Zhanlue yu guanli* (Strategy and administration), no. 4 (2001), pp. 95–108.

29. www.cinfo.org.cn/dtgj/liudongrenkou/017/htm2002/9/2; *Liberation Daily*, September, 10, 2001; Han Jialing, "Beijingxi liudong ertong yiwu jiaoyu zhuangkuang diaocha baogao," pp. 10–18; *Beijing qingnianbao* (Beijing youth daily), May 10, 2002; Du Wenpin, "Liudong renkou zinu jiaozhiguan cunzai de wenti zi jiaoyu ganyu"; Lu Shaoqing and Zhang Shouli, "Chengxiang chabie xia de liudong ertong jiaoyu."

30. www.cinfo.org.cn/dtgj/liudongrenkou/017/htm2002/9/2; *Beijing chenbao* (Beijing morning news), November 22, 2001; *Beijing qingnianbao* (Beijing youth) August 2, 2002.

31. Han Jialing, "Beijingxi liudong ertong yiwu jiaoyu zhuangkuang diaocha baogao," pp. 10–18; *Beijing chenbao* (Beijing morning news), November 22, 2001 (www.people.com.cn/GB/kejiao/230/5650/5651/20011122/610768.html2002/9/1); *Renmin ribao* (People's daily), December 26, 2001 (www.people.com.cn/GB/guandian/182/6549/20011226/535353.html2002/9/1).

32. *Liberation Daily*, September 10, 2001.

8

Educational Stratification and the New Middle Class

Jing Lin

China's rapid economic growth has brought about profound transformation in the social landscape. The old social class categories have been replaced with fluidity, and social groups have been greatly diversified. Redistribution of resources and wealth under the framework of a market-oriented socialist economy have caused the rise of new strata of people, and in this process access to political, economic, and educational power have been determining factors in one's "making it" or not in the upper echelon of the society. As education has become a screening mechanism for social mobility, a newly formed "middle class" is exerting their influence in education to attain an advantage in the competitive economy.

This chapter studies the formation of a new middle class in China and critically examines the influence they exert on education. The chapter starts with defining and identifying the new middle class, discussing the debates on their existence and their features in the social context of China. The chapter pays special attention to the rise of a large number of elite private schools, which respond to the demands of the new middle class for high-quality education. The features and characteristics of these schools are outlined. The chapter points out that not only does the new middle class have access to an exclusive form of education, they have also gained wide access to elite public schools and universities that once touted themselves as only accepting students "based on merit." Although the new middle class is making inroads into all kinds of spheres, the chapter argues that the stratification of educa-

Small class size, bright classroom, and individual attention: this is what attracts the parents of the new middle class to elite private schools

tional opportunities has disadvantaged the urban working class and rural peasants who are being suffocated by the escalating rise of tuition and fees. In terms of educational reform, the chapter pinpoints crucial changes in educational practices as a result of the new demands made by the middle class, such as changes in the mission of schools, curriculum, teaching approaches, school culture, school administration and management, and so forth. The chapter finally reflects on the implication of the rise of the new middle class on the formation of civil society and the building of democracy in China.

The chapter draws from the empirical data the researcher collected from field work in China in 1993, 1995–1997, 1999, and 2001–2004. During these years I visited a large number of schools, which include elite public schools and ordinary schools, elite and ordinary private schools, and private and public universities. The cities visited included Beijing, Shanghai, Shenyang, Dalian, Guangzhou, Guilin, Kunming, Zhengzhou, and Xi'an and covered eastern, central, and western China. Visits covered major metropolitan and medium-size cities, as well as some rural townships. Interviews were conducted with presidents of public schools and private universities, and with school principals, founders, teachers, and students of private schools.

Education and the Middle Class

Education has long been viewed as a mechanism for equalizing opportunities and opening doors to social mobility. However, in reality education does not automatically provide upward mobility for all. Studies have pointed out that schools stratify students based on their socioeconomic background.[1] Bowles and Gintis argue that education serves the role of training students to adopt the required attitudes and attributes for serving the needs of a hierarchical capitalist economy.[2] Other studies find that schools track students systematically and often by family background.[3] The consequence is that students from working-class families are tracked in large numbers to more vocational streams of instruction, leading to a future of low-paying work and low social status.

American schools value middle-class culture, thus advantaging children from a middle-class family background as they acquire habits and basic skills in schools. This notion extends to behavioral norms and language codes.[4] In this sense, children of the middle class are said to have more "cultural capital" to succeed in schools.[5] Academic tracking in schools favors the middle class and reinforces the cultural capital they possess and continue to accumulate.[6] The high tracks lead to college and university whereas the low tracks result in lesser jobs that require lower skills. In short, education plays a key role in stratifying society.

In the United States, children living in suburban, wealthy neighborhoods attend public schools that are taught by better-paid teachers with more diverse curriculum. Elite private schools open their doors to middle- and upper-middle-class families who can afford the tuition. Entering an elite private school means not only receiving a higher-quality education but also helps the children form an exclusive web of social relationships that give them future social capital to advance in society.

Access to colleges and universities is also heavily influenced by socioeconomic background, especially as the cost of higher education continues to rise. Students from a lower-class background attend community colleges in greater numbers or enter middle-level state colleges and universities rather than premier elite universities.

China's New Middle Class and the Role of Education in Stratifying Society

In industrial countries, 80 percent of the population consider themselves to be middle class. In income, they take home from $25,000 to $100,000 annually.[1] The middle class is often defined as having a distinct lifestyle and access to certain goods and services. As a group with financial assets, skills, and education, they can even become a stabilizing force for a developing society.

Economic reforms in terms of management and ownership have in recent decades resulted in the rise of a middle class in the formerly socialist countries, including Russia, the Ukraine, and China. Equal distribution of resources and egalitarianism under a socialist paradigm has been replaced by widening gaps in income and wealth among different groups in these countries. A report indicates that some 8 to 20 percent of Russia's 145 million people qualify as middle class.[7]

In China, especially for three decades during the reign of Chairman Mao Zedong (1949–1976), the middle class was nonexistent. In the early 1950s, a socialist state ownership system was established by the communist government, forcefully eliminating private ownership and turning all private properties and businesses in the country into state-owned units.[8] Two major groups were formed: The "people's" classes that the Chinese Communist Party (CCP) relied on (party members, workers, peasants, revolutionary cadres, and soldiers), and the "class enemies" (a wide range of social groups, defined by their property and business ownership before 1949 and their political attitude and affiliation after 1949). The two groups received differential treatment in education and other services and benefits. The former were favored politically, economically, and educationally, whereas class enemies suffered discrimination and intense persecution, especially during the Cultural Revolution.

The economic reform and opening up launched by Deng Xiaoping's government in 1978 constituted a bold measure to save the country from economic bankruptcy. Private entrepreneurship was reintroduced into the economic system and dramatically affected production activities in both urban and rural areas. Individuals were gradually encouraged to establish private businesses while state-owned companies and institutions were given greater autonomy and held accountable for their own survival. Foreign investment grew rapidly, resulting in the establishment of tens of thousands of Sino-foreign joint enterprises. Rural industrial enterprises mushroomed, as well as urban private businesses and factories. Government organizations also entered the market, setting up new companies. As a result, a myriad of new ownership patterns appeared, including shared ownership, state-private collaborative ownership, contract ownership, renting ownership, state ownership with private management, and so on. New ways of thinking, new concepts of management, and new business relations, although resisted along the way, were adopted for the sake of enhancing market competitiveness and modernizing the country.

In the early and mid-1980s, although the majority of urban residents earned 3,000 to 8,000 yuan a year, a number began to earn 10,000 to 50,000 yuan. By the early 1990s, a million millionaires were said to exist in China. By early 2000, the urban rich became noticeably richer while the ranks of the urban poor grew larger. According to Zhu Guanglei,[9] economic reforms ushered in a great wave of industrialization, as hundreds of thousands of rural industrial enterprises urbanized the country. In 1998, the number of peasants working in rural industrial enterprises reached 130 million, joining the 150 million urban workers. Meanwhile, more than 100 million peasants migrated from the rural areas to urban cities and coastal areas in search of jobs, providing low-cost labor. The tremendous tide of industrialization changed the eastern part of China significantly, and the influence quickly spread to central and western China.

With the dramatic change of the social landscape, urban social stratification was transformed. The urban working class, once called the most reliable force by the CCP, was dividing into blue- and white-collar sectors. The better-educated white-collar workers employed by foreign companies or joint ventures received salaries three to ten times higher than blue-collar workers. In Shanghai, 40 percent of workers were said to be white-collar workers, while in other cities the number was significantly lower.

As the entrepreneur class emerged, they joined managers of state enterprises who had accumulated significant personal assets during the reconstitution of ownership and restructuring of management of the state organizations. Managers leading the once-state-owned enterprises increasingly acted like CEOs of privately owned businesses. Government officials of all ranks, totaling thirty million, often enriched themselves during the reform through kickbacks and bribery. Furthermore, employees of government organizations formed a public servant stratum with sources of income outside of their regular salary and exerted tremendous influence on the country's social and economic system.[10]

The classification criteria for social stratification dramatically changed.[11] Politically based criteria were gradually replaced by a combination of new and old indicators: wealth (income, business ownership); educational level; occupational employment in enterprises, government agencies, and other sectors; and urban/rural residence. The class system is fluid yet stratified by possession of political, economic, and intellectual capital.[12] Those with higher learning and education credentials were promoted in government and generally had more opportunities in finding high-paying jobs in Sino-foreign joint ventures. University professors and young graduates established new companies in the technical sphere. A professional stratum with knowledge of English and computers appeared in finance, sales, and real estate. In contrast, a new urban poor formed, including those laid off from state-owned enterprises with less than junior high school education and aged in their forties and fifties. Excluded from most opportunities for upward social mobility, they were joined by millions of rural migrant youth and adults workers in low-paying manufacturing jobs.

Chinese sociologists engaged in the study of China's stratification system classify the emerging occupation system as follows: government and social administrative officials; managers; private business owners; professionals and technical personnel; public servants; individuals running private industrial and commercial businesses; individuals working in service sectors; individuals working in manufacturing; peasants; and unemployed urban residents, laid-off workers, and semiunemployed people.[13] Li Qiang identified four major interest groups: those who have been major beneficiaries of reform, those who have benefited somewhat, those who have been harmed somewhat, and those who have been condemned to the bottom of the society.[14] He especially stresses that in modern society, occupation has become the main demarcation of an individual's social status:

> One's social status, whether high or low, is quite precisely reflected in one's occupation. A person's occupation reflects not only economic, wealth and income status, but also reflects a person's position in the power structure and prestige categories. Hence there is a great match of one's social class status with one's occupation. Furthermore, most people rely on their education level to gain access into the occupational structure, hence education in modern society has become the main screening mechanism for social stratification.[15]

Research through the years reveals that China's new middle class contains these groups: first, private entrepreneurs and business owners, including those operating small to large businesses in major cities as well as those running factories or engaged in large-scale production of all kinds of agricultural products in rural areas; second, white-collar workers working in foreign companies or China-foreign joint venture enterprises; third, intellectuals who consult or own their own high-tech companies; fourth, university faculty members and teachers in good primary and secondary school in major cities; fifth, those who work as real estate agents, stockbrokers, entertainers, and so on; and sixth, high-income state enterprise managers, government officials (public servants), or those government officials who garner large incomes from bribes and taking advantage of their relational networks.

However, there is also a latent middle class that penetrates all sectors of society.[16] They include people who garner income that can double or triple their paychecks through bonuses or other income outside their regular job. These include government employees, bank clerks, schoolteachers, university faculty and staff, police, small business owners, peasants with possession of special skills, and so on. They own their apartments and can afford large consumer items as well as travel holidays and international brand-name clothing. They generally possess properties, have major savings in banks, live a life of relative comfort, and have received tertiary or higher education.

In the early 1990s, the estimate is that they comprised 5 to 10 percent of the population. The overall characteristic of the middle class and latent middle class is that they have a significant level of autonomy in choosing and purchasing services, including education.

In the 1990s, the middle class were generally voiceless in the political arena, but they have gradually gained ground as they have become an important force in the local, regional, and national economy. In the Party Congress and the People's Congress conferences in 2002 and 2003, owners of private enterprises were elected representatives, joining other Party representatives in giving the government suggestions and voicing criticism on issues of concern.

The rise of the middle class also signifies that the gap between social classes has been dramatically enlarged. By 1994, a decade and a half after the economic reform led by Deng Xiaoping was launched, the poorest 20 percent of the families owned only 4.25 percent of the total income, whereas the wealthiest 20 percent owned more than 50 percent of the total income.[17] By 1998, fifty-eight million people lived below the poverty line, making less than 300 yuan a year. In 2004, a significant number of rural people were earning less than 300 yuan a year. Urban unemployment has brought disasters to many families. Tens of millions workers have been laid off as a result of problems such as low efficiency, low-quality products, and poor management in a large number of state-owned enterprises. With the restructuring of the economy toward exportation, in formerly well-off cities such as those heavy industrial cities in northeastern China, millions of laid-off workers could not find anything to do. Regional gaps between coastal China and western China enlarged. All these contribute to the complex picture of social transformation and stratification of classes under the economic reform.

The debate about the existence of a Chinese middle class began in the 1990s. Research conducted in 2001 by the Chinese Academy of Social Science that surveyed 6,000 participants in twelve provinces indicated that 7 percent of the Chinese population met the criteria of a middle class (in occupation, income, lifestyle, and personal identification), totaling sixty million of the population. The new middle class is concentrated in urban areas. Twelve percent of major city residents are said to belong to the middle-class group. Of them, 11.8 percent are government officials, 22.1 percent are business managers, 9.8 percent are private business owners, 23.9 percent are employees of government agencies, and 32.4 percent are professionals. The representation of the middle class is reflected in the following categories: 57.1 percent of private business owners, 55.6 percent of government officials, 50 percent of managers of state-owned enterprises, and 35.9 percent and 15.8 percent of professionals and government workers, respectively. By gender, 59.3 percent are male and 40.7 percent are female, and by education, 72.5 percent have a postsecondary-level education or above.[18]

The rise of a new social class will have an impact on many sectors of China's society. It is predicted that in the next five years, the new middle class could swell to 200 million people. Others argue that the pyramid-shaped class structure is creating instability and that an olive-shaped class structure would be conducive to social stability and prosperity.[19] Some hold that the new middle class will inspire more admiration for Western lifestyles, enlarge its private space, incur suffering from work-related stress, and show a decreasing interest in politics.[20]

The Middle-Class Impact on Education: Access, Treatment, and Outcome

The middle-class influence on education became evident at the beginning of the 1990s. My research indicates that members of the middle class realize that their children will have greater opportunities if they receive a high-quality education and if they are taught new skills highly demanded by the market economy. They wish for their children to have abilities other than just academic ones, so that they can adapt to the rapid changes characteristic of the era of globalization. Chinese public schools have been characterized by poor teaching quality, poor facilities and equipment, low educational spending, large class size, rigid curriculum, and a disconnection of school learning from society. A small number of schools, called "key schools," have advantages in all of the above-mentioned aspects due to the fact they have receive preferential treatment from the government. Yet less than 5 percent of public schools are key schools, and access is extremely competitive. The rising middle class has created a demand for more of this kind of schooling, and the demand is being met by private elite schooling. After a decade of development, private schools charging high fees are seen all over urban China, attracting students mainly from the middle class.

Since 1985, in the name of restructuring China's education system, the central government has been shifting the burden of educational funding to local governments, which in turn exert pressure for revenue generation on local schools. Urban public schools find themselves receiving less than 60 percent of their funding from the government, and rural schools even less. The shortfall in revenue forces schools to become entrepreneurial and find ways (such as offering after-school classes and doing business) to supplement their income. Doors of elite schools have opened to those who can pay. A new framework has emerged in which good education costs more and has became a market commodity. This new paradigm benefits the middle class and the latent middle class, providing them with more choice and enabling them to gain access to more forms of schools that provide quality education. The egalitarian notion that education is to be free and equal for all, and strictly meritocratic, has been replaced with the commercialization of education, which sees education as a commodity for trade.

Elite Private Schools: Access, Curriculum, and School Culture

One example of the middle class's influence on education is reflected in the rise of a large number of elite private schools in the 1990s, which responded to the demands of the new middle class for high-quality education.

Under the state-ownership system, no private schools were allowed to exist in China. In the early 1980s, a small number of privately founded schools began to appear, along with the relaxation of control in the country's politics and economy. At the beginning they were remedial, temporary schools or adult learning institutes. Gradually they increased in number in response to the tremendous needs in the society for all levels of education. Private education underwent an explosive development in 1992, when the economic engine stalled by the student movement in 1989 was set into motion again by Deng Xiaoping's south China tour speech (affirming China's continuous intention to reform). At one point there were 70,000 private learning institutions in the country. In 2001, statistics provided by the Ministry of Education indicate that the total number of private learning institutions was 56,274, of which 44,526 were private kindergartens, 4,846 private primary schools, 4,571 private regular secondary schools, 1,040 private vocational schools, and 1,291 private higher-learning institutions.[21] The private universities have more than a million students.

Among the private schools, elite private schools especially cater to the demands and affordability of the middle class. These were once dubbed "schools for aristocrats," a name picked by a school founder to create a dramatic advertising effect. Implicitly, these schools provide conditions that aim to give the children of the new middle class an education that puts them in front of others in academic learning and habits of life. The first elite private school was set up in 1992 and, soon afterward, many others came along. Locating mainly in major cities and townships, these schools operate a boarding system with excellent learning and living conditions and a low teacher–student ratio. Classrooms are decorated colorfully, and teachers are required to pay attention to students' individual differences. These schools charge tuition and fees that range from 20,000 yuan to 50,000 yuan a year, an amount equivalent to several times to more than ten times the annual income of an ordinary family in the early 1990s. The schools also charge a "school construction fee," which can range from 30,000 to 50,000 yuan, and some schools charge even more. Teachers are hired through competition; a portion are retired teachers and public school teachers working part-time. The teachers receive higher pay than public school teachers and are held responsible for providing the best education possible to their students.

The schools not only strive to provide education in the government-designated curriculum areas but also aspire to prepare students for globalization and development in science and technology. They stress the need to give the middle-class children exposure to advanced science and technology. Thus in these schools there is great emphasis on learning English and computer science. In order that the children can take advantage of all kinds of opportunities, the schools make it their central focus to help students develop in a well-rounded manner. They hire dynamic and well-known teachers who have worked as professionals in music, arts, sports, and other areas. The range of activities in which students are involved includes classical music, ballet, piano, gymnastics, fashion, painting, band, and calligraphy, to name just a few.

The elite private schools had an average of 500 to 1,000 students at the beginning, yet their size has gradually increased to about 2,000 students on average. Founders include private business owners, individual entrepreneurs, retired principals and government officials, democratic parties, returned overseas Chinese, real estate companies, state businesses, and government organizations. Taking advantage of the government's policy for private schools, they usually acquire land at much lower than the market price, pay lower taxes, and construct modern, spacious, and artfully designed campuses to attract parents.

The other features of these schools are standardized running tracks, heated swimming pools, gyms, piano rooms, large libraries and reading rooms, computer labs, and employment of foreign instructors teaching English to the students from an early age. Some schools also establish relations with foreign schools, sending their students overseas for short-term classes to "experience the high development of Western countries." Some schools stress the importance of integrating Eastern and Western virtues and the need to learn independence, creativity, compassion, and cooperation. Many promise the parents that their students will be sent to study abroad right after graduation.

Clearly, the schools are affordable only to the middle class. Our research found that the majority of the children of elite private schools come from families of business owners, private entrepreneurs, government officials, managers of state enterprises, urban white-collar professionals, and overseas Chinese doing businesses in China. These middle-class parents foot a fortune to make sure that their children learn more than other children, acquire newer knowledge, learn more actively and creatively, and learn in a better-equipped environment. The children are expected to have much more social and cultural capital to start with after having studied in such a school environment.

The government has been wary of this kind of school, especially with regard to the criticism that the well-to-do family can buy high-quality education, hence undermining the notion of public education as a common good. This concern has led to a wavering attitude by government officials, who choose to be ambiguous and conflictual in their policy. Most elite private schools have been met with discriminatory measures from the government, such as exclusion from consideration for model schools and refusal to recognize their teachers' seniority when the teachers want to return to public schools. However, some local governments have also adopted supportive measures, as these schools lessen the incredible competition for quality education.[22]

More than a decade has passed since the first elite private school was founded. New ones have been opened whereas old ones have closed down. The schools that have survived have built up their own unique organizational culture and a reputation that attracts parents. They are found in cities and townships in eastern China, and central and western China. One can say that without the existence of a middle class, the elite private schools would not have survived and prospered.

Access to Elite Public Schools

The new middle class also gained wide access to elite public schools as China's public education became widely commercialized. These schools were called key schools in the 1980s and 1990s, and were established in the early 1980s. The government rationale was to concentrate the limited resources available for training China's highly needed talents and to establish role models in teaching for other schools.[23] Originally, there were key elementary schools and key secondary schools. The stratification of schools from the primary and elementary level up drew such severe criticism from society that in the early 1990s key elementary schools were no longer called that. However, the system basically has remained intact as the former key elementary schools maintain their advantage by their possession of a group of highly qualified teachers selected from a vast region and much better facilities and equipment. The schools are often located near residential areas of high-ranking government officials, who can send their children to these schools free of charge.

In the late 1990s, key secondary schools were also reidentified for similar reasons. Local governments found other names, such as "model schools," that could attract and recruit students from across the region, province, or nation. These schools comprised only about 4 percent of China's public schools, yet they boasted that they had the best teachers, the best students, the best reputation, and the best equipment. In the annual highly competitive national university entrance exam, they often claimed a 95 to 99 percent admission rate. Eighty percent of the students who study in these elite public secondary schools come from families of intellectuals and government officials.

In the early 1980s, admission into the key schools was largely based on examination scores. However, the withdrawal of central and local governments from funding the full cost of education forced ordinary public schools to become business enterprises. This opened wide the opportunity for elite public schools to generate a huge amount of income. Elite public secondary schools took advantage of their social prestige and enrolled extra students (beyond the number permitted by the government), many of whom did not meet the admission criteria. They charged fees from 6,000 to 20,000 yuan a year, and some schools even charged a lump sum of 80,000 to 100,000 for three years of study.

Elite primary schools followed suit. A key primary school in Beijing is known to charge 80,000 yuan and another even 140,000 yuan for an "out-of-district" student's six years of education. This amount is affordable only to a small number of households. In the morning, parents drive their children to school in Mercedes and even more expensive cars.

This type of practice increased access for the children of the new middle class to high-quality public education and guaranteed them a jump on other children, whereas children from the working and peasant classes have been kept outside, with only a tiny number making it through on their outstanding academic achievement. Their chance of social mobility through elite schools remains slim.

Access to Public Universities

Similar practices have been adopted by public universities that once only accepted students based on their academic merits. In the 1980s, public universities provided education for free to all students, regardless of their background. Students were also assigned to jobs by government organizations. Although public universities were allowed to accept nonresident fee-paying students (all their regular students were provided room and board), the number was usually very small. In 1997, Chinese public universities started to charge tuition and fees to students, and the amount has increased from 2,000 yuan per year to about 4,000 to 6,000 yuan per year by 2004, excluding the cost of living, board, and transportation. This change makes higher

Table 8.1

Increase in Enrollment in Public Universities

	1996	1997	1999	2000
No. of public universities	2,149	2,107	1,905	1,813
No. of students (in 1,000s)	5,662	5,884	7,143	9,097

Source: Adapted from National Educational Development Research Center, Ministry of Education (2001), *2001 Green Paper on Education in China.*

education easily affordable only to the middle class and the latent middle class. For the working-class and peasant-class families, the amount is a fortune. Although efforts have been made to provide financial aid and loans to students from low-income families, the families still need to put up nearly all their savings, as the financial aid is far from comprehensive. Stories of peasants having to sell their only assets such as cows and houses, or even resorting to selling their blood to gather the necessary amount for tuition, are reported every year. Many families have to borrow from relatives or take one or two children out of school in order to support the child who looks most promising.

Starting in 1998, China's public universities dramatically expanded their enrollment, increasing admission by more than 30 percent a year (see Table 8.1). By 1999, the gross enrollment rate of the cohort age (eighteen to twenty-one years old) group at the higher education level had reached 10.5 percent. In 2002, the ratio was 15 percent. Public universities went from having five million students enrolled in 1997 to having about sixteen million students studying in much more crowded classrooms and hurriedly built campuses. The enlarged enrollment greatly benefits the new middle class, as fees charged are affordable for them. In 2004, 75 percent of the students who reached the admission line were accepted into universities.

Meanwhile, public universities are establishing so-called second-tier colleges that take advantage of the resources, reputation, and facilities of their universities. These colleges, numbering more than 300 in 2003, charge tuition and fees just like any other nongovernmental school and are operated with fewer restrictions from the government. The colleges enroll students from a wide range of academic achievement levels by significantly lowering their admission criteria, thus enabling a large number of students from middle-class families to receive higher education comparable to that provided by public universities.

Access to Private Higher Education

The new middle class also finds wide access to higher education through nongovernmental universities. China now has about 1,300 nongovernmental colleges. They offer programs in highly demanded or popular subjects such as English, computer science, business management, information technology, international trade, accounting, law, and so on. They charge a tuition that ranges from 6,000 yuan to 8,000 yuan per year, and some programs and colleges charge over 10,000 yuan a year. The universities also charge students dormitory fees, and students have to pay for their food and transportation. The overall cost can range from 15,000 yuan to 20,000 yuan a year for a student. Again, the middle class has a huge advantage. In 2003, more than twelve private universities had an enrollment of over 20,000 students, and the number continues to increase.

The private universities usually admit students who have very low scores. Considered to be second-class universities, they strive to connect their programs to the needs in the economy and establish their niche through teaching students practical skills and the ability to adjust to market needs. Because of these schools' low admission threshold, the new middle class essentially can find their children a university to go to no matter what their scores are.

Because of the increase in numbers of the new middle class, private universities have undergone great expansion. In the beginning, private universities founded in the early 1990s had but a few dozen to a few hundred students studying in rented classrooms. High demand from society saw the universities snowball into institutions with several thousand students in a few short years. By 2004, more than a dozen had enrollments of 20,000 to 35,000 students. These institutions are attended by children from all class backgrounds, yet the middle-class students have a better learning environment: they can choose to pay a higher fee and stay in a dormitory with only two to four students; they can have a computer installed on their desk and eat much better food in the school canteen; they have an easier time finding jobs after graduation as their parents have prepared them with more economic resources and a social network to locate jobs. Although middle-class parents would rather send their children to a public university with a better reputation, they use private universities as a last resort for their children who have low academic achievement.

Access to Senior High School Education

Since 1986, China has implemented the policy of nine-year compulsory education. The Compulsory Education Law stipulates that no fees will be charged for basic education for children from ages six to fifteen, and government officials are held accountable for ensuring that all school-age children in their jurisdiction enroll in school.

However, senior high school education is considered to be outside the range of the government's responsibility, and the shortage of senior high schools, not to say good-quality ones, is staggering. Public senior high schools have become a bottleneck in China's educational development, as their numbers are far from meeting the needs of society while both primary education and higher education have expanded greatly.[24] There is a saying in China that it is even harder to get into a good senior high school than a good university, for there are simply not enough senior high schools. Less than 30 percent of rural children can advance to senior high schools, and nationally less than 50 percent of all students graduate from senior high school. Many schools are run like private businesses, for they charge a high amount of tuition and fees to all students even though they are called public schools. Reputable senior high schools charge parents from thousands to hundreds of thousands of yuan a year, and even county-level senior high schools are asking no less than 3,000 yuan a year. The high cost has been driving working-class and peasant-class children away from senior high school education, which in turn excludes them from a huge number of job opportunities that require a certain level of education.

The Disadvantage of the Urban Working Class and the Rural Peasant Class

The economic restructuring taking place in China has resulted in large number of layoffs. In 1996, laid-off workers comprised 8 percent of all workers; in 1997 this number was 13 percent, and in 1998 it was 17 to 18 percent. This means of every six employees, one was laid off. The situation varied in different places. Liaoning Province was the highest with 22.4 percent, and Hubei was the lowest with 16 percent. In 1996, the laid-off workers were paid 77 yuan a month, and in 1997, 83 yuan a month, comprising 15 percent of the nation's average salary. By 2004, half of the laid-off workers had not found a job. They are paid 200 to 300 yuan a month, an amount that is just enough to survive. Overall, the country's unemployment rate in industry is 10, and in some places 20, percent.

Poverty has been widespread in rural areas in China. While provinces in the eastern coast of the country (Zhejiang and Jiangshu Province, for example) have seen peasants becoming prosperous by running small businesses and selling their land for large development projects, peasants in central and western China still linger in poverty. In my research trips, I found that many children in western China could not continue their schooling, as their per capita income is only 300 yuan a year and schools often charge fees that parents cannot afford. Overall, rural residents take in less than one-third the income of urban residents.

The widespread unemployment in urban areas and the poverty in rural areas have effectively marginalized a large group of people. Their lack of resources in education is perpetuating their social class status.

Stories abound that when a highly talented child from a peasant's family receives the admission notice from a university, anxiety and worry set in, instead of joy and hope. The family not only has to use up its savings, the parents also have to borrow door-to-door from relatives and friends. Similar stories are heard of laid-off workers. The cost of paying over 10,000 yuan a year for a child's education in senior high schools or universities is way beyond their means. Many families are even finding it hard to afford the 300 to 500 yuan of fees charged by schools. Slums are being formed in affluent cities like Shanghai where working-class people, many without jobs, see their children trapped in low-quality schools with no way out.

The Impact of the Middle Class on School Reform

The access of the middle class to all forms of education also generates greater parental involvement in education. Middle-class parents are very active in their children's education in elite private schools, which also try to involve parents. The schools usually hold meetings with parents once or twice each semester, and some schools provide direct phone lines for parents to inquire about their children's learning and living experiences in the school. Because of parental pressures, elite private schools strive to maintain their student clientele by providing a diverse curriculum and paying attention to individual differences. Admitting students who come with various levels of intellectual ability, the schools search hard to find creative ways to teach the students and encourage them to build self-confidence. For low-performance students, for example, extracurricular activities are provided to generate a spark of confidence, enabling students to see that they have talents just as other students do. The fact that the elite private schools gather students from high-income families also forces the schools to find ways to build collective consciousness and form a community of learning and interdependence while ridding students of bad habits such as arrogance, snobbishness, wastefulness, and selfishness.

The middle class is especially keen on the new opportunities created in China's opening to the world and globalization. According to Wen Jun,[25] ten major development trends exist in today's shift toward globalization. Jun lists the globalization of transportation, information, science and technology, economy, trade, and management and administration and includes globalization of culture, values, competition, and international social problems.

To meet the challenges of globalization and harness an advantage in competition for opportunities, the middle class has had a direct effect on the course offerings and learning culture in elite private schools. The schools all look to English proficiency and computer literacy as basic requirements, and they also strive to drill into their students qualities such as independence, creativity, imagination, social participation, and mutual dependence. In higher education, the new middle class essentially determines program offerings by flocking to hot (*remen*) subject areas regardless of cost. They render educational institutions as "service providers" rather than ivory towers. The new middle class also is the force that breaks the government's monopoly on education. The opening of various types of schools and the availability of all kinds of programs increase choices for parents, as well as enhance the diversity of education in China. Although the Ministry of Education still exerts tremendous influence on all levels of education, it is not a monopoly anymore. All kinds of social forces are involved in the provision of education, affecting schools' missions and characteristics. The schools are more service oriented than ever, driven by the needs and preferences of the new middle class.

Implications and Conclusion

Based on the National Statistical Bureau's study published in 2002, the average assets of urban families in China were 228,300 yuan per year. Of those surveyed, 48 percent of the households had average assets between 150,000 and 300,000 yuan. If this is used as the criterion to measure middle-class status, then 200 million Chinese people, or 18 percent, qualify as middle class. What exactly defines the middle class? Some people have emphasized the population's own perception, others have looked at income, and still others take into consideration wealth, occupation, and education. Regardless of the different criteria, it is widely agreed that a new social class is being formed in China. Some scholars estimate that in the 1990s this middle class comprised 5 to 10 percent of the population, and others estimate it will be about 15 to 20 percent by the first half of 2010.

However, scholars have gravely warned that China's social class structure is pyramid shaped, which is creating dire consequences such as social upheaval. In the government report for the sixteenth conference of the communist government in 2003, the call for an emphasis on increasing the middle-level income stratum was brought up for the first time.

Enlarging gaps between the rich and poor have worried many people. *Forbes* magazine in 2001 wrote that the richest fifty people in China owned U.S.$10 billion of assets in 2000, whereas in the same year the net income of a family in six poor provinces averaged only 1,464 yuan. This indicates that the assets of the fifty richest people in China are equivalent to fifty million Chinese peasants' net annual income. Sociologists worry that clashes between classes could intensify and become China's biggest problem in the decade to come. The peasants, at the bottom of the society, are losing land and dealing with low prices in agricultural products, an inability to find jobs in cities, and the loss of human resources to cities and more developed areas.[26]

China's middle class, although enlarging in rank, is still in the beginning stage of formation. According to Tian Weidong,[27] this group of people, as compared to the middle class in developed countries, still lacks a solid economic foundation for independent existence. They do not yet have their own independent financial system, and they rely strongly on government- and state-owned businesses for resources and investment opportunities. In addition, although they share similar a mode of production and lifestyle, they have not formed a shared class psyche and consciousness. They have a mixture of identities based on their former position in China's long public state ownership system, and their new role and values in a capitalist economy are still forming. Furthermore, they do not have a national network and a political party that represents their interests. The article mentioned, written in 1997, remains largely true today.

In the great transformation of China's society and economy, many previously privileged positions no longer exist, as the urban working class has experienced,[28] and new challenges face people every day. This creates a sense of imbalance, loss, and helplessness, and there is a strong mentality favoring short-term gain. Education in the transitional economy is inadvertently playing the role of guiding people with the hope that if one has a good education, one has a future. This mindset drives the tremendous demand for all forms of education by all sectors of the society, and the new middle class has a clear advantage in the competition.

It is evident that the new mentality of the government needs to switch from encouraging a small number of people to become rich to that of helping all people and elevating all members of society to become equal and prosperous. Given the critical role of education in placing people in different social class categories, educators need to bring the issues of equality for all to the center of attention. This means that educators need to push for increases in funding in education and call for a shift from focusing mainly on development and expansion toward equalizing opportunities. The unemployed and the Chinese peasants need advocates.

Inequity of educational opportunity is a widespread phenomenon in China. There are inequalities between regions, between ethnic groups, between genders, and between rural and urban areas. The new middle class is composed of various groups, from different regions and ethnicities and both genders. Overall, they have the conditions necessary to garner access to quality education in China: they possess economic power, if not intellectual or/and political power. The concern is that these three powers have tended to reinforce each other, thus intensifying the stratification of social classes. Education is becoming the gatekeeper in the country for social and economic mobility, as well as the political arena. It is not difficult to see that those who are left behind in the economic reform and opening up will be disadvantaged continuously, whereas the new middle class will strengthen their advantage and perpetuate their power and privilege through access to quality education.

On the other hand, the new middle class has facilitated the formation of civil society. China's private education development is a grassroots movement, with schools overcoming all kinds of obstacles to provide choice in education. Private schools and universities contribute to the diversity of social services in the country and render schools to be much more responsive to social demands. The new middle class expands the autonomy of education by forcing schools to be creative and flexible.

The challenge is to enlarge educational opportunities by providing assistance of all kinds to poor families, increasing the number of schools, and placing a cap on tuition and fees for the poor. It is obvious that the Chinese government cannot avoid the issues of the poor and must take an active role in maintaining affordability of education to the lower echelon of the society. While a country is striving for prosperity, the dream of providing for the common good should never be given up. Thus, in the next decade or so, it is imperative that the needs of the disadvantaged social groups in China become the top priority of the government's education policy.

Notes

1. Teachers tend to judge students' academic abilities based on their class background. See Ray C. Rist, "Student Social Class and Teacher Expectations: The Self-Fulfilling Prophesy in Ghetto Education," *Harvard Educational Review,* no. 40 (1970), pp. 411–451.

2. Education is not neutral, and schools mold students according to the needs of the capitalist economy. See Samuel Bowles and Herbert Gintis, *Schooling in Capitalist America* (New York: Basic Books, 1976), pp. 84–148.

3. Tracking is believed to teach students different types of knowledge and hence give them different life chances. See Jeannie Oakes, *Keeping Track: How Schools Structure Inequality* (New Haven and London: Yale University Press, 1985).

4. Kathleen Benet DeMarrais and Margaret D. LeCompte, *The Way Schools Work: A Sociological Analysis of Education* (New York: Longman, 1995).

5. Pierre Bourdieu, *Language and Symbolic Power* (Cambridge, MA: Harvard University Press, 1991).

6. Oakes, *Keeping Track.*

7. "Russia's Middle Class: It Has Emerged from the Rubble of 1998. But Can It Grow and Prosper?" *Businessweek Online,* October 16, 2000 (www.businessweek.com:/2000/00-42/b3703093.htm?scriptFramed).

8. See Lin Jing, *The Red Guards' Path to Violence* (New York: Praeger, 1991).

9. Zhu Guanglei, "Ten Major Trends in Social Stratification in the Chinese Society at the Crossing Point of the New Century," *Nan Kai Academic Journal, Philosophy and Social Science Edition,* no. 1 (1998), pp. 1–9, 59.

10. Zhu Guanglei, "Ten Major Trends."

11. For a systematic study of social class transformation and the rise of private education, see Jing Lin, *Social Transformation and Private Education in China* (New York: Praeger, 1999).

12. As social class formation is still shifting due to the marketization of the Chinese economy, the latent middle class may become either middle class or working class, depending. The middle class can be dramatically enlarged if it is taken to include the latent middle class. See Jing Lin and Heidi Ross, "Potential and Problems of Diversity in China's Educational System," *McGill Journal of Education,* vol. 33, no. 1 (1998), pp. 31–49.

13. Lu Xueyi (chief ed.), *A Research Report on Modern China's Social Class Stratification* (Beijing: Social Science Documents Publisher, 2002).

14. Li Qiang, *Zhuangxing shiqi de Zhonguo shehui fencing jiegou* (China's social stratification structure in the transition period) (Harbin: Heilongjiang People's Publisher, 2002).

15. Li Qiang, *Zhuangxing shiqi de Zhonguo shehui fencing jiegou,* p. 3.

16. Jing Lin and Ross, "Potential and Problems of Diversity."

17. Cai Xiaohua, "How Should We Understand and Deal with the Problem of the Gap Between the Wealthy and Poor?" *Ningbo University Journal, Humanity Edition,* no. 2 (1997), pp. 46–52.

18. Li Chunling, *Zhongguo shehui xinshi fenxi he yuce* (Analysis of China's social trend and prediction) (Beijing: Social Science Documents Publishing House, 2004).

19. Zhen Guozhong, "How Far Away Are We from the Rise of a Middle Class?" *Wisdom Consulting* (zhinang) *Finance and Economic Report,* February 2003.

20. Zhang Wanli, "The Rise of the Middle Class and Its Social Function," *Twenty-first Century Economic Report,* December 27, 2003.

21. Ministry of Education Development and Planning Bureau (www.edu.cn/20011105/3008194.shtml).

22. Jing Lin, *Social Transformation and Private Education in China* (New York: Praeger, 1999).

23. Ibid.

24. Jing Lin and Yu Zhang, "Educational Expansion and Shortage of Secondary Schools: The Bottle Neck Syndrome," *Journal of Contemporary China,* vol. 15, no. 47 (2006), pp. 255–74.

25. Wen Jun, "Ten Major Development Trends in the Global Shift Toward Globalization," *Chinese Soft Science,* no. 8 (1997), pp. 45–49.

26. Lu Xueyi, *Dangdai shehui jieceng yanjiu baogao* (Research Report on Modern China's Social Class Stratification) (Beijing: Social Science Documents Publisher, 2002).

27. Tian Weidong, "My Own View on Private Entrepreneurial Class," *The Theoretical Forefront,* no. 12 (1997), p. 16.

28. Jing Lin, *Social Transformation.*

List of Contributors

Ben Jiao, a Tibetan anthropologist, took his first degree at the Central University of Nationalities in Beijing before earning his M.A. and Ph.D. from Case Western Reserve University in the United States. He is currently associate professor and vice director of the Institute for Contemporary Tibetan Research at the Tibet Academy of Social Sciences, China. His research has focused on various areas related to Tibet's development, including marriage and the family, educational development, rural health care, Tibetan oral history, socioeconomic and cultural changes in rural pastoral and agricultural areas, and international NGO development programs. He has worked on a number of international and national research and development projects over the past 16 years and has published numerous papers about his research findings.

Sonam Gyatso is a development expert at the Tibet College of Agriculture and Animal Husbandry and at the Tibet Agricultural Development Office. He has worked in the area of poverty alleviation for ten years, especially in rural nomadic and agricultural areas of Tibet, and his projects include education, animal husbandry, water resources, agriculture, and community development. At the same time, he has conducted various academic research and produced papers on his findings.

Emily Hannum is assistant professor of sociology at the University of Pennsylvania. Her research interests include education, social inequality, poverty, and child welfare. Since 1998, she has directed the Gansu Survey of Children and Families, a longitudinal research project that investigates family, school, and community factors that support children's education and healthy development in rural northwest China. She is analyzing Gansu data to investigate mechanisms linking rural poverty and educational outcomes. Recent articles include "Market Transition, Educational Disparities, and Family Strategies in Rural China: New Evidence on Gender Stratification and Development" (*Demography*, 2005); "Global Educational Expansion and Socio-Economic Development: An Assessment of Findings from the Social Sciences" (with Claudia Buchmann, *World Development*, 2005); and "Trends in Children's Social Welfare in China: Access to Health Insurance and Education" (with Jennifer Adams, *China Quarterly*, 2005).

Julia Kwong is professor of sociology at the University of Manitoba. Her area of interest covers broad areas of China's development including education, minorities, corruption, and aging, but her main interest is in education. She is interested in exploring how Western theories can inform our understanding of developments in China and how understanding China's development can enrich or modify our theoretical understanding of social changes. Her interest in education includes the curriculum examinations, educational inequality, and the interaction of social forces in Chinese society. Her articles have appeared in the *International Journal of Education, Comparative Education Review, British Journal of Sociology,* and *Canadian Review of Sociology and Anthropology.* Her major works include *Chinese Education in Transition, Cultural Revolution in China's Schools,* and *Political Economy of Corruption in China.* She is currently studying private schools in China as part of the global trend toward privatization in education.

Jing Lin is an associate professor at the University of Maryland, College Park, in the area of international education policy. She received her doctoral degree from the University of Michigan–Ann Arbor in 1990. From 1991 to 1999, she worked as a faculty member at McGill University in Canada. Jing Lin has done extensive research on Chinese education, culture, and society. In particular, she has systematically studied social changes in China and educational reforms taking place in the country since 1978. She is the author of four books: *The Red Guard's Path to Violence* (1991), *Education in Post-Mao China* (1993), *The Opening of the Chinese Mind* (1994), and *Social Transformation and Private Education in China* (1999). Jing Lin's other research focuses include peace education, environmental education, and spirituality education. Her forthcoming fifth book, *Love, Peace and Wisdom: Education in the 21st Century*, is a synthesis of her work in these areas.

Gerard A. Postiglione is a professor at the University of Hong Kong, where he has been director of the University of Hong Kong's Wah Ching Centre of Research on Education from 2000 to 2005. His research focuses on how sociology can inform educational policy in improving access and equity, and he has been a research consultant on this topic for many organizations, including the Asian Development Bank, United Nations Development Program, the Academy of Educational Development (USA), and the Department for International Development (UK). He has delivered policy recommendations to the Chinese government on ethnic minority education. He was also senior consultant to the Ford Foundation/Beijing on educational reform from 2000 to 2001. He is co-editor of the journal *Chinese Education and Society*. His works include *China's National Minority Education* (1999), *Asian Higher Education* (1997), *Education and Society in Hong Kong* (1991), *Hong Kong's Reunion with China* (1997), and *Education, Social Change, and Regional Development: Mainland China, Taiwan and Hong Kong* (1995).

Heidi Ross is professor of educational policy studies and East Asian studies at Indiana University. Ross publishes widely on education and gender issues and secondary schooling in China, and has served as president of the Comparative and International Education Society and director of Asian studies at Colgate University. She is currently working on several projects, including the contributions of U.S. liberal arts schools to teacher education, the development of girls' secondary schooling in China, the development and implementation of "gender sensitive" curricula and environmental education in Chinese elementary and secondary schools, and an analysis of the concept of social capital in the context of the educational and social experiences of Chinese students and their families in rural and urban schools.

Vilma Seeberg is associate professor of International/Intercultural Education at Kent State University, where she teaches graduate courses in international and multicultural education as well as undergraduate courses in social foundations of education. She has published on various aspects of Chinese education, and her work includes *The Rhetoric and Reality of Mass Education in Mao's China* (2000), the second of two books on basic education in China. She has guest edited an issue of *Chinese Education and Society* on university reform, tuition, and financial aid, and contributed articles to many publications. Her intellectual interests include social theory of education and inequality, Chinese studies, girls' education, and development education. Her work draws from the fields of sociology, anthropology, comparative international education, and political science. She serves on boards of the American Association of University Women and the Comparative and International Education Society.

Jin Xiao is associate professor in the Department of Educational Administration and Policy, Faculty of Education, at the Chinese University of Hong Kong. She received teacher training in Chongqing Normal School and then settled down to educate youth in the countryside, where she was a director and literacy campaign instructor as well as substitute teacher. She finished her university education at the Beijing Broadcasting Institute and then worked at Yunnan University. In 1991, she completed her Ph.D study in adult and continuing education at Michigan State University and then worked as a researcher with Michigan Partnership for New Education for two years before moving to Hong Kong in 1993. Her interest of research has been human resource development and education reform in social and economic transition in China. She has published extensively in a number of journals, including the *China Quarterly*.

Shengchao Yu is a consultant to the World Bank on rural health sector reform in China and holds a Ph.D. in demography from the University of Pennsylvania. Her research area is population and development, and her recent work has focused on health inequalities by gender among children in India, children's health and schooling in China, and rural health care access in China. Current projects include an impact evaluation paper on a health sector project in China, collection of large-scale survey data on health reform in rural China, detailed analysis of new and existing data sets on how health reform in rural China can improve health outcomes and reduce inequalities in access to health care, and documenting differential trends in maternal and child mortality reduction across different parts of China. She has also conducted research on health and economic development for the World Health Organization.

Index